SELECTED LETTERS OF
EDWIN MUIR

EDWIN MUIR, 1955

SELECTED LETTERS OF
EDWIN MUIR

Edited with an Introduction by
P. H. BUTTER

1974
THE HOGARTH PRESS
LONDON

Published by
The Hogarth Press Ltd
42 William IV Street
London WC2N 4DG

*

Clarke Irwin & Co. Ltd
Toronto

All rights reserved. No part of this publication may be reproduced, stored in a retrieval system, or transmitted, in any form, or by any means, electronic, mechanical, photocopying, recording or otherwise, without the prior permission of The Hogarth Press Ltd.

ISBN 0 7012 0385 4

Letters © Gavin Muir 1974
Introduction and Notes © P. H. Butter 1974

Printed in Great Britain by
Cox & Wyman Ltd
London, Fakenham and Reading

CONTENTS

INTRODUCTION	*Page* 7
ACKNOWLEDGEMENTS	11
CHRONOLOGY	13
LETTERS	19
APPENDIX	213
INDEX	215

INTRODUCTION

Edwin Muir was a quiet, shy man, whose life was comparatively uneventful; who took no great part in public life, founded no new school of poetry, and enunciated no new system of ideas. Why, then, are his letters of interest? Most obviously for the light they throw on his own and others' writings. We know that we must trust the tale not the teller, and not take the intention for the deed; but what a poet says about how his poems came into being and about what he thought he was doing in them is still more interesting, and usually more enlightening, than what anyone else says about them. Muir waited for poems to knock on the door, knocking from the deeper levels of the mind on the door of consciousness, coming up at first often as lines, sometimes as ideas, sometimes as dreams. The pace must not be forced. 'I hoped that it might have completed itself,' he wrote to Eliot while his poem 'Prometheus' was in course of formation. The poem is to complete itself; but this does not mean that the poet does not have to work on it—as the state of his MSS shows. The critical intelligence must be used, but in the service of imagination. It may be said that something like this is the experience of most poets. But I think there is a real difference between those poets who are content to use experience fairly raw and those who, like Muir, use it only when it has been 'cooked', often for a long time, beneath the surface. The review which, he wrote in 1949, came closest to his own feelings about his poetry was that by Kathleen Raine of *The Labyrinth*, in which she wrote that he 'evokes with quiet sureness the archetypes that lie latent in each of us. One has the sense not so much of reading his poems as of reliving them, for he has the bard's gift of speaking the dreams of his tribe. Such poetry still comes from Ireland, Wales and Scotland, where racial memories are relatively undisturbed, and the gods not too far away for the poet to call back.' What knocks on the door of the poet's consciousness and seeks to complete itself through him is more even than the distillation of one man's experience. Muir's inheritance helped, but his own patience and integrity were also needed to enable him to speak from and to a deeper level of experience than all but a very few poets of his time reached.

The letters contain some good criticism of others' writings, and add something to the published works by showing Muir's views in process of formation. In the letters to Sydney Schiff, for instance, we see him worrying at length (there are many more letters than are selected here) over writers, such as Lawrence and Wyndham Lewis, about whom he was uncertain. He was scrupulously anxious to see and to pay tribute to the good qualities of writers whom he found in some ways antipathetic. Though his own poetry was traditional in form he was always on the look-out for merit of new kinds, for the growing points in literature. No critic has been less influenced by jealousies or narrow party views. In letters to his friends we see the warmth and generosity of his response to their work.

Secondly, the letters add something to the *Autobiography* by showing him feeling his way imaginatively towards some understanding not just of books nor just of himself, but of life. At first it may be disappointing that they do not more fully represent the range of his interests and experiences outside literature. For his life was curiously representative of the life of modern man. As a child in Orkney he grew up in a small, close-knit rural community with an ancient, mainly oral culture shared by a whole people. As a boy he was suddenly pitch-forked into the modern world in industrial, competitive Glasgow. He saw the life of the slums, though he did not live in them, and endured for almost twenty years the boredom of routine work. He lost his early religious faith, and turned as a protection to the philosophy of Nietzsche; at the same time, incompatibly, he was actively involved in various left-wing organisations—the Clarion Scouts, the I.L.P., the Guild Socialist Movement. His earliest writings were more about politics and philosophy than literature. His inner conflicts and sense of alienation led to nervous breakdown and a course of psycho-analysis. Restored to inner wholeness by his marriage and the discovery of his proper vocation, he saw in Europe in the twenties the aftermath of one world war and some of the premonitory symptoms of the next— the inflation, the anti-semitism. In the thirties he was keenly aware, through friends and relations, of the effects of unemployment at home and of rising tyrannies abroad. Again in Europe after the Second World War he saw a new birth of freedom in Czechoslovakia and its extinction by the Communist coup. His mature poems deal with the state of

Europe with more imaginative perception and at a deeper level than most of the work of the more overtly political poets. In spite of his recovered faith his last poems are dark with the fears of our time—of atomic war, of the pollution of the world, of the beating down of Everyman under inhuman systems. He experienced deeply the distresses of our century—the loss of faith, the alienation and inner division, the threat to human freedom and dignity; and was involved in or came close to many of the modern attempts to deal with or escape from these distresses—Nietzscheanism, psycho-analysis, left-wing politics, return to nature (the simple lifers in Germany), free love (the Bohemian artistic set in St Tropez), progressive education (A. S. Neill). He was well qualified, therefore, to see beneath the story of his own life the fable of man—of man falling into division, both within himself and from others, and seeking to recover the lost unity. For his account of the story and the fable we turn, of course, to his *Autobiography*. The letters do not significantly alter the picture, nor add much new detail. But they add something by their sense of immediacy; we see him in process of discovering things, not just telling us about them long after. If they seem to be concerned mainly with books, this was not an escape from life. In finding his vocation in literature he did not leave behind his other interests, but found the way, proper for him, of dealing with the problems, both personal and social, with which life had faced him. Early in the twenties he was praising American critics for having, unlike the British, a general end, a concern for 'culture in general', not just for the particular book they were writing about. In writing a series of essays on modern authors he wanted, though he doubted his competence, to examine 'the assumptions on which people live as well as those on which they could conceivably live'; at least to see 'where the straw is being blown. . . . For if we cannot discover from our literature where we are, then it seems to me we shall never discover it.' Art for art's sake was meaningless to him. Literature 'faces life more completely, both the good and the bad, than any other expression which the human spirit has thrown out'. 'Only those who face the great issues of life, who enter into and therefore suffer with humanity, the struggles of their time, the whole thing, great and small, and put their witness, as if it were their signature, to it, can attain that joy which the great writers have felt.' From the writers of our time we ought to be able to discover where we are, where the straw is being blown. But that is not by itself enough. 'The mere portrayal of the sufferings of existence, the mere questioning of fate' is not sufficient to be the whole equipment of an artist; 'for people cannot live by it, they must come to a stage where they make a judgment, value, call it whatever one will.' Muir was not content to record and question; he felt his way by imagination to the discovery, or rediscovery, of values to live by. What these were I will not try to sum up; for if one speaks of his belief in immortality, Incarnation, the imagination, etc., it will make these things sound like abstractions or dogmas, which they were not for him. Immortality was a state of being, something experienced; Incarnation something seen – in his parents as he remembered them, and in works of art and people around him in Italy. God was a presence; Transfiguration not just a story of a distant event, but the manifestation of 'that transmutation of life which is found occasionally in poetry, and in the literature of prophecy, and sometimes in one's own thoughts when they are still'. As Neil Gunn wrote to me, 'time and acceptance are not in the nature of philosophic abstractions but realities experienced in Muir's inner being. A poet's essence must also be the essence of his poetry. And in fact the essence is always there, any "lack" being due to the reader's blindness. I am tempted to say more about this, because an intelligent reader may well be blind, until, reading on, he forgets himself, then *sees*, and enters in. I know of no poet of my time, not even Yeats, who so intuitively pierced through human obscurities to this ultimate light.'

This piercing through to the ultimate light was not an abandonment of social concerns in favour of personal salvation. For Muir 'the decay of the idea of man in the fiction of the present century, ... the supersession of the old conception of humanistic man by a new species of natural man ... is bound up with dictatorship, and helped to make it possible'. The poet's best contribution, to the social as well as the personal needs of the time, is to revive a more adequate conception of man and to keep alive imagination.

'A poet's essence must be the essence of his poetry.' Of none is this more plainly true than of Muir. His life and his works are all of a piece. The best of the letters have the same clarity and quiet elegance found in his published prose; all convey something of himself. For his admirers their chief value is simply that we hear again his voice speaking in them.

ACKNOWLEDGEMENTS

I gratefully acknowledge the help of those who have provided me with letters, whether included here or not. The letters included have come from the following sources:

Letters to Professor Aitken, Mrs Mott (daughter); to George Barker, Humanities Research Library, University of Texas at Austin (hereafter referred to as 'Texas'); to Hermann Broch, Yale University Library; to Van Wyck Brooks, University of Pennsylvania Library; to George Mackay Brown, University of Edinburgh Library; to Richard Church, Texas; to John Buchan, Queen's University at Kingston, Ontario; to T. S. Eliot, Mrs T. S. Eliot; to John Lehmann, Texas; to Bettina Linn, Professor Laurence Stapleton, Bryn Mawr College; to H. L. Mencken, New York Public Library; to Willa Muir, item 100 from Mrs Muir (now seems to be lost), others from St Andrews University Library; to Philip O'Connor, New York Public Library, Berg Collection; to David Peat, Mrs Peat (widow); to Kathleen Raine, National Library of Scotland; to Sir Herbert Read, University of Victoria, British Columbia; to Sydney Schiff, British Museum; to Mrs Smallwood, Chatto and Windus; to William Soutar, National Library of Scotland; to Stephen Spender, Texas; to Mr and Mrs George Thorburn, Mrs Ross and Mrs Abenheimer (daughters); to James Whyte, National Library of Scotland; to Professor J. Dover Wilson, National Library of Scotland; to Oscar Williams, Houghton Library, Harvard University; to others, the addressees.

CHRONOLOGY

1887 (May 15) Edwin Muir born in Deerness on the Orkney mainland, son of James Muir, farmer (b. 1833), and Elizabeth *née* Cormack (b. 1843). There were five older children—Jimmie (b. 1876), Willie (b. 1877), Johnnie (b. 1879), Elizabeth (b. 1881) and Clara (b. 1883).

1889 Family moved to the Bu, a hundred-acre farm on the small island of Wyre in Orkney. About five years later moved to another farm in Wyre, Helzigartha.

1895 (or early 1896) Family moved to Garth, a farm four miles from Kirkwall on the Orkney mainland. E.M. went to Kirkwall Grammar School. Friendship with Stanley Cursiter. Family began to break up—the brothers and Elizabeth going away to work in Kirkwall, Edinburgh and Glasgow.

1900 (or early 1901) Farm given up; father, mother, Clara, E.M. moved into Kirkwall. E.M. experienced 'conversion' under influence of revivalist preacher.

Winter 1901-2 Moved to Glasgow, where Jimmie and Johnnie had work, to a flat in the Crosshill area. E.M. worked as clerk in central business area, walking to work through the Gorbals. In September 1902 his father died of a heart attack, and in October 1902 Willie, who had come home ill from his lawyer's office in Edinburgh, died of tuberculosis. E.M. got work for a year as apprentice chauffeur on an estate at Kirkmichael in Ayrshire. Came home to find Johnnie suffering from tumour on the brain, of which he died after much pain in November 1906. In February 1907 his mother died. Loss of religious faith.

1907 Living in lodgings and working in office of beer-bottling factory. Became active socialist—member of Clarion Scouts, later of I.L.P. and of Guild Socialist Movement.

About 1909 Began to read *The New Age*, of which A. R. Orage had become editor; and to read Nietzsche in Oscar Levy's translation.

1912–14 Clerk at bone factory at Greenock, lodging at Gourock. Friendship with David Peat, and with Bob and Ned Scouller, with whom he formed branch of National Union of Clerks. Began in 1913 to contribute to *The New Age*—immature verse and a dialogue on 'The Epigram'.

1914 Returned to lodgings in Glasgow and to work in shipbuilding office in Renfrew. Rejected for Army. Active in Glasgow branch of National Guilds League.

1916 Began to contribute 'We moderns' (epigrams) to *New Age*. Friendship with Francis George Scott and with Denis Saurat.

1918 *We Moderns* published under pseudonym 'Edward Moore'. An American edition, with introduction by H. L. Mencken, was published in 1920. Meeting with Willa Anderson. Beginning of friendship with John Holms.

1919 (June) Married Willa Anderson. Moved in September to London. After short time in office became assistant to Orage on *New Age*; wrote drama criticisms for *The Scotsman* and reviews for *The Athenaeum*, edited by Middleton Murry.

1920 Course of psycho-analysis under Maurice Nicholl; dreams and waking visions recorded.

1921 Began to contribute to the American *Freeman*, to which he was introduced by Mencken and of which Van Wyck Brooks was literary editor. Prospect of regular income from *Freeman* enabled Muirs to leave London in August for Prague via Germany. In Prague until following March; friendship with Karel Čapek.

1922 (March) Moved to Dresden, and then to nearby Hellerau, where W.M. worked in school run by A. S. Neill. Began to write poetry.

1923 (May) Moved to Forte dei Marmi, where they shared house with John and Dorothy Holms. (August) E.M. to Salzburg Music Festival, joining F. G. Scott. (September) E. and W.M. to Lucca. (October) To Salzburg. (December) To Vienna.

1924 (March) *Freeman* ceased publication. Moved to Sonntagberg near Rosenau, where Neill's school had moved. Began to make living by translating from German—plays by Gerhart Hauptmann. Writing *Chorus of the Newly Dead*. (July) Back to Britain. After brief stay with Sydney Schiff, went to W.M.'s home town, Montrose, where they got to know C. M. Grieve, who was working on the local paper. Reviewing for *The Nation and the Athenaeum* (until 1928). *Latitudes* published.

1925 (January) To Penn, Buckinghamshire, close to the Schiffs. (October) Back to Montrose. W.M. had miscarriage.
First Poems published.

1926 (March) To St Tropez. Writing *The Marionette* and translating *Jüd Süss*. (October) To Menton.
Chorus of the Newly Dead and *Transition* published.

1927 (May) Returned to England. Took house at Lingfield, Surrey. (October) Son Gavin born.
The Marionette published.

1928 Until 1933 ceased regular reviewing; but continued with much translating. *The Structure of the Novel* published.

1929 Moved to Crowborough, Sussex.
Began translating Kafka.
John Knox published.

1931 Began translating Broch.
The Three Brothers published.

1932 (May) Went to PEN Conference in Budapest. Meeting with Broch in Vienna. (December) Moved to Hampstead.
Six Poems and *Poor Tom* published.

1933 (January) Began regular novel reviewing for *The Listener* (continued until 1945). (May) Went to PEN Conference at Dubrovnik. (August) Gavin's leg broken in accident. (September) Holiday in Orkney.

1934 (Summer) Went to PEN Conference in Edinburgh; then went on journey through Scotland recorded in *Scottish Journey*, ending in stay in Orkney, where Muirs thought of settling.
Variations on a Time Theme published.

1935 (August) Move to St Andrews.
Scottish Journey and *Social Credit and the Labour Party* published.

1936	Devised St Andrew's Day programme for BBC (1936–45—considerable number of talks and other programmes for BBC). *Scott and Scotland* published.
1937	*Journeys and Places* published.
1938	Beginning of friendship with Professor Alec Aitken. Broch came to stay.
1939	(March) During illness of W.M., experience of reciting Lord's Prayer, realisation of Christian faith. *The Present Age* published.
1940	Financial difficulties; no demand for German translations; attempts to get teaching post. Member of Home Guard. (Autumn) Went to work as clerk in Food Office in Dundee. *The Story and the Fable* published.
1941	(Spring) Ill—heart strain; had to give up job at Food Office and rest completely for six weeks. Later in the year W.M. dangerously ill; underwent operation in January 1942; slow recovery.
1942	(March) Got work with British Council in Edinburgh, organising programmes for International Houses. Family moved to Edinburgh in summer.
1943	*The Narrow Place* published.
1945	Went to Prague to be Director of the British Council Institute.
1946	*The Voyage* published.
1947	Received Honorary Doctorates from Universities of Prague and Edinburgh.
1948	(February) Communist take-over in Czechoslovakia. (July) Returned to Britain. Nervous break down.
1949	(January) Went to Rome to be Director of the British Council Institute. *The Labyrinth* and *Essays on Literature and Society* published.
1950	(July) Returned to Scotland to be Warden of Newbattle Abbey College at Dalkeith.
1952	*Collected Poems 1921–1951* published.
1953	Awarded C.B.E.

1954 Increasing worry over Newbattle; pains in chest. *An Autobiography* published.

1955 (Summer)   Went to Harvard to be Charles Eliot Norton Professor. His lectures were published in 1962 as *The Estate of Poetry*.

1956 (May)   Returned to Britain; found house at Swaffham Prior near Cambridge; visited Orkney to gather material for a BBC programme; settled at Swaffham Prior.
Awarded grant for three years by the Bollingen Foundation to write a book on Ballads.
One Foot in Eden published.

1957 Russell Loines Award for Poetry from American Academy of Arts and Letters.

1958 (February–March)   Went to Bristol University as visiting professor. (June) Received Honorary Doctorate from Cambridge University. Ill—water on the lung.

1959 (3 January)   Died.

I: TO JEAN LEITCH

> c/o Blair
> 7 Granville Street
> Glasgow
> 24 March, 1919

Dear Jean,

I received your letter this morning, and it made me ashamed, for it made me realise how unworthy I am of you; and it made me sad when I realised that I will not see much of you on this earth, though I will think much of you. Yes, that is very sad, Jean, for you are the noblest soul I have ever known, and inexpressibly dear to me because of that and because you were unconscious of it. I have no fear for you in the troubles of this life, for I know a soul as innocent as yours cannot suffer wrong; you have a charm, dear Jean, that will preserve you always, not from suffering, for that is the lot of all of us, but from the suffering of those who sin against what is highest in them. When I read your letter this morning I was kneeling in spirit at your feet with a reverence as great as I have ever felt. You will let me say this, now that we are not to see each other? Had I been meeting you I might have been ashamed to say it (and what a petty quality that is in me!), but now that I am not to meet you, my lips are unsealed. You know the story of the great Italian poet, Dante, and his Beatrice? He only saw her once or twice during his life, and I don't know whether he ever spoke to her; but all his life she inspired him and he speaks of her in the accents of the most exalted love. Is that not beautiful? You have made me understand it. Jean, I, too, am afraid. We inspire each other and become transported to a higher world, a world where our poor wings are not strong enough to keep us poised; and yet it hurts us to be dashed down to the earth again. I, as well as you, cannot bear that that should happen. I must think of you and myself as we were in the moments when we did dwell in that higher world: I *do* think and have always thought of you in that way, Jean. It has often seemed to me that love such as ours can never reach its true expression in marriage, but only in

---

1 Jean Leitch had been a friend of Muir's for several years. Realising that they were not suited to be more than friends they had parted soon after the end of the War, but had recently met by chance at a dance, where he told her of his plans to go to London. They had arranged to meet again, but she wrote cancelling the engagement. This was his answer.

high dreams and in some act of great renunciation whenever the one needed the other. Jean, if you are ever in trouble, let me know: I beg it as a pledge of the trust you put in me. I, also, promise, and I shall not lose touch with you. Though I will not see you, except when Fate decides so, I shall love to think you are living and breathing in such and such a human habitation. I hope I have not made you sad by my letter, dear Jean. It was sweet to meet you at that dance: it is sweet to know that you will be thinking of me, and that I will be thinking of you, and that we understand. May Fate give you what you deserve, dear Jean.

Yours always
Edwin

2: TO H. L. MENCKEN

c/o *Thorburn*
5 Jardine Street
Kelvinbridge
Glasgow
13 July 1919

Dear Sir,

Dr Levy has written me saying that you were very pleased with my little book *We Moderns*, and that you were trying to find a publisher for it in America. He added that you might yourself 'introduce' it. I am more grateful than I can say for this generosity. The recommendation by yourself would give it a welcome which without that I am afraid it would have little chance of receiving. So far

---

2 *H. L. Mencken (1880–1956), journalist, editor, critic, was at that time one of the most influential men of letters in America. Verse by Muir began to appear in* The New Age *in 1913. 'We Moderns', aphorisms in the manner of Nietzsche, by 'Edward Moore' appeared in* The New Age *about fortnightly from November 1916 to September 1917, and were then published in England as a book, still pseudonymously, in 1918. Thanks to Mencken's influence* We Moderns *was published in America, under Muir's own name and with a preface by Mencken, in 1920. Dr Oscar Levy was editor of the complete English edition of Nietzsche's works (1909–12). A. R. Orage (1873–1934) was editor of* The New Age *from 1907 to 1922. For G. K. Chesterton on* We Moderns *see his* Fancies versus Fads *(Methuen 1923) pp. 117–23.* Expository Times *Vol. XXIX (August 1918) pp 485–6 discusses Muir's ideas on original sin.*

about 550 of the English edition have been sold, and although both Dr Levy and Orage have told me to my surprise that this is a good sale for the particular kind of book, I own to a decided disappointment with it. I thought the public whom I wished particularly to reach was a little bigger than that. Very likely it is smaller! I've come to the conclusion from a knowledge of some of the readers I've heard of! Do you know if the intellectual atmosphere of America is any freer than that of this country? I am not thinking of sales at all, but I am hoping that it is.

Dr Levy said that you had been making some enquiries about my age, my occupation and so on. If you don't mind, I'll just reply to them myself. I've just newly reached my 32nd birthday, and I was 28–29 when I wrote *We Moderns*. From the very moment when I first became acquainted with Nietzsche (when I was about 22) I have been more attracted to him than to any other writer. He has *spoken* to me as no one else has. I suppose everyone who has understood Nietzsche in any degree at all must have felt that. The kind of life I had lived before I met him also pre-disposed me, I have no doubt, to listen. I was born up in the Orkney islands in the north of Scotland, where my father was a small crofter. We all came to Glasgow when I was 14; my brothers, who were older than me, went into warehouses and I was sent into an office. Within four years, my father and mother and two brothers were dead, and I was left to fend for myself. Very bad health supervened for a while, and it was when I was emerging from it that Nietzsche came my way. He discovered a number of things for me. I began to write in my spare time. I sent some bad verse to *The New Age* which was unfortunately published with the result that it was not until I was 28 that I began to find a provisional medium of expression, and launched out in *We Moderns*. I'm still in an office, and my occupation gives me a little leisure and the freedom to write what I like. A little while ago I made an attempt to get into journalism, but there appears to be no place there for me in this country, and such places as I did see were not more enticing than an office. May I ask if there is a greater opportunity in America for original work in the journals and reviews? Do you think my work would be accepted if I sent it to some of the American reviews? I am certainly going to make an attempt to dispense with my clerical work, for it is, from my point of view, a sheer waste of time if I can make a living by writing. If you would be so kind as to give me your candid opinion of the literary market in America—and especially what can be made by writing for the better journals—I should be much obliged.

I've been so grateful for the kind reception you have given my book, and for your enquiries, that I find I've told you much more than I intended! It has been my rule since the beginning, and I intend it still to be so, to make my work stand on its own feet, and not to let *the public* know that it was written by tinker, tailor, soldier, clerk or anything else. There is too much of that, I feel, and I should very much dislike to have any of my private interests made public.

Thanks once more for the interest you have taken in *We Moderns*. I've been rather fortunate in the matter of appreciation if not in the largeness of my public. Dr Levy has been most generous in his encouragement from the very beginning, and Orage, although, naturally, his views are not at all similar to mine, has been very appreciative. The praise I've got in reviews has been rather peculiar. G.K.C. has rather broad-mindedly blessed the book, and I had my biggest and one of my best notices in *The Expository Times* a Christian monthly!

Yours sincerely,
Edwin Muir

3: TO MR AND MRS GEORGE THORBURN

chez Mme Mala
20 Nubřeži Legii
Smichov
Prague
8 February [*1922*]

Dear Lizzie and George,

... In spite of more expense than we expected both Minnie and myself are very glad we left Britain, life here is a hundred times more pleasant; there is not the constant atmosphere of calamity and anxiety which there is in London or Glasgow; and the continental peoples seem to have such a knack for making everything pretty

3 Muir's sister Elizabeth was married to George Thorburn, a house painter in Glasgow. Freeman: *an American weekly of high quality, to which, on H. L. Mencken's recommendation, Muir had begun to contribute in 1920. It was the prospect of a regular income from it that enabled the Muirs to leave London for Prague in the summer of 1921. A selection of Muir's* Freeman *essays was published in* Latitudes *(1924)*. Minnie: *Mrs Muir*.

that one is constantly being delighted or surprised as one walks down the streets. Even in Germany, where things are supposed to be so bad, I was absolutely astonished at the difference between Berlin and London. In Berlin there was a feeling of cheerfulness, of comfort, of contentment, especially of hope for the future, that came like a breath of fresh air after London. We sailed from Leith on the 31st August last, arrived in Hamburg two days later, took train to Berlin, stayed there the night, and came straight down to Prague, through Dresden, next day. Germany as I saw it from the train is the most clean, neat, orderly and efficient nation that one could imagine. Everything looks as if a hose had just been turned upon it: there are the most delightful little villages, and, especially in the South between Dresden and the borders of Czechoslovakia, the scenery is very romantic and beautiful. It was a lovely autumn afternoon when we saw it first from the train, which ran along the banks of the Elbe, by this time quite a small river, for two or three hours. Czechoslovakia (the old Bohemia) is also beautiful in the north, but incredibly dry and dusty; the train, which in Germany seemed to be running on a vacuum-cleaned carpet, immediately began to raise whirlwinds of dust as soon as it got into Czechoslovakia. But Prague is a very clean town, and of course a very beautiful one. Its situation is somewhat like Edinburgh's, with a castle on the top of a rock standing by itself; only where the Princes Street Gardens are in Edinburgh there is a fine river in Prague, the Vltava crossed by about a dozen of stylish bridges, one very old one dating from the 14th century. All round the Castle, or the Hrad, (which is the Czech name for castle) there are old palaces and monasteries and churches so thick and so close together that one can hardly count them. Some of them are now being used as Government offices of the Republic, others have been turned into dwellings for the people; the ground floor of some of them are now restaurants. All this part of the town is called the Mala Strana (literally, small side). Opposite it, on the other side of the river, is the Stara Město (old town) which is also very charming, full of Renaissance houses, in the Baroque style. The rest of the town is comparatively modern; but the buildings have far more style than they would have in Britain, are more solid and very conscientiously finished. The air in the town is as a rule very dry and stimulating; in summer very hot, and in winter very cold. To show how cold it is—the river has been frozen over for two months and the ice is about a foot thick. But you do not feel the cold as much as in Britain: the air is so much drier.

The theatres are a revelation, though I cannot make much of the language yet. At present they are producing works of Shakespeare, Molière, Alfieri, Goethe, Calderon, Marlowe, Synge, Yeats, Wilde, Ibsen, Chekov, and a host of others. In addition to this there is opera. And the town of Prague is about half the size of Glasgow! Then there are orchestral and other concerts practically every night in the week, all of them cheap.

I have not been working so hard as I did in London; but I have just about finished a series of articles for the American *Freeman* which I hope to get published there—the editor says he will try and arrange it. Then I am trying to concoct a book of lyrical philosophy to contain partly narrative, partly aphorisms and partly poetry. How it will work out I don't know. Both Minnie and I have been much better in health than we were in London. . . .

Yours affectionately,
Edwin

4: TO MR AND MRS THORBURN

bei Frau Dr Neustätter
Hellerau
Dresden
Germany
15 December 1922

Dear Lizzie and George,

I hope you'll forgive me for being so long in writing. I am as bad at doing so as ever, and have scarcely sent a line to Britain, except to *The New Age* since I left it. The thought of Xmas is making me take up my pen again, and a little home-sickness which comes over me now and then. I like Germany and the Germans very well; they're very kind and very simple people; but for one brought up in Scotland there is no place like Scotland, and I've become intensely sentimental about that country at intervals ever since I left it.

We've been in Dresden now since the beginning of April. It is

4 poetry. 'Re-Birth' and 'Ballad of Eternal Life' (later much revised, and re-named 'Ballad of the Soul') appeared in The New Age *in June and July 1921.*

a very pretty, but a very bourgeois town; there is a fine art Gallery, with a fine collection of Rubens and Rembrandts, an opera house which was at one time the finest in Germany, and which is still very good; a state theatre where the acting is intensely bad; any number of concerts, and cabarets which are really pleasant and unoffensive, and where the Germans, for a sum a little less than a penny, can sit of an evening drinking schnapps and listening to singers of comic songs, who are amazingly like the English ones. We live at Hellerau, a little village about two miles away from Dresden, set on the edge of a pine forest which stretches away for seven miles. The central interest of the village is an Eurhythmics School for teaching dancing, in which there are girls from all the nations in Europe, Germany, Sweden, Russia, Finland, Hungary, Czechoslovakia, Yugoslavia, Bulgaria and Belgium. There is connected with it, a 'free-school' for children, run by A. S. Neill, the author of *The Dominie's Log*, in which Minnie now teaches for a few hours a day. There are naturally, with this atmosphere, the usual complement of Communists, vegetarians, simple-lifers and so on. Among the youth of Germany there is a very strong movement called the Warder Vogel (Warder Birds) of young people who live as simply as possible, go walking in bands every week-end in the woods, singing old German songs, and sleeping at nights under the trees. They are of all ages from 14 to 20; they are out against their parents' authority and do as they please; but, unfortunately they are a bit too serious, regard smoking, drinking, the cinema and fox-trotting as inventions of the devil. Nevertheless, they are promising as a protest against the Germans' terrific respect for the law. In Germany in summer you will see public roads lined with cherry trees hanging with cherries, (the property of the State), and though there are any number of children about, these cherries are not picked. There is something rather fine about that, though to the Scotch it seems more than human.

Living is in most respects terrifically cheap in Germany; except for such things as clothes, boots, and now, books, which are almost as dear as they are in England. A pint of beer is less than a penny; I get good Virginia cigarettes, better than 'Gold Flake' for 12 a penny; you can have good Rhein Wine for about 3*d* a bottle—it costs about 5/- in England. Our bill last month for our rooms and all our food was for the two of us less than £3, and we lived fairly well. The people in general, however, are much poorer than the English papers make one think. The working class is relatively well off, on account of the strength of their unions, but the middle class is very hard put to it to keep a roof over their heads and feed themselves. There is a general bitterness against the Versailles Treaty and the French, who are hated, but a disposition to be friendly to the English who, for some reason, are rather liked. I've met a lot of interesting Germans, have made some progress in German, and read a good deal of German poetry. Minnie speaks the language almost like a native.

I've been writing a lot of poetry again, two samples of which you might have seen in *The New Age*. I have collected 12 of my poems, three in Scotch, and have sent them to Heinemann in London for publication, but have received no reply yet. I am in negotiation for the publication of a volume of essays in America (they have appeared already in the American *Freeman*, a very good journal) and I am preparing a volume of aphorisms which I intend to try my luck with in London in the next few weeks. If any or all of these projects come off, I may reap a little fame from them, especially the poems, which are easily the best things I have yet written.

I was glad to see that the Labour Party had such a haul in Glasgow, and that the personel was so promising. Things must be pretty bad, with so much unemployment. I hope you have managed to ride the storm successfully. How are the children? I'm enclosing a small cheque for £2 for their Xmas....

Yours affectionately,
Edwin

5: TO VAN WYCK BROOKS

Hellerau
18 December, 1922

My dear Van Wyck Brooks,

... I'm very glad to recognise your pen in *The Freeman* again after an absence of some months. The temper of your work, for the task you have, I take it, in hand—the bringing of America culturally to her senses—is, I think, absolutely right. Such criticism as yours is more living than any one can find in England, because you have an end for America, and work towards it: whereas in England the critic

---

5 *Van Wyck Brooks (1886–1963), American literary critic, was literary editor of* The Freeman, *and Alfred Jay Nock was one of the editors.*

has no general end, under the impression, mistaken it seems to me, that nothing, for culture in general, remains in that country to be done. This state of things (I mean in my country) is due almost certainly to the fact that the English critics are a class who, beneath their reading and equipment, have the prejudice of the English man in the street that culture does not matter. The English critics cannot see culture for the books, or rather for the one book or one writer they are immediately concerned with, and while certainly they deal very competently sometimes with their immediate subject, this lack of a general conception is a bad fault in them—having something profoundly to do with English indomitable self-satisfaction. But at any rate I am far enough away from it here no longer to be acutely hurt by it. Your criticism—I think you can have no idea how refreshing it is in comparison.

I am continuing to write, as you advised, for *The Freeman*, and Mr Nock has been so good as to tell me that he likes my work very much. I am going to send in a few days a further set of aphorisms and an essay on a young, almost unknown, Scottish writer, George Douglas, who died some years ago, after having written about the best novel of the last fifty years, *The House with the Green Shutters*....

Yours sincerely
Edwin Muir

6: TO VAN WYCK BROOKS

Hellerau
18 April, 1923

My dear Van Wyck Brooks,

... I have in my mind at present an essay on the assault in modern literature on the humanistic tradition: I mean the new savagery, shallow but powerful, in the works of such people as Kipling, Lawrence, O'Neill, the German Expressionists and so forth, which I shall try to appraise from the standpoint of its human validity, that is, from the standpoint of humanism. All this I should like to show not as the appearance of something new but as the disappearance, the defeat, of something immemorial: therefore a

6 '*The Assault on Humanism*' *appeared in* The Freeman *on 27 June. Brooks did not welcome the suggestion of a very long article on Hölderlin, but accepted a short one which Muir sent in June.*

weakness, and a weakening of the grasp which the total humanity of the world has upon itself. I have also in mind the notion of writing about the German poet, Hölderlin, who, neglected for a century, has had in the last five years in Germany a sort of renaissance which he entirely deserves. Although you are rather against long articles I should like to do this at some length, perhaps at such length that it could appear as two successive articles in *The Freeman*. Hölderlin's ideas are such as, apprehended to-day, would be fruitful, and make for that realisation of the spirit of humanism for which all of us are working. Can I possibly quote him in German? I should of course append translations, too, preferably in prose. I have also other ideas, and if the present volume is published, I already see another lengthening before me....

Yours very sincerely
Edwin Muir

7: TO VAN WYCK BROOKS

Casa Pellizze
Forte dei Marmi
(Lucca)
Italy
21 September, 1923

Dear Van Wyck Brooks,

... I am agitated at present by the old problem—really a practical one, it seems to me—of the romantic and the classical.... At any rate my next volume will be about Romanticism;[7] and I only discovered that the other week, when I suddenly realised that all the authors I have been writing about for you in the last few months have been romantics, and that those I shall think of writing about are also romantics. These will go into the volume, along with my conception of Romanticism. I equate it more or less with the entire modern way of regarding the world. The classical writer, it seems to me, is the man who sees life in this world simply and completely as in this world. The Romantic is the man who sees life against a background which one may call variously infinite possibility, heaven or the future. It is a new way of regarding the world to which mankind

7 Essays on 'The Meaning of Romanticism' appeared in three numbers of The Freeman *in December 1923 and January 1924.*

is not yet adapted; a struggle to break through into a new sphere of life. From its incompleteness, for it is not yet come to its full development, as Classicism has long ago, springs all that is weakly, sickly and neurotic in it. But I believe, on the other hand, that it is capable of coming to its perfection: that the sickliness, etc., are not essential and eternal attributes of it. Being more incomplete and not adapted, it is more dangerous for those who essay it than classicism; and that is why almost all the great romantics either died young or became sentimental in self-defence. It is the reason also why Goethe turned at last to classicism. The real symbol, in no religious or ascetic sense, of Romanticism, seems to me to be Christ. The force which threw him up threw up also the whole imperfect system of life which we call romantic. But he was only a part of it; one among many romantics. I hope this hasty generalisation will not appear wild to you; I cannot put in all the steps which would make it more convincing. But with this thesis I will begin my volume; and I hope, if you think well of it, that it may appear in *The Freeman*. But I have still to consider the matter for a while, and I will first send you essays on other things.

We leave this place now in almost a week's time, and we shall go first, I think, to Salzburg, which in autumn should be very auspicious for working....

With kindest regards

Yours sincerely
Edwin Muir

8: TO MR AND MRS THORBURN

bei Frau Antner
7 Hahngasse
Wien IX
Austria
20 December 1923

Dear Lizzie and George,

... How are you all getting on? Write and let us know whenever you have time. The Scottish election results, combined with the recent temper of the Glasgow group in Parliament, gave us quite a

8 The Scottish Nation: *a weekly, issued by Grieve from Montrose from 8 May to 23 December 1923. Ethel and Irene: the Thorburns' daughters, later Mrs Ross and Mrs Abenheimer.*

thrill. Things have changed enormously since I lived in Glasgow, only a little over five years ago (It seems far longer). The Scottish members should make a move for Scottish Home Rule, and then they would have the field to themselves. Do you know if that idea has taken hold of the Socialist parties in Glasgow or not? There's a man C. M. Grieve, a Socialist, running the idea in *The Scottish Nation*—a very bad paper which I sometimes see. When I see things stirring up so much I would like to be back to take a hand in the work. We will certainly (DV.) be back in Scotland to stay next summer. We'll try to get a small cottage in the Pentlands, not far from Edinburgh, and when we're there you must come for a while and see us.

... Here in Vienna there are lots of literary circles that we're beginning to know. We've met Louis Untermeyer, the American poet, a very nice man, and a chap of the name of Pierre Loving, also an American, a student of dramatic art. We hope shortly to meet Schnitzler, and perhaps Hugo von Hofmannsthal, and it is possible that we may get free seats for the opera and the various theatres. Minnie speaks German now as if she had been born to it, but I speak it much worse, although I can converse, and understand easily everything that is said. ...

Good luck to you all. Perhaps in a few years Scotland will be a Socialist republic. I shouldn't wonder: things are moving so fast. A happy Christmas and a Guid New Year from us both, and don't forget to include Ethel and Irene. Give the same to Clara and Jimmie, too, when you see them, and tell them we're doing quite well. Love from us both

Yours affectionately,
Edwin

9: TO VAN WYCK BROOKS

bei Frau Hauser
28 Schlösselgasse
Wien VIII
28 January, 1924

My dear Van Wyck Brooks,

... The books have come; and many thanks for them; and for the others which you promise. I think that in this lot Huxley's book alone calls for extended notice. It is fundamentally a very bad book very brilliantly done; no health from beginning to end: a very sad business; but I shall try to be fair. I enclose an essay on Thomas Hardy which I do hope you will like. It strikes me as being much better than the articles on Romanticism which I feel at present are horribly unsatisfactory. I was very glad you liked the dialogue, and I have in mind at present a half dozen or so which I shall execute as I find time.

It was very interesting to hear that you had met Orage. I was for about a year and a half his assistant on *The New Age*, but although I have the greatest regard and liking for him, I have never been able to sympathise very much with the wild goose chases he periodically goes away upon. I'm afraid that in another few years it will be something else than Gurdyeff's [sic] Institute that will be saving the world for him. He is a queer mixture of the most admirable good sense and a bizarre lack of judgment. As a man I have the utmost admiration for him: and that, after all, is the chief thing. He has had a struggle for many years against odds, and he has maintained his integrity. One must take a thing here and there from him; but I have had to be careful all the time I have known him not to take too much. I know very little about the Gurdyeff School, except what my instinct tells me, and I distrust deeply everything of the kind. Orage is really much too big a man to be drawn into a circle of

9 Huxley's book: presumably Antic Hay. *Hardy: an essay 'Novels of Mr Hardy' appeared in June in the* Evening Post Literary Review *(New York). The dialogue: 'Edwin Muir and Francis George Scott: A Conversation,' published in* The Freeman *on 19 December 1923. Orage: after giving up the editorship of* The New Age *in 1922 had spent over a year at Gurdjieff's institute at Fontainebleau before going to America, where he lectured on Gurdjieff's system.*

cranks like that; but the fact is that he has often been drawn in. It is his particular weakness.

I gave your regards to Louis Untermeyer, who asks me to say that you have always his, and now doubly so, in the sending of them. I like him very much: he is one of my acquisitions since I came here, and one of the best and most likeable people I have ever met. Excuse this garrulousness.

Yours sincerely
Edwin Muir

10: TO VAN WYCK BROOKS

Wien
13 February 1924

Dear Van Wyck Brooks,

Many thanks indeed for your splendid letter. Although it was written the day before the type-written notice announcing the cessation of *The Freeman* it has not arrived until this morning. My last letter was in reply to the notice, but I must write again in reply to this, to say how much I appreciate your kindness and how much I prize the friendship which through our correspondence we have struck up. I hope we shall not lose sight of each other, though whether I shall ever be in America is a question I cannot answer to myself. It would be an immensely interesting experience (perhaps the most interesting that remains for a European) and, fortified by what I have read in *The Freeman* I do not think I should be disillusioned, at any rate America seems to me to be a terribly hard place for a writer to live, but at the same time a distinctly inspiring one after England, which is a mere standing pool. I think your American writers have more to them, more *character*, than the English (I mean the present day English), though the English have normally more everyday wisdom, and are more instinctively and readily on the spot before all sorts of things. But no, they are not so interesting as your countrymen are. Forgive me for rushing off and on like this. You say that if I were in America I would probably have a fine position. That interests me very much; and it is infinitely

10 In his previous letter about the cessation of The Freeman *he wrote that three-quarters or more of his income had been derived from it, and asked for advice about getting work.*

kind of you to tell me so. The difficulty is that I could only risk staying in America if I had a job: I would find it impossible on a freelance basis; and I have no idea how jobs in America, on reviews and so on, are to be procured. I should like to stay in America for a few years: I should like to have a steady job for a few years, until some more poetry and my novel have time to get finished; but I don't know how such things are done, though I should love to do them.

I do sincerely hope that the cessation of *The Freeman* will not strike you a very heavy blow pecuniarily; we are all struck pretty hard, I take it, in our feelings, and in our hopes for the growth of culture and humanity, by its cessation. For myself I had a sort of personal feeling for it, and its disappearance is like the disappearance of a friend. I am sorry if, in the first shock last week, I wrote too much about myself. Immediate anxiety is always selfish, but I am once more reasonable and hopeful; and I cordially hope that all my colleagues, whose work I enjoyed reading so much every week, will have the best of fortune....

But I can't quite believe yet that *The Freeman* is going to cease. A miracle, or a gift of unknown gold is bound to come before the best review in America or England is allowed to die. For it is easily the best. At least we must hope until the last moment.

With every kind of good wish
Yours ever sincerely
Edwin Muir

PS It occurs to me, though I almost blush to mention it, that perhaps I might lecture my way into America. I am not a good speaker, but on the other hand, I am not strikingly bad. In my youth I used to do quite a lot of speaking for Socialist Parties. But really I disapprove of the whole lecturing blight, except as a last resort; and it may well be that Americans (even those who go to lectures) are now sick of going. It might be fun, however!

11: TO SYDNEY SCHIFF

>Internationale Schule,
>Sonntagberg,
>Rosenau,
>bei Amstetten,
>Austria
>7 May, 1924

Dear Stephen Hudson,

Thanks more than I can say for your letters and *Richard Kurt*. I had intended to write you further about *Tony* but when *Richard Kurt* arrived I thought I would read it first, half expecting it would alter the more critical part of my note upon *Tony*. And it has done so; and on a further reading I wish to retract what I said in the way of perfectly sincere fault finding. And I want to express again my admiration for what you attempted—successfully—in that book: your revelation with such a subtle simplicity of Richard's character as seen by Tony, of Tony himself, and of the paradoxical but human relation between the two. As for *Richard Kurt* it seems to me to be the most mixed in quality of all your books. There are very fine things in it: your portrait of Elinor (with her you are magnificent in the three books she appears in), and your portrait of Virginia, which, being more subtle, (the character demanded it) is still more a tribute to your art. The first, describing the later, more enigmatic relations between Richard and her have a wonderful skill, and always a kind of skill which acts itself singly to serve the truth. As a whole—I am

> 11 Muir attracted the attention of Sydney Schiff *(1868–1944; wrote as 'Stephen Hudson')* by a review in The Freeman *(5 March 1924)* of his novel Prince Hempseed. *Knowing nothing of Schiff he hailed him as 'this promising young writer.' The elderly and quite well-known Schiff, amused by this and pleased by the penetration of the review, wrote thanking Muir for it, sending his* Elinor Colhouse *(1921)* and Tony *(1924) and asking for criticisms of them. Muir answered on 15 April; and Schiff, having now read* We Moderns, *sent more letters and his earlier novel* Richard Kurt *(1919). A wealthy man Schiff wanted to help the Muirs by providing them with a bungalow near his home at Chesham in Buckinghamshire; but, wanting to go to Scotland and to avoid accepting patronage, they at this stage declined. When later they did go to live near Chesham they paid their own way.* Lavrin: *(1887–); Professor of Slavonic Languages at Nottingham University 1923–53, author of many books on Russian literature; a friend of the Muirs since their London days.*

sure that you know this yourself best of all—the book is much more unsure and much less economical than those which you have written since. One of the things which struck me first of all in *Prince Hempseed* was the success with which you seized upon the essential—I do not mean the expected, on the contrary; but at any rate on the thing which one at once recognised to be important. This gift, which is a sort of just intuition, you have in an unusual, a distinguished, degree; it must be, I can only think, the quality of an unusually understanding mind. In addition to it I was struck by your economy: a sort of round treatment of the episodes, and then a bee-line to the next. Economy, I wish I had it. These things I admired enormously in *Prince Hempseed*, and I admired them also in *Elinor Colhouse* and *Tony*; and it is in these that I think you have made such splendid progress since *Richard Kurt*. But in the matter of style—but all this you are bound to know—your development has been as clear. No very distinct idiom, or at any rate an imperfect one, comes to me through the writing of *Richard Kurt*; but your idiom is unmistakable in *Prince Hempseed* and *Tony*, and an idiom is something, I fancy, that one cannot lose, once it has been found. As mere writing, these two books delighted me. *Richard Kurt* did not; but all the same it has the qualities which since you have refined and pruned until now they shine with their own light. But by its truth and seriousness the book is a significant one, and one which has moved me deeply. Thanks once more for sending it: unfortunately all I can do in return for an artistic experience, is to send you my opinion.

What can I say in reply to the many kind things you say about *We Moderns*. I know that there is some merit in it; but I feel more and more that it is in the last degree raw, immature, and an expression of a lamentable bad-taste. Thank you for pressing through all this—forbidding enough—to whatever is good in it. And in the English edition you will have a further shock; you will find an appendix of ill-natured couplets full of bumptious conceit, written I really cannot tell why, because I am not ill-natured, and have no ill-will, so far as I know, for anyone alive. Probably it was my profound unhappiness of that time coming out in this queer way; for I did not sting to wound, but I almost believe, like the scorpion in a kind of desperation, when he feels himself in a circle of fire. My life had been a continuous enemy of my inner development. At 14 I had had to begin work in a commercial office—hours 9 to 6; at 18 I was thrown upon the world to live on the 14/– a week that I earned at the cost of ill-health and psychological misery: and I am still a little surprised to this hour that all this time I read, learned to love music, and being a Scotsman, speculation, without knowing for years a single person to whom I could speak of these things. I had had fourteen years of this when I wrote *We Moderns*, and though towards the end of that time I had come to know, even in Glasgow, some people who were in my own case and who had some of the joy of life, I was all that time at continual variance with the work which from 9 to 6 each day was my only conceivable fate. Fortunately a year later I met my wife, but for whom I might still be in that melancholy circle. She shook me out of my unavailing struggle, and gave me courage to come down to London and tempt fate, on, I think between us, £13. Life became far better for me (although she had to make a good many willing sacrifices): but in London, too, we found that to live, we could only write things which kept us from our work; dramatic criticism, reviewing for certain papers and so on. So, in 1919 [actually 1921], acting on the advice of Janko Lavrin, we threw everything up and went to Prague. And that accounts for the reason why I am in Austria, now. We stayed in Prague for a little, then we went to Dresden, where we were more happy than we had ever been before; then we were in Italy for six months and now we are in Austria. This has meant for me leisure for the first time in fifteen years, and I have not yet exhausted all the fruits of it. We do not teach in the school here, which is run by a delightful Scotsman, a friend of my wife. We are boarders and friends of the dominie, to whom we are very attached. And Sonntagberg is in a very beautiful position, at the beginning of the Austrian Alps.

I have been caught into this rigmarole of reminiscence by a desire to account for what you may not like in *We Moderns*. I think you will like *Latitudes* better; at any rate it is better written and has more cohesiveness. But I feel that not yet have I found satisfying expression in prose. You ask what my literary plans are. Most definite is another volume of essays, a good few of which are already written: I think better than anything I've yet done. That, at any rate, I know I can do. Then there is the novel I mentioned; whether it will be a success is still a mystery to me. The idea is not so bad, but it requires more skill than I've been able to acquire yet. I am going to call it *Saturday*: and my subject is, in fact, that day, which in an industrial place like Glasgow, and to the bulk of the people in the

British Isles, has an atmosphere quite different from that of every other day. I am going to try and render this atmosphere, suggesting as a background the other working days in the week. The feeling of pathetic freedom which workmen have on the day when they stop work at 12 instead of 6 I know well, for I have felt it myself. There will be a central figure: and in him will be worked out the gradual disintegration of the day as it is consumed: the hope of the morning, the freshness of the afternoon after work, and then the gradual loosening and demoralisation of the evening, the slipping of happiness through one's fingers. To finish it, I shall have a chapter, being the reflection and judgment of the chief figure on the day, an extract from his diary. The story should be about 50,000 words; quite short; and I have half of it already written in rough draft; but I know it will all have to be written again and differently. The idea is good, and sooner or later I hope to cope with it.

I have this in mind, and I have also an idea for a poem, which I shall call *Chorus of the Newly Dead* (a good deal of it is written). I wished to get a certain pathos of distance in contemplating human life and I found this the most unconditional way. In this 'chorus' there will be types like the Saint, the Beggar, the Idiot, the Hero, the Mother, the Rebel, the Poet, the Coward, and they will all give some account of their lives as they see it from eternity, not in Heaven or in Hell, but in a dubious place where the bewilderment of the change has not been lost. There will also be choruses for all the newly dead in which some kind of transcendental judgment will be passed on these recitals as they arise. The atmosphere I am aiming at is one of mystery and wonder at the life of the earth. There will be no dogmatic justification, and as little mere thought as possible; no mention of the name of God, but an assumption of infinite and incalculable powers behind the visible drama. Yet I hope that in the end a feeling of gratification will be given by the poem as a whole. The theme is fearfully ambitious—I am conscious enough of that—but I feel that there is nothing for me but to attempt it in what moments of inspiration may come, even if it takes me years. My technique is more adequate now than it was in any of the poems which I sent you, and my expression is more free: I am getting more out.

But enough about myself. I do not know how to thank you for your offer to let us have the bungalow. That is very, very kind indeed; but—you will not regard this as ungrateful, I am sure—I do not know that we can accept so much. We should like to see you there for a day or two as we go through England to Scotland; but in any case, we must go to Scotland for a time; we thirst for it, and that probably means that we need it. But I thank you again and again for the kind thought; and I'm looking forward eagerly to seeing you, and your wife whom you say means so much to you. I am, too, peculiarly happy in that way. My wife has made possible what work I have been able to do these last two or three years to satisfy my own taste, and has given me the happiest years of my life. You ask me to say what age I think you are; but I am sorry to say that this question has been spoiled for me by hearing by chance from a youth here from London that you were between 40 and 50. It was a youth of the name of Rolf Gardiner, very nice and enthusiastic, a great admirer of D. H. Lawrence. I don't think he knows you, or you him. But I think from your books I would have set you down as younger; indeed a little over 30; and I think it is nice that your books should have given me that impression.

You have read many things which I have not, but I shall read them some day. Rivière I have not read at all, for instance, though I believe he is very fine: of James—this is one of the most glaring holes in my reading—I have only read two books, and of Proust I have read only *Swann*—but with tremendous admiration, marvelling at it. He is wonderful, a unique genius. Mann's *Tonio Kröger* and *Der Tod in Venedig* I know; and the former is truly exquisite. I have read Schnitzler and Hofmannsthal, and I admire, I think inordinately, the early poems of the latter. And lately I have discovered two other Austrian writers of uncommon gifts, Richard Beer-Hofmann and Georg Trakl—the latter died young in 1914. What do you think of *Ulysses*? I have been going over it very carefully, and I am convinced that with all its perversity, it is a great work.

My main find in German literature has been Hölderlin. Perhaps you know him, but if you do not, would you let me send you his poems? I am interested in Rimbaud's poems at present—truly an immense genius. But before I close I find I will have to thank you again, for *The Criterion* you mention. We shall be here, I think, until the end of June. And this reminds me that I, too, admire very much T. S. Eliot's poetry, especially in his early period.

All good fortune with your work,

Yours,
Edwin Muir

12: TO SYDNEY SCHIFF

Sonntagberg
Sunday [June, 1924]

Dear Stephen Hudson,

Forgive me for being such a long time in replying to your last letter and in acknowledging *The Criterion*, which you so kindly sent me. Both my wife and I have been writing from morn till night this last week translating these Hauptmann plays, typing them and correcting, and it has completely tired us out. I really think it has not been the labour which has exhausted us so much as the stupidity of the original. We did not choose Hauptmann for translating (we would never have thought of doing so); it was the publisher's suggestion. There's only one play now to do, and we are taking a rest before we begin it, and I have an opportunity of writing you.

I think your story in *The Criterion* is very beautiful, in its way I think the most beautiful thing of yours I have read. Please forgive me if I do not want to add anything further to that opinion; the story is so delicate and pure—in a high sense—that I should hate to have to give it attributes. Very, very fine indeed! I suppose there's no doubt that the main character is Proust. Your idea of telling the story through his attendant was an inspiration; in the telling you avoid so successfully the various pitfalls which are strewn over a theme so pathetic as this, that one doesn't notice you avoid them. But all this strikes me as not being worth saying; and what must strike a reader of your story is its beauty both of spirit and execution....

I had not thought you were 57! I had imagined you were between 40 and 50, as someone told me. It is selfish of me to say so, but your greater age has given me more courage, for I have been feeling now and then in this last year that I have nothing to show for my years—I am 37 now, and sometimes I have a feeling (very silly)

---

12 *Impoverished by the failure of* The Freeman *the Muirs had accepted the invitation of B. W. Huebsch to translate three plays* (Indipohdi, The White Saviour *and* A Winter Ballad) *by Gerhart Hauptmann (1962–1946) for a hundred dollars a play. Later in 1924 they translated also Hauptmann's novel* The Island of the Great Mother. *Schiffs' story is 'Celeste', published in* The Criterion *Vol. II, No. 7 (April 1924). The poems by Muir referred to may be 'Horses', 'Ballad of Hector in Hades' and 'Remembrance', all first published this summer.*

of being left behind when I see men under thirty who have half a dozen books behind them. My development has been very slow; but I suppose that's as it must be. There is no getting past things such as these, and I think one is always to be congratulated if one—at one period of life or another (it doesn't matter much which)—brings one's gift to its proper perfection, as, it is clear to me, you are doing. It is quite a surprise to me that your name is not Stephen Hudson; it was a name which somehow or other went with your work. And, as it means all that, I shall always think of you as Stephen Hudson.

I hope your work is getting easier to you now. I have been able to do nothing since the translating began, except a few poems—three, which I think are good; but in another month I hope to return to the novel and really see if I can do anything with it. I agree with you in what you say about a political standpoint for artists—political as you define it. And things are so bad at present that I think that standpoint must be a very simple one, the simpler the better. I've felt this for some time. The younger literature, as represented by writers like Aldous Huxley, is really fundamentally an anarchic literature, a literature without orientation; and being that always strikes me involuntarily as being in a final sense silly. I don't think anyone can face the simplest of life's problems with an attitude like Huxley's, and if one can't do that then the attitude may be clever, effective as an attitude, fashionable or anything else, but it is foolish. It seems to me that people have come to the stage now—with all this habit of taking life as a joke, but without gusto—when it's necessary, almost as a paradox, to say that life is worth living. It's a mark of practical wisdom in any case, just as the doing of the other thing is the sign of foolishness—making a man a fool in the literal Biblical sense. Of course I don't assert that Huxley and writers of the same school are deliberately perverse; possibly they can't avoid their attitude: it may be their fate, or something very unhappy and arid in this time which speaks through them: in which case their fate is horribly sad. But I find I am rambling on in a very unsatisfactory way....

Yours sincerely,
Edwin Muir

Thanks very much for showing the poems to T. S. Eliot. I'm very glad you've done so. I wonder if he will like them? I don't think so.

13: TO SYDNEY SCHIFF

81 High Street
Montrose
Scotland
2 August, 1924

My dear Stephen Hudson,

We have got settled here at last with thankfulness, and now we shall have the satisfaction of sitting down to a good term of work. I do not know how we can express our thanks to you both for your wonderful intuitive kindness while we were with you, and the encouragement and refreshment which you made us experience—for it was an experience such as very few human beings can give to others. I have had new ideas about my novel since I left you and quite a surge of them about the volume of criticism the idea of which I owe to you, and I know now that I have only to get over a certain amount of immediate work to get to these and undertake them. All this quickening I put down to the few days when we were all together, which were full of quiet delight for both of us. . . .

Scotland has been a sad disappointment to us after all the longing we had for it, so shut in, unresponsive, acridly resolved not to open out and live. For our own sake we shall not live here for long, not more than two months I think, if we can help it. But this sounds worse than I had intended. We love the landscape here, and the lingering twilights, if not the people, and we shall get a solid amount of work done. Willa will be engaged on her book on women, and I shall have all these things I have mentioned. . . .

Yours ever,
Edwin Muir

13 The Muirs left Sonntagberg on 8 July, and stayed with the Schiffs on their way through England to Mrs Muir's mother's house in Montrose. Muir then began work on a series of articles on contemporary writers, which were published in periodicals and then in Transition *(1926). Mrs Muir's essay* On Women *was published by the Hogarth Press in 1925 and by Knopf in America in 1926.*

14: TO SYDNEY SCHIFF

Montrose
6 October 1924

My dear Stephen Hudson,

... So *Myrtle* is finished at last. I am glad and I send you my congratulations. I hope it may appear very soon. I agree with you about almost every work of art being too long, even those of Stendhal, which I adore. Lawrence's are certainly all too long, except perhaps some of his short stories, where he gets, for him, really impersonal form. *Ulysses* is certainly far too long, I think, even admitting that its bulk in itself has a sort of aesthetic value. Joyce, it seems to me—my opinion of him is always changing—is *au fond*, a very meretricious artist, a getter of effects, and quite incapable of attaining the simplicity which is the condition of the most real and great art. (I don't mean simplicity of mind, but of spirit, singleness, sureness). I think I have made quite a valuable discovery regarding him—that he is primarily an artist in words, that he is more interested in language than in his subject matter, and that his interest in the one gets between us and the other—a very fundamental sin against art, it seems to me. I hope by the time I come to write at length about him I shall have ceased to be astonished by him, for at the other side of that astonishment (which he exerts all his histrionic genius to arouse) I fancy I shall find a great amount of sham work. This is my reaction at present, from a too great admiration, I know, but there is no doubt some truth in it, which I will be able sooner or later to set in proportion.

I agree, too, with almost everything you say about poetry. The neat, felicitous, epigrammatic kind of poetry bores me or else gives me a kind of trivial pleasure, which is so insignificant that it is really worse than boredom. At least my poetry cannot be said to have excellence of form! It has no felicities, and I dislike felicities from the bottom of my heart—they give me a faint sickish feeling. I don't know whether this feeling is justifiable objectively, but I think it is; neat poetry is a kind of poetry in which a disagreeable kind of personal superiority is asserted, and as poetry is concerned in my mind with great themes and is the response of the individual mind to those at the few moments when it is raised above itself that assertion of superiority is false psychologically, repellent and foolish. Humility is better, though I don't like the expression of humility in art, but simplicity can never be wrong. In among my other jobs I have been writing poetry too, in the last few weeks; I am glad of it, for it gives me a more intense life than any other kind of aesthetic expression, and is bound, too, as you say, to make my criticism more alive. I am building up gradually, out of these various moments, a large poem, *Chorus of the Newly Dead*, which in some little time now may be proximately finished. When it is, I shall send it to you, if you wish. . . .

Yours ever,
Edwin Muir

15: TO SYDNEY SCHIFF

Summerhill,
Lyme Regis,
Dorset.
1 January, 1925.

My dear S.H.

This is my first letter of 1925, and it is to wish you both from Willa and me all good fortune in the New Year. May you do all you wish to do. With our getting a cottage for ourselves once more we feel that the new year is in reality a new beginning for us.

We have decided to get our furniture shifted on Monday, and that will allow us to go up to London on Saturday and to take a run out on Sunday to see the cottage and to find out what, roughly, we need in the way of utensils and so on. It should not take us long to get settled.

Your point about Lawrence's persistent patches of great writing is, I think, very just, but I think with an absolute justice which one cannot uphold unconditionally in literary criticism. I found myself in this difficult position with Lawrence, that I had pointed out his faults, among these formlessness, haste, lack of objectivity; and then, in consulting my total reaction to him, I discovered that what I had

---

15 *The Muirs had moved down from Montrose to spend a week with A. S. Neill at his school, Summerhill, before going to the cottage Schiff had found for them at Penn, near his house at Chesham in Buckinghamshire. Muir's essay on Lawrence appeared in the American* Nation *on 11 February and in* Transition. *For Lawrence's own comment on it see 'Accumulated Mail' in* Phoenix *I pp. 801–4.*

said did not do justice to that, and I knew, too, that where I had been most moved by Lawrence's genius was in isolated passages of splendid divination, where a really extraordinary power of vision came through. It would not have been fair to close the essay without some acknowledgment of these. Considered purely from the standpoint of art these passages are actual blemishes, for they are not on the same plane as the rest of the works where they occur; they stick out like isolated peaks, and spoil the pattern and destroy proportion. Yet Lawrence's genius is most essentially seen in them; they are fine, wherever they may occur, and I have no doubt in my mind that he should be given credit for them, if not as an artist, as a man of great natural power. I think of such passages as the wallaby hunt and the fight between Jack Grant and Easu in *The Boy in the Bush*. Do you agree with this? I was again in continual difficulties with the essay on Lawrence chiefly because, like you, I am profoundly repelled by a great many things in his work. I tried to make allowance for this feeling of repulsion, and to see, putting that aside, what fruitful elements there were in his novels. I should have to write a long essay, perhaps to examine most of the assumptions on which people live as well as those on which they could conceivably live, to do that properly. It would be to write a statement and criticism of the whole modern standpoint—not by any means clear yet to anyone at all, certainly not to me—from which such work as Lawrence's and Joyce's and a great number of other writers, among them Freud's, arises and takes its temper and shape. That would be well worth doing, it might be useful to our generation, but it would be a task involving stupendous labour, mostly of divination and thought about conceivable possibilities of life; and I am not ready for it yet, and perhaps never may be. This series of essays, at any rate, should give me some idea of where the straw is being blown. If that cannot, nothing will, for if we cannot discover from our literature where we are, then it seems to me we shall never discover it. By we I mean of course the modern world in toto, not any individual artist, for an artist, I think, should always know where he is. . . .

Best love from Willa and me to you both

Yours ever,
Edwin Muir

Very many thanks for all you have done about the cottage. You have been very kind. Willa says she is looking forward very much to it.

16: SYDNEY SCHIFF

White Gates,
Beacon Hill,
Penn, Bucks.
1 February, 1925.

My dear S.H.

Thanks more than I can say for your letter about the 'Chorus'. The poem fulfilled all my dearest wishes for it in evoking a response from you of that kind. It has been a long labour for me to get it so far finished as it is now. I have only been able to work at it at certain moments and in certain moods; and I must depend upon these now for completing it, and giving it the inevitability of expression which I desire. What you have seen will then be the largest portion of it, but I have sections in my mind which will alter the whole atmosphere of the poem. I should have said this to you before I gave the poem to you, but it is difficult to put these things in words other than those they will find in the work itself. As you say, I want to give some of the suffering and tragedy of life; and that is almost as far as I have got with the poem. But I also wish to give some sense of triumph in and above the suffering and tragedy; I wish, accepting all these things, to affirm life, to use Nietzsche's expression. To do that it is necessary to realise the suffering first, to open my eyes to everything that seems hopeless, helpless, inexplicable. This, at least up to the figure of the harlot, is all that I have done thus far. The poet begins the new movement, away from suffering to its transmutation and the Hero emphasises that movement; but I have another figure, I don't know what to call him, perhaps the Mystic, in which all life will be affirmed. Then there will be a grand final chorus—this is what I must prepare for—which will sum up everything and adumbrate some of the glory even of those who pass through life apparently deprived of what it can give, the beggar, the harlot, and so on. That, at any rate, is the poem as I have conceived it, and what I shall try to make it. The mere portrayal of the sufferings of existence, the mere questioning of fate—that, with nothing further to back it, is, I think, what most people, without knowing it, understand as romantic—I mean romantic in the bad sense. It is an invaluable thing to the artist, I think, as a weapon, it makes him realise life more deeply, gives him one direct *aussicht* into existence. But as his whole equipment it is bad, for people cannot live by it, they must come to a stage where they make a judgment, value, call it whatever one will. So that the romantic in this sense would be a man who expressed an attitude to life—a perfectly genuine one, too—but not a principle of life, not something by which one can live. That is, I think, what Leopardi and Baudelaire did, great men as they were. What do you think of this? I am convinced of it.

Willa is *very* much better. She has been out walking—she can move about without pain; and we are both very happy about it. Very soon I think she will be quite all right again.

Janko Lavrin was out seeing us today. We had not seen him for more than 4 years. He is a dear chap.

I am reading some of Valéry's poetry just now. He seems to me to be almost, perhaps quite, a first-rate man. It is the first of him I have read. I fancy you know him much better than I do. Do you admire him? But I must stop.

Love from us both,

Yours ever,
Edwin Muir

17: TO SYDNEY SCHIFF

Penn
28 February, 1925

My dear Sydney,

I have intended several times to write you since Wednesday, but I have been so taken up with immediate work that I have had no time until now, although our talk has often been in my mind. Your view of life—as you saw it on Wednesday—did trouble me quite a lot. I returned here feeling unusually—for me—despondent; and this feeling lasted all that evening and part of next day. But by now I have become glad—for my own sake—that we had that talk; for it has shown me that my faith in life is very strong, stronger than I had any conception of. And I have no doubt in my mind—though it cannot be demonstrated—that this faith is a good thing. This I do not need to demonstrate to myself. But it is a curious thing that you, who I am certain have somewhere very deeply a faith in life, should have been the cause of shaking me, and then more firmly re-establishing me on this point.

I have no doubt at all that life is full of suffering, of injustice, of meannesses, of weakness, of hypocrisies; but I know that these things are not to me in the least arguments for or against life. I do feel all this misery very keenly; but I feel in it, too, a sort of splendour, in love, hatred, anger, loss, despising and being despised, life death, desire and everything. Seen deeply enough the life of the most ordinary human creature, who has to feel or bear all these final things, seems to me portentous, past all theorising, all relevance to optimism or pessimism. So that for myself the affirmation of life is not conditioned by my having to think life a happy business, and it has very little to do with love, except that love which is an attempt to comprehend, to imagine, everything, terrible as well as pleasant. I believe you are perfectly right as an artist in trying to see life, suffering, degradation, as it is. I do not know whether you know Keats' wonderful lines in the second *Hyperion*, but to me it is the innermost revelation of the artist:

> None can attain this height [that is, the artist's
>   height]
> Save those to whom the misery of the world
> Is misery, and will not let them rest.

And Goethe said the same thing in 'Wer nie sein Brot mit Thränen ass', and Shelley again and again. Indeed, I think that almost all the artists of all ages have said the same thing. I do not think really, that our own age is so much worse than others, except perhaps in the lower vitality of artists and poets, and in lower vitality generally. Morally, in such things as cruelty, meanness, duplicity, lack of courage, intellectual honesty, freedom of mind, sensitiveness, I do not believe we are any worse than we have ever been before, and it may be that we are a good deal better. Perhaps our chief misery is that we are a period of transition, that nothing quite full-grown can come to us, that we are striving for what we do not rightly know—in other words, experimenting. The joy of an artist who, like Shakespeare and his contemporaries, has all the means of art fresh minted to his hand, new and yet perfect, we cannot know. But periods of that kind can come very seldom. One may come in the generation to follow ours if the experiments of this age are successfully prosecuted and should open out a new opportunity. Or one may come like 'a thief in the night' as such things do often come. At any rate, with all the disadvantages, I would far rather live in this age which can show Joyce and *Ulysses*, than in the last one, which could show nothing better than Shaw. This is very rambling. I know the expense of spirit in this waste of shame which our generation is; the mysterious spiritual destruction of such really fine and gifted natures as Eliot, the spiritual twisting of Joyce, the distortion of everything, the chaos between the fall of one set of values and the discovery of another. All this is not to be denied. But I should like to quote Keats again, out of one of his letters. 'As to the poetical character [he might have said the artistic] it lives in gusto, be it foul or fair, high or low, rich or poor, mean or elevated—it has as much delight in conceiving an Iago as an Imogen'. And even old Wordsworth, defending Burns' obscenity in 'The Jolly Beggars', said something of the same kind.

This is a very rambling letter, and the only thing it is intended to show is that a realistic vision of the world is not incompatible with joy, and that there is joy even in the vision. I cannot say why this should be, but it is. Moreover, your view of life at present is simply the result of your temporary feeling of impotence before your work. I have had that feeling over and over again; I have felt that I could never write anything worth writing, never write again at all; but that is simply a phase, without objective value in the least, and it always passes. Goethe felt it again and again, and he recommends pottering about as the most profitable way of spending a day in which one cannot get the best work out of oneself. And that is obviously a very wise thing to have said, with a whole lifetime of experience behind and written by a man who took his work probably more seriously than anyone else has ever done, except perhaps Keats. Moreover you are in the happy position of being able to do this. I know, all the same, the difficulty of being idle when one wants to be doing something; it is a torment.

There, I have written a long, rambling but quite sincere letter. I do wish you were reinstated in your more happy attitude to the world. You will be whenever you get into the stride of your work again, and you will probably get into that when you have ceased troubling about it.

Please do not bother at any rate at the mistaken idea that you have depressed either of us. We were depressed for a day, I more than Willa, but now that is as if it had never been, or rather we are the better for it. If you were only the better of it, too, we should be really glad. All good luck and best love to you both.

Yours ever,
Edwin Muir

18: TO SYDNEY SCHIFF

Penn
8 May, 1925

My dear Sydney,

What can I say about your letter except that fundamentally, completely, when you talk about your attitude to life, I agree with you? Of course all great art is a wrestling with life, a facing, realisation, of everything in the artist and in the world outside him that he can see and that torments him and is a problem to him. From that surely comes the joy and the freedom which we find in great art. We feel that Shakespeare never turned aside from anything, and not because he did not suffer—he must have suffered monstrously—but because he had a passion greater than his suffering. We feel this too about Proust, to take an example much nearer us. I agree, too, that the people who only take art seriously, and not life, and especially themselves, can never produce significant work. And I feel absolutely sure of this, that only those who face the great issues of life, who enter into and therefore suffer with humanity, the struggles of their time, the whole thing, great and small, and put their witness, as if it were their signature, to it, can attain that joy which the great artists have felt; which I believe Baudelaire and Dostoevsky must have felt as much as Mozart. In Strachey, because there is no Sturm und Drang, because he disliked Sturm und Drang too much even to overcome it, as the artist must, there is no joy. And on this plane of judgment I may as well agree with you that Virginia Woolf is not a figure of sufficient importance to warrant a difference of opinion between us. She does not face the problem, and it may be that when I write my final essay in this series I may have to put her down along with Strachey and Garnett among the forces which are imposing a premature and hardening limitation on contemporary literature—fencing it off into a small perfection which is a denial of further progress. I shall have to come to some conclusion about this as I go on. I do still think that she has more breadth and humanity, more comprehension and seriousness, and less fastidiousness in the bad sense than you will admit. But I do not believe that this is a fact of very much importance in view of the finally important values you have written about. Yet what would you say of Jane Austen or of Madame

---

18 *Virginia Woolf:* this was not Muir's final opinion. See letter 105.

de Sévigné in view of these values—which, I think are masculine values? And Virginia Woolf is a woman: that, it seems to me, is of supreme importance.

About Lewis I have never come to satisfactory conclusions; except unconsciously, where I know I dislike him. But when I decided that I did not want to write about him in this series of essays it was because I thought he had published nothing sufficiently finished to give me a clear view. I find him interesting—there are very few evil, positively evil, figures in our literature at present, and positive evil has an inspiring quality. But Lewis's evil strikes me as being the effect largely of a limitation; he does not seem to me to realise it; he strikes me in the very midst of it as being self-righteous, as imagining that he is right and all the world wrong. And on the other hand there is no joy, no innocence, in his evil, as strangely enough, there seems to have been sometimes in literature. There is rather a sort of satisfaction at proving the whole world to be as unhappy as himself; the world is his enemy, and his satisfaction is to reduce it to humility. When is evil really great? When it is sublimely conscious of itself, as it was in Baudelaire and Dostoevsky; or when it is happily unconscious and innocent, as it was in Cellini and Stendhal. In both these cases we are in the realm of freedom; but Lewis is not free. He is unhappy, and he uses his intellect to conceal this from himself; not only to make his unhappiness appear the norm, but to make it almost admirable. There is a devastating absence of joy in his work, something wall-eyed and self-willed; and that can only come from weakness, it seems to me. His prose is formless; *Tarr* is a mass of tags, some of them splendid, some of them affected, none of them showing a clear mastery; all of them showing a hesitating even if an arrogant mind. Am I being biassed? At least this is what I feel. As for freedom, I feel he is far beneath even Lawrence, slip-shod and tawdry as he sometimes is. I feel that he has as many terrible inhibitions as Joyce has, but that, unlike Joyce, he will not acknowledge it. His arrogance takes the form of justifying himself intellectually, just as Joyce's takes that of showing himself as he is. I do not see how it is possible that he should develop, except intellectually, and his intellect in that case will gradually kill his artistic development. I hope I may be wrong; for his force and his sincerity within certain limits are magnificent.

As for your last point, what can I say? To myself I make no contradiction when I say that the artist should not be solitary and that his centre should be within himself. It is like saying that we are mankind and yet individuals. You mentioned the other day how galling it sometimes is that we cannot talk to all sorts of people; that we are cut off by modern life from all sorts of experience. I take this to mean finally that we all have a tremendous impulse to be united with humanity in some way; we get it, according to our natures, in becoming drunk, in joining societies, in becoming socialists, in working for 'humanity', in a hundred different ways. Union is as essential as separation, and the most profound union that can exist is that between a man and a woman in love. But the most essential thing in that union, it seems to me, is the unconscious out and in flowing of life between the two, which postulates both a physical and a spiritual correspondence between them, and is very like a process of nature, and is in any case as old as the hills. But this process strikes me as more like a free give and take, the freedom of two people who are united in one thing (their feeling towards each other) than like a unity. What is it that gives one thoughts, images and so on, in the centre of oneself? It is one's unconscious which is one's own from the cradle, but which a great experience can set free—a union with someone one loves, for instance. If marriage can do that, it does not matter how extreme may be what you call the tyranny of love, it is an entirely good thing. If it does not, then it is not good. But this is a very crude statement of the subltest thing in the world. I do not agree here with your terms, and I have tried to put mine clearly.

Love to you both,

Yours ever,
Edwin Muir.

19: TO SYDNEY SCHIFF

Summerhill
Charmouth Road
Lyme Regis
1 September, 1925

My dear Friend,
 ... I am very glad that you are once more getting on well with your book. All success to it. I'm glad too, that you like the essay on Eliot so well. I really think it is one of the best in this series; one of the most just perhaps because in Eliot's case I found it peculiarly difficult to be just. I sincerely hope that he himself will not feel hurt by it; the effect of all criticism such as this which is perfectly sincere and disinterested should be ultimately to help a writer, make him reconsider himself and be prepared against his deficiencies. I only wish I had someone who could do this for the things I write, but almost all criticism is either the kind of praise which does not help at all, or the detraction which is mere misunderstanding. It is only among my personal friends that I have found any help or guidance—Willa, yourself, and to a great extent Holms—and this help is immensely valuable, for some of our qualities and some of our limitations we cannot see for ourselves until they have been pointed out by someone else. This is what criticism should do, and I am more and more convinced that criticism is almost more than anything else, moral courage, frankness without bitterness, character—far more of these than I have. It should tell us the truth about ourselves, the only sure way of helping us. But I am always getting led away by these themes.

19 Eliot: In a letter (6 October 1925) to Schiff, Muir wrote 'This morning a very nice letter arrived from Eliot, in which he mentioned my essay upon him [which had appeared in The Nation and the Athenaeum *on 29 August], thought it very good, disagreed with it, but said it had been useful to him. In short, it was an astonishingly nice letter, such as I would not have expected from anyone I had criticised in such terms, and very honourable to Eliot, proving him to be a very exceptional man.' John Holms (1897–1934) became a friend of Muir's in 1919; Muir described him as 'The most remarkable man I ever met (*Autobiography *180). Rickword: Edgell Rickword, one of the editors of the* Calendar of Modern Letters, *perhaps the best literary periodical of the time, to which Muir contributed. Muir had been recommended to Rickword by Schiff.*

Rickword is very pleased with my 'Zeit Geist' article and hopes to insert it in the October issue. This is all to the good, though in reality it should have been twice as long. I have not been so idle since coming here as the beginning of this letter suggests. I have been brooding over a fairly long poem (I have written parts of it) of which I hope a great deal. It is partly the change of scenery and life which has inspired this. Also I have been browsing among Neill's library of books on psychology, and found them of great use. Certainly it seems more clear to me than ever that if we are to have any revaluations of values, it must come from a study of psychology, conscious and unconscious. Yesterday and today I have not felt very well—the result, I think, of overstraining myself while swimming, but now I am waking up again, and this letter is the first proof of it. I think we will be here still for almost a fortnight; it is so good for us in every way that it would be a pity to come away. Almost all the visitors have departed now except ourselves and Neill's staff, so that we will be able to work in quiet.

All good health and fortune to you both, and love from Willa and myself.

Yours ever,
Edwin Muir

20: TO SYDNEY SCHIFF

Montrose
17 December, 1925

My dear Sydney,

At last I have found time to write you. Tuesday I spent mostly in bed, for I did not sleep a wink coming up during the night in the train, and yesterday my friend Neill was with us all day; Willa is growing slowly but steadily better, and I have not written about her because today she wishes to reply herself to Violet's very very kind letter. I am feeling very hopeful now about her and about us both, and we are really, in spite of her illness, very happy.

I was very much impressed by the things you said in your letter.... Your statement that you have been 'literally growing up

20 Muir had been down to London to see his American publisher, B. W. Huebsch, for whom the Muirs were to translate Feuchtwanger's Jüd Süss, and to investigate the possibility of lecturing in America. Mrs Muir had had a miscarriage early in December.

with your work', that this presents difficulties as well as rewards—this is, I feel, the mark of all true creative living, and I think anyone who endures it is happy, is privileged, when he can give it the second-life, the victory, of art. I have often said to you that I value my poetry more than my criticism (though I think that the latter approximates far more closely to excellence of form); and it is for this reason, that I feel art is for me the only way of growing, of becoming myself more purely; and I value it for myself, I know it is my *good*, the only real good for me, and the personal feeling, the personal integration seems to me more and more the thing that really matters. Given that, other things will become right, for one will be alive and have therefore some sort of criticism of life. And it does seem to me, however uncertain the future may be, that this being alive, this capability of renewing oneself (which you spoke of on Sunday and which goes along with what you say in your letter) is the thing which chiefly matters. I think you are profoundly true when you say that this state is not finite, that it 'seems to have an unlimited extension at both ends'; and your saying so makes me convinced that you are in the preliminary state for creation again, that this feeling will not rest until it has been resolved. Can an equilibrium be reached? Or if it is reached is it anything more than a point which becomes once more a point of departure? I cannot think so, and I cannot wish it so. There is something constant in us, I feel; but we can only feel it when we are growing through creation, and when the habitual has no longer any power over us. These things you have touched upon are so deep that my personal response to them at this moment seems to me quite inadequate: they are things to which one's personal response will always perhaps appear inadequate. ...

Yours ever,
Edwin M.

21: TO SYDNEY SCHIFF

La Vetille
St Tropez
Var
France
11 May, 1926

My dear Sydney,

Many thanks for Wyndham Lewis' book, which I have found very interesting, which I agree and disagree with in about equal parts, and which gives me a more kindly feeling for Lewis than I have had yet. It is, of course, an extremely badly put together book; it has none of the classic virtues, though Lewis seems to be on the classical side; it is at times tedious, almost always garrulous, and the jocularity here and there is, I think, lamentable. But the occasional observations are, I think, valuable: and, most important of all, Lewis is always dealing with real issues. This, it seems to me, is his most valuable gift in this book: his eye for real things, things so real, in fact, that I feel that he felt himself compelled to write about them, seeing that the professional writers, economists, etc., were not doing it. Had he marshalled his arguments in order, had he attained coherency, I think it would have been a wonderfully good book. Yet I disagree myself quite flatly with his main assumption: that freedom is not desirable, and that it can be reduced to the terms he uses, and that it is dying, or dead, or, indeed, can die. It would take a very long volume to show why I think this is so, but anyhow that is my conviction. It seems to me that Lewis, out against rhetorical conceptions, is incapable sometimes of distinguishing the rhetorical from the genuine. Some of the things he exposes as rhetoric are rhetoric, but some are not rhetoric at all, but genuine feelings, implicit in human nature, in everyone, even those who intellectually deny them. But it is, much as one may disagree with parts of it, a remarkable book, the book of a very remarkable man, and, one feels a very magnanimous one. I am glad therefore of the opportunity of possessing it, and I must thank you for only another addition to your great kindness to me....

My novel is becoming more clear every day; though I think

---

21 Lewis's book: The Art of Being Ruled. *My novel:* The Marionette. *Mrs Muir's projected novel was* Imagined Corners. *translation: of* Jüd Süss.

there may be quite a struggle when I sit down to it. We have been doing prodigies in translation. Only 24 pages remain now out of the 610, and when they are done we are going to take a week's holiday before we sit down to our novels.

Willa and I send our best love to you both.

Yours ever,
Edwin Muir

22: TO SYDNEY SCHIFF

St Tropez
23 June, 1926

My dear Sydney,

... No; I do not doubt for a moment your sincerity; I think the whole conception of the book more profound than that of any other written by any living writer; but there it is, for me the presentation is not adequate to the conception. You say, 'I am not speaking of its literary qualities; I am speaking of its internal truth and sincerity.' But to me truth and sincerity are literary qualities; if they were not, literature would be a very poor business; they are simply essential in all true literature, and in literature have their highest power. Truth can always be told in literature; it cannot always be told in actual life, though it should be told there as much as possible. I admit the sincerity of your conception, but I do not feel that it has come through in your presentation in the unconditional form in which it comes through in your other books. But I have no doubt in my mind about the final success of your finished work. I think it will be your justification, and I most sincerely admire your work as you know. I wish you all success.

But I must say something, too, about your charges against me, and try to clear them up. Art for art's sake has simply no meaning to me, and I doubt whether it ever had any meaning. Why art exists I do not know, any more than I know why humanity exists; but I know that its existence is one of man's justifications for existing at all. It is one of the proofs of man's victory over nature, the world and himself. It is man's most successful attempt to defy life, more successful than religion or than philosophy, because more complete,

22 *Schiff had been nettled by Muir's criticism that* Richard, Myrtle and I *(1926) is lacking in complete sincerity (in the sense here defined).*

embracing a greater number of realities, both happy and terrible. It faces life more completely, both the good and the bad, than any other expression which the human spirit has thrown out. How you can think, therefore, that I or anybody at all who considers his words, can believe in art for art's sake, I simply cannot understand. As for being a romantic, I agree that I am, at least if you admit that all the part of literature which is interested in the undeveloped and potential part of the human spirit is romantic. And in that sense I think you are a romantic too. I am not much concerned with the label. Classical literature is a very good thing if we could be classical; it is like asking a man to be calm when his house is burning. All this does not mean, of course, that we should be indefinite and sloppy; it only means that we should be true to our experience in the world of transition and therefore of instability and possibility in which we live. But by romantic I know you mean something very different from this; I do not know quite what it is. The word in any case, I have as little use for as I have for classical. Certainly I get a great deal more out of the romantic poets, Wordsworth, Shelley, Keats and the rest, than I get out of Johnson, Fielding, Smollett and Swift, simply because they are still the more full of possibility and potentiality: just as I get more out of Germany than out of France, though the latter literature is in many ways the superior. . . .

Much love to you both from Willa and myself, and the best of good fortune.

Yours affectionately,
Edwin Muir

23: TO SYDNEY SCHIFF

Villa Soleil
Rue Pietra Scritta
Menton
10 November, 1926

My dear Sydney,

... Yes, I have read Sacheverell Sitwell's book, and like it as much as you do. *Vogue* sent it to me; unfortunately the time they gave me to consider it was not long: and my review is quite

23 *Sacheverell Sitwell's book:* All Summer in a Day. *Osbert's book:* Before the Bombardment.

inadequate though sympathetic. The book, so original and packed it is from beginning to end, would need at least four times as long as any ordinary good book needs, if one were even to discover its beauty and truth. I think it is almost as startling and originative as *Ulysses*, and far more successful in achieving what it sets out to do. I only wish it had appeared a year ago, so that I might have added another chapter to *Transition*, and perhaps as well have modified my diagnosis of contemporary literature. It is one of the most hopeful books the last few years have shown; it awakens, as few books of our age do, a feeling of sympathy, a positive feeling which is quite beyond mere reaction. It was only after my review was written that I realised the full beauty and the absolute newness and originality of the book; and I am still returning to it and getting something more out of it. I think what you say of Proust is right, although Sitwell's world is quite different from that of Proust. Osbert's book, though astonishingly good, is in a different class, I think; but I don't want to say anything against it, for it is nearly as good of its kind as it could have been. Yes, I do think the Sitwells are doing magnificent work, for their generation. Though I have liked Sacheverell's work always, this book is a surprise; Osbert's is wholly so. . . .

Yours ever,
Edwin

24: TO B. W. HUEBSCH

Menton
10 November, 1926

My dear Huebsch,

I received your letter this morning and hope you have not troubled to reply to my wire. I am despatching the novel in manuscript to-day by separate post, registered. It should reach you about the 13th or 14th, that is in good time. I hope you will like the book. It is less a novel than a sort of metaphysical or symbolical tragedy, and at the same time a perfectly straightforward tale. My hope is that the human significance of the book will transpire through this.

24 B. W. Huebsch was the publisher of The Freeman *and of the Muir's earliest translations, and was the publisher in America of Muir's first volume of poems and of his first novel,* The Marionette, *referred to here. After severe criticism by John Holms of the second half this novel was extensively rewritten during the next two months.*

Some parts of it you may find rather horrible, but the theme dictated this, and there was no getting out of it. If you have time to give me your impressions of the book before you leave London, I should be delighted; but I have no idea how your time may be taken up. I think, in the event of your liking the book, it would be advisable on publication to safe-guard the cinema rights; for I have an idea for a film, in many ways, of course, differing from the story, but using it in a different way which I think could be made effective. . . .

Yours sincerely
Edwin Muir

25: TO MR AND MRS THORBURN

Menton
21 November, 1926

Dear Lizzie and George,

I am sorry to have been so long in writing you. I intended to last Christmas, when we were in Montrose, but not with enough money to go either to Edinburgh or Glasgow. But we had a rather bad time: Minnie had a miscarriage, and I was down for some time with something which seemed to be appendicitis, but which passed off. We came down to the south of France in March in no very good state of health; but now we are quite well again, after a summer of very hard work. I am sending you two books of mine which have appeared this year; and I have just finished another, a novel, which the publisher likes, and which should appear in the Spring. It may bring us in some cash, and then I hope, wherever we are, you will come and spend a holiday with us.

We have only been in this place, two miles from the Italian border, since the beginning of October. It used to be called Mentone in the geography books. Before that we were living in a little fishing village called St Tropez; a rather primitive, but pretty place, where most of the inhabitants, I believe, are Communists. It was very hot in summer, and we could not have supported it, except by bathing in the sea, which was so warm that you could stay in for a long time. We translated a huge German novel there, 150,000 words; and I wrote my novel; and Minnie wrote about half of one she is still writing. There were two huge snakes in the grounds of the house we

25 *two books of mine:* Transition *and* Chorus of the Newly Dead.

rented at 13/- a week; and Minnie killed two scorpions which the kitten was playing with. Figs grew along all the roads; there were grapes everywhere; but the heat, for us, was sometimes unspeakable. Menton is a much more civilised place, and we are enjoying the change, though now it has been raining for about a month solid.

How are you getting on? We only see from the papers what a state Britain is in, and we are very glad for the time being to be out of it. If it were not that I feel I am doing work now that justifies itself, I should like still to be taking an active part in the Socialist movement, for it is unbearable sometimes to look on and do nothing. But one can't do two things, and it is better to try to become a good writer than to be a bad writer and a bad Socialist. I am of course a Socialist and shall always be one; but I can't do anything, not because my hands are tied, but because all my energy is going into something else. Intellectually I think we are on the eve of great things, and my hope is that that in its turn will set social changes moving. Write and let me know what you are doing, how you are all in health; and give my love to the children. I feel ashamed of myself for not having written long before this; but I have written to hardly anybody; and I have been writing so hard at my novel that it has quite tired me out, and left nothing in my head.

Love from us both, and may you be having better fortune than the times.

Yours ever affectionately,
Edwin

26: TO SYDNEY SCHIFF

Menton
19 April, 1927

My dear Sydney,

... Now for the main subject of your last letter, Lewis. I sent for *The Enemy*, and I have had *The Lion and the Fox* from Holms. They have both given me, the first especially, a much greater regard for Lewis than I have had before. The criticism of Joyce is certainly far and away the best thing I have read upon him; it is a brilliant and decisive piece of work. It has set me to reading *Ulysses* again, and I find that it has cleared up a great number of things for me; has shown me that a large part of the book is atrociously written, for one thing, and that it is packed with sentimentality, for another. About Stephen I agree entirely, but I feel that Lewis is altogether wrong about Bloom, who I still think is the greatest character in contemporary fiction. Lewis takes him as a Jew, but I never think of Bloom particularly as a Jew, but as a human being, like Shylock, who is much more human than Jewish. One must always do that finally, I think: we know that the Karamazovs are Russian, but it is because they are human that we understand them and they move us. And if Lewis says that there has never been a Jew like Bloom, the only thing one can reply is that there have been quite a number of human beings like him. This I feel as strongly as I did before I read Lewis's criticism; on this particular point it has not touched me at all. But everything else I think is extraordinarily good.

---

26 The Enemy: *The first number (January 1927) contained Lewis's* The Revolutionary Simpleton, *the major part of his* Time and Western Man, *published later in the year. Lewis attacks the ideas on time put forward by A. N. Whitehead in* Science and the Modern World *(1926)—for reasons suggested in the following extract (p. 192):* 'The artist whose chosen material is a static one is expressing by that choice a philosophy; as much as the musician with his more emotional material is committed to another. Literature lies half-way between the two: but it is more static than it is the reverse. It suits it really as little as it does painting to blur its outlines in a restless flux. So literature suffers ... by the invasion of a fanatical doctrine of "time" and "motion".' This Quarter: *an international periodical. Novel by Feuchtwanger:* The Ugly Duchess. *The Muirs had received £300 ('truly generous terms' it seemed to him when offered) for* Jew Süss, *and had not shared in the great success of that book.*

I have taken this up first because it was the thing that struck me most. The Shakespeare book is I think brilliant in parts, but as a whole sadly inadequate. To prove his thesis Lewis can do little more than cite among the great tragedies *Othello*, among the secondary ones *Troilus and Cressida*, and among the worst *Timon*. But to *Lear*, *Antony and Cleopatra*, *Hamlet*, and *Macbeth*, the fox argument does not apply at all. Lear was not destroyed by a cunning fox, a man of the world, but by the ruthless she-wolves, his daughters, almost as great as himself. Antony was destroyed by a fault in his own character, or by the single passion which ate up all the others, leaving him defenceless. Hamlet was destroyed by himself; Macbeth by the consequences of his own acts. Yet these four plays, with *Othello*, are the pinnacles of Shakespeare's work. So it is no wonder that in spite of many fine things the book should be irritatingly self-contradictory, and extremely inconclusive. I doubt whether anyone will consider it very highly in ten years' time.

Much the same, I think, will be the fate of *The Enemy*. It will be outdated in a very short time. The best things in it are first rate, I think; the passage on Joyce, that on Pound, the character of the revolutionary simpleton. But the whole Time-Space business is to me (at any rate) grotesque. Lewis never enquires whether it is true; all that he asks is whether it is a good thing for him to believe. But whether it is a good thing for him to believe or not will not alter its truth, which will remain unchanged. There is this further contradiction, a very interesting one. Lewis is all out for the intellect, and attacks Whitehouse [sic] and the others because, according to him, they are attacking it. Yet if you put Whitehouse and Lewis side by side you will find that Whitehouse has all the intellectual strictness and rigour, and that all the looseness of statement, the incapacity to argue from cause to effect, is Lewis's. To turn from Whitehouse to Lewis is to turn from a man who thinks to one who feels; from a classic, in Lewis's terms, to a romantic. These terms mean really very little; but Lewis has wasted a great deal of time on them, as if they really stood for important things. He has wasted a great deal of time on Gertrude Stein, too, who is not clever, as he says, but a very simple and stupid woman. He has wasted, finally, a great deal of time on *This Quarter*, which is of no account whatever. All this, I think, is very curious: to attack the Time-Space theory, which can only be refuted by a new scientific discovery; to attack Whitehouse for degrading the intellect when as a matter of fact his intellect is a very efficient one; to take Gertrude Stein seriously when she is only a foolish woman; to produce the fox as the key to Shakespeare's greatest tragedies when it can only be discovered in one. All his main positions are absurd, and only in his particular observations is great power of mind shown. So it is when he is seeing particular aspects of a problem that you feel; Here is a man of first rate powers; but as soon as he tries to see the problem as a whole you get a solution which is either cheap, or childishly simple, or obviously untrue. This is roughly the conclusion I have come to about him thus far. I think on the other hand that he is developing rapidly, and I recognise his great powers where they are expressed. I shall certainly follow whatever he might write this year; the novel especially will interest me. His drawings I found quite horrible, and the more so because one feels he does not know what he is doing in them. In spite of all this I must finish by saying that I did admire, that I felt the presence of an unusually honest and vigorous mind and personality, and that that mind and personality are no longer antipathetic to me as they used to be. His candour is on such a large scale that it raises the temper of one's mind. If I have pointed out so candidly what I consider his faults, it is in disappointment and not in dislike.

You asked about Holms. He is staying in Menton now with his wife, and making slow progress with a novel which may go to 20 or 30 thousand words. There is little outward change in him, and I am afraid his difficulties will be considerable for some time.

We have been asked by Secker to translate another novel by Feuchtwanger, and this time we have been able to arrange royalty terms of 5 per cent, so that we may be able to share in the success of the book, should it be successful. I shall not be able to get on to my next novel until after we have finished with it.

I have kept the most important part of my news to the last. Willa is going to have a baby. She has had a very bad time of it for a month or so now, with sickness, but she is already a great deal better. We should both have preferred that it should not have come at this present time; but if Willa is to have one it would be better that it should come sooner rather than later; and our prospects for the coming year in the way of money are better than they have ever been before. I shall be glad when her sickness is entirely over; nature seems to inflict a great deal of stupid suffering on women. However, she like a dear is cheerful, and only complains because she cannot do as much work as usual. We send our love to the both of you, and hope we may see you some time this summer. *The Marionette* will come out in the beginning of May, and I will send you a copy then.

Yours ever,
Edwin Muir

27: TO GEORGE THORBURN

Menton
14 May, 1927

Dear George,

... When we were in Scotland last time we heard a lot about Scottish Nationalism from C. M. Grieve (Hugh McDiarmid) who wrote *A Drunk Man Looks at the Thistle*. It seems a pity that Scotland should always be kept back by England, and I hope the Scottish Republic comes about: it would make Scotland worth living in. Grieve is a strong nationalist, republican, socialist, and everything that is out and out. He thinks that if Scotland were a nation we would have Scottish literature, art, music, culture and everything that other nations seem to have and we haven't. I think that would probably be likely; but I feel rather detached, as I've often told Grieve, because after all I'm not Scotch, I'm an Orkney man, a good Scandinavian, and my true country is Norway, or Denmark, or Iceland, or some place like that. But this is nonsense, I'm afraid, though there's some sense in it, as Lizzie will agree....

Yours ever,
Edwin

28: TO VIOLET SCHIFF

*The White Cottage,
Dormansland,
Lingfield, Surrey.
8 November, 1927*

My dear Violet,

I should have written before, but I have had so much anxiety about Willa both before and after the event that I have not been able

28 Violet Schiff: née Beddington, wife of Sydney Schiff and sister of Ada Leverson.

to attend to my friends' natural anxiety. The baby was born on the Saturday before last, the 29th October: it is a boy. Willa had a very bad and severe time; the labour pains lasted about 65 hours: she was twice under chloroform and twice under twilight sleep; and when it was all over she was absolutely exhausted, she suffered from chloroform poisoning on top of the rest. But she has now quite definitely taken the turn; she is glad now that it is over, that it has happened; and she and the baby are both getting on well. I never had any idea before that birth was so terrible, or could be so terrible. But it is over and past, and we are both free for the first time for months from anxiety.

The reason that the baby was so soon born was because it had to be induced. It was not due for another fortnight or three weeks, but had it been left till then it would have been too big, and there would have been danger. . . .

Love to you both,

Yours ever,
Edwin Muir

29: TO JOHN BUCHAN

The Nook
Blackness Road
Crowborough
28 June, 1929

Dear Mr Buchan,

It was very generous of you to write me so warmly, and I am proud of having won such high praise from you. I am very grateful, in particular, for your saying that I leave Knox a great figure, for much as we may dislike Knox that seems to be the end of the matter; and yet, good as many of the reviews have been, no one seems to have given me credit for acknowledging his greatness but yourself.

My appendix on Scotland is, I cordially agree, inadequate; and I can only explain both its tone and its brevity by my surprise at the

---

29 *John Buchan (1875–1940), later Lord Tweedsmuir, was then M.P. for Scottish Universities. In Appendix A of his* John Knox: Portrait of a Calvinist *(1929) Muir wrote:* 'What Knox really did was to rob Scotland of all the benefits of the Renaissance. Scotland never enjoyed these as England did, and no doubt the lack of that immense advantage has had a permanent effect.'

generalisations of other writers, and writers of great talent, and by the certain fact that my knowledge of history was far too scanty to gratify any but the most obvious generalisations. This is not an excuse, but only an explanation. Thank you once more for your very generous praise.

I hope you have now quite recovered from the discomfort and strain of the Election.

Yours sincerely,
Edwin Muir

30: TO SYDNEY SCHIFF

Crowborough
8 July, 1929

My dear Sydney,

I have been intending to send you a copy of my Knox for some time, but I had mislaid your London address and did not know quite how to find you. I am sending a Knox by the same post as this; I hope you will find it interesting enough to look through. The book should have a general interest, I think, but it was more particularly written for the purpose of making some breach in the enormous reverence in which Knox has been held and is still held in Scotland, a reverence which I had to fight with too in my early days (so that I really feel quite strongly about it) and which has done and is doing a great deal of harm. It is astonishing (and has given me a great distrust of biographies) that all the worst utterances and doings of Knox which I have mentioned have all been quietly suppressed by his former biographers.

I am very glad you are in such a health-giving place, though sorry it has not more interests. Is it not possible to find some place that combines the two? Yes, I said something of going abroad, but now we have taken this quiet little house for three years, and are going to settle down in it. We have been working really hard to pay off the expense; translated three German books in the last three

---

30 Translations by the Muirs appearing in 1929 were Feuchtwanger Two Anglo-Saxon Plays, Hauptmann *Dramatic Works* Vol. IX, 'Ludwig Renn' War, *Ernst Glaeser* Class of 1902, *Hans Carossa* A Roumanian Diary; *and in 1930 Kafka* The Castle, *Rheinhardt* Life of Eleanora Duse, *Feuchtwanger* Success, *Carossa* Childhood. *Muir's next novel was* The Three Brothers *(1931), and Mrs Muir's* Imagined Corners *(1931).*

months, and are now beginning another. In fact, I don't think we have ever been so busy before. However, we're going to have a reward shortly. Heinemann has offered me an advance to write a novel; it should give us fairly complete leisure for four or five months; and Willa is going to take advantage of it, too, to finish her novel, long since begun, and well under way. I am greatly struck with what she has written of it, and by the whole scheme. My own novel has been in my head for over a year; none of it is written yet, however, but I will be able to sit down to start what I have already thought out. It will be in a completely different style from *The Marionette*—not at all fantastic.

You ask me whether I have come across anything moving recently. By great good fortune I have. I don't know whether you have ever read Rilke's *Die Aufzeichnungen des Malte Laurids Brigge* and Franz Kafka's *Das Schloss*. I came across them both about the same time, and I was more moved than by anything I have come across for a long time. Rilke's poetry I really don't much care for, subtle and supremely skilful as it is, but this strange prose work certainly proves that he was a man of genius. The atmosphere is very curious, half Baudelairian, half Dostoevskyan, the psychology really subtle, and the style superbly brilliant and incisive. I was quite thrilled by the book, and I think you might like it. Kafka's book is still more strange in its atmosphere; it is a purely metaphysical and mystical dramatic novel; the ordinary moral judgments do not come in at all; everything happens on a mysterious spiritual plane which was obviously the supreme reality to the author; and yet in a curious way everything is given solidly and concretely. The book was left unfinished when Kafka died a few years ago. We are translating it for Secker. I don't know whether you would like it or not, but it appeals particularly to the part of me which wrote *The Marionette*. It is quite unique, and I think first class of its kind.

About English things I know less, for I have given up reviewing for the time being, to my great relief. I read Huxley's *Point Counter Point*, however, and thought it easily the best thing he has yet done. I think that he may yet go far. *Elizabeth and Essex* disappointed me. I have not seen Sacheverell Sitwell's new book, but from the reviews it seems no advance, Joyce I have given up, and Stein has always seemed to me a stupid woman with good intentions. Lewis is hammering away at something or other, but he has not divulged to his readers what it is: perhaps he does not know himself. Yet I feel that probably the next ten years will reap the benefit of all this confusion, these tentative beginnings, and that then even Gertrude Stein may have proved to have done something of importance. But there seems to be little use of bothering one's head about it at present.

I think your difficulties in writing are a quite temporary matter: all writers have them, and while one has them they are horrible enough, but with a little waiting they go by: the thing that retards the flow most, I think, is forcing it; it will come of itself. . . .

Love to both of you from both of us,

Yours ever,
Edwin Muir

31: TO MR AND MRS THORBURN

Crowborough
23 July, 1929

Dear Lizzie and George,

We're very glad that Ethel and Irene can come for a month and we'll try and make them enjoy themselves as much as possible. . . .

Who do you think I've just been interviewing on account of having written the Knox? Lord Beaverbrook! He's enchanted by it, and disagrees completely with it. He's offering me work, but how that comic incident is going to turn out yet I can't say: I'll write you later on. It's the most comic thing that has ever happened to me yet, but I rather liked the old rascal. . . .

Yours affectionately,
Edwin

32: TO SYDNEY SCHIFF

Crowborough
11 April, 1931

My dear Sydney,

I'm so sorry to have been so remiss and ungrateful both towards Violet and yourself for your lovely letters about my story. They cheered me up more than I can say, and encouraged me and made

31 Muir declined the opportunity of working for Beaverbrook.
32 my story: The Three Brothers *(1931). Another one:* Poor Tom *(1932).* Hermann Broch: The Sleepwalkers *(1932).*

me think again that I was capable of writing something good, which I could never have gathered from the reviews, except for three or four of them. The book, I should say, has been a pretty complete failure publicly, and there's little more to be said about it; so I have started on another one which I am writing at odd moments during the intervals of translating and which already seems to me to be much better. I have a feeling—which may be a false one however—that only now am I really finding myself as a writer. I hope it is true! . . .

I can understand that the translating of Proust must have been a fine experience. Translation does take one close to a writer, closer probably than anything else, and when the writer is a great one, like Proust, one is bound to gain an intimate insight into the workings of the human mind at its best which is really valuable, and is worth all the immense difficulty that has to be encountered. We are translating a novel at present by a new German writer, Hermann Broch, which seems to me really first rate, and very beautiful, and not unlike Proust in its great truth and psychological subtlety. I have thought since we began it how immensely you will like it, and when it appears, perhaps in June, I will have a copy sent to you at once. It is really exciting, really new, and consummate as a work of art. *The Trial*, a wonderful book too, is being postponed for the time being, but only postponed.

We're really very happy again, and really well, and the little boy is rapidly getting well. He is becoming more interesting every day, his mind opening out in all sorts of naïve and surprising ways, like a little tree quite unconsciously putting out its buds. He's very fond of singing to himself, and quite spontaneously fond of his parents—thank God. We're very happy at the thought we can see you again so soon.

Our love to you both,

Yours affectionately,
Edwin

33: TO JAMES WHYTE

Crowborough
10 September, 1931

Dear Whyte,

Many thanks for your letter. I did not think that there was much immediate hope of an economically self-supporting Scottish literature—and it may be that there isn't ever any ultimate hope of it. You are on the spot, and far more in touch with things than I am; and your findings—with which I can do nothing but agree—are pretty hopeless. But if there is no ultimate hope of such a consummation—or even no hope of it in our life-time—I think I am clear too on this further point; that Scottish literature as such will disappear, and that London will become quite literally the capital of the British Isles in a sense that it has never yet quite been; that, in other words, it will become our national capital in just as real a sense as it is the capital of an ordinary English man to-day. How long it will take for this to happen it is impossible to say—a few centuries, or only one, what does it matter? 'Hugh MacDiarmid' will become a figure like Burns—an exceptional case, that is to say—an arbitrary apparition of the national genius, robbed of his legitimate effect because there will be no literary tradition to perpetuate it. Scottish literature will continue to be sporadic—and being sporadic, it will be denied the name of a literature, and it seems to me rightly so. But for myself I feel so detached, when I look at this possibility objectively, that I cannot even quite exclude the thought that this resolution of the Scottish spirit, its disappearance finally into a larger spiritual group, to which it would inevitably contribute much, may be a consummation to be hoped for. At any rate, all things seem to me to be working for it: the fact that Scottish energy has gone mainly into international forms of activity, finance, industry, engineering, philosophy, science—forms of activity where one's nationality is irrelevant; the fact Scotsmen have helped to shape the industries of so many other countries and neglected their own: their almost complete blindness or indifference to the forms of activity in which the spirit of a nation most essentially expresses itself—poetry, literature,

33 James Whyte was editor and financial supporter of The Modern Scot, *a quarterly issued from St Andrews from spring 1930 until 1936. Both the Muirs contributed to it. Muir's essay on Stevenson appeared in it in October 1931.*

art in general: all this, looked at from outside might almost make us imagine that Scotland's historical destiny is to eliminate itself in reality, as it has already wellnigh eliminated itself from history and literature—the forms in which a nation survives. But the really awful phase is the present one: we are neither quite alive nor quite dead; we are neither quite Scottish (we can't be, for there's no Scotland in the same sense that there is an England and a France), nor are we quite delivered from our Scottishness, and free to integrate ourselves in a culture of our choice. It was some such dim feeling as this that made me take up the question. The very words 'a Scottish writer' have a slightly unconvincing ring to me: what they come down to (I except Grieve, who is an exception to all rules) is a writer of Scottish birth. But when we talk of an English writer we do not think of a writer of English birth: we hardly think of such things at all. A Scottish writer is in a false position, because Scotland is in a false position. Yes that's what it comes down to; and now that I think of it, that is what fills me with such a strong desire to see Scottish Literature visibly integrated in a Scottish group living in Scotland for that would make the position unequivocal, or at least would be a first step towards doing it; it would not merely be a gesture, or an expedient, but a definite act, and therefore with a symbolical value. England can't digest us at the present stage, and besides one does not want to be digested—it is a shameful process—one wants to be there. And there is no there for Scotsmen. And the idea that there might be is, I feel sure, a dream. Like Scottish Nationalism and the great digestive act, Scotland will probably linger in limbo as long as the British Empire lasts. It seems inevitable.

All the same, at suitable opportunities, and when I feel like it, I am going to have a shot at advocating an indigenous Scottish school of literature in Scotland. I'm glad that you are thinking of writing an editorial about it. I think it should be pressed in the B.B.C. Don't you occasionally speak for them? The weekly review I pin little faith to: it would be inadequate for the purpose in any case. And I don't know why I brought the matter up at all except as a protest. It will have no effect in my own life, which will go on pretty much as it has gone, except for the possible accident that I may manage yet to write something better than I've written so far. Which is quite a praiseworthy wish.

I'm enclosing an Essay on Stevenson which I hope you will not feel obliged to accept. It is rather long; I have sent it also to the American *Bookman* who I think will take it, but probably will not print it for a couple of months. But if you do take it I'm afraid I shall have this time to make the condition that it is paid for—the simple fact being that I need the money. So please decline it with a free mind, if for any reason you don't want it; but in that case will you return it as soon as possible, for I would send it somewhere else.

We'll be very glad to see you in November. Could you come down for a day? My wife's in a nursing home at present recovering from an operation; but by that time I hope she will be in better health than she has had for several years.

With kind regards

*Yours
Edwin Muir*

34: WILLA MUIR TO HELEN CRUICKSHANK

*Crowborough
26 May* [*1932*]

My dearest Helen,

This is a private, unofficial account of many things which we do not care to put into an official report. Generally speaking, first: we were never so glad to leave any country as to leave Hungary. The official welcome, the official sprees, etc., were all very grandly and lavishly done, but the psychological tension behind it all oppressed us almost to misery. (1) Barely a fortnight before the Congress the Hungarian PEN was riven in two by Nationalist, or rather, by Chauvinist interests. A prize founded by Rothermere for the best Hungarian book was awarded by the then existing PEN Committee (President, Kostolanyi) to a book which everybody admitted to be really a good book. The Government however intimated that

34 Helen Cruickshank: poet, secretary of the Scottish Centre of PEN. Toller: German poet and playwright; a refugee from Nazi Germany, he committed suicide in New York in 1939. Horthy: Admiral; after the brief Communist régime under Bela Kun, Regent of Hungary from 1920 to 1944; anti-Communism led him in the end to support of the Axis blok. Bethlen: Count; organiser of counter-revolution against Bela Kun; Prime Minister from 1921 to 1931; not the holder of the real power in 1932; later refused to co-operate with Nazis. Ould: International Secretary of PEN.

this book was not to get the prize, since it was merely a study of peasant life and in no way furthered the Chauvinist aspirations of Hungary. The Government added that should the PEN persist in awarding the prize to this book it would not grant a single pengo for the International Congress. Result, uproar, and the resignation of all the members of the PEN who put good literature above propaganda. Resignation of Kostolanyi (who is a fairly good poet). Appointment of Berceviczy as President—an old reactionary (half deaf and with a voice no one could hear). Appointment of an ex-Minister, a purely ornamental Government wire-puller called Von Pekar, as the second member of the Representative committee, a man who never has written anything, and probably never reads a book: a big fat blighter with stars and orders and a white moustache, who can eloquently say nothing of interest, and say it in five languages. At the last moment, because of the general literary protest, reappointment of Kostolanyi as a kind of third associate to these two, at least until the Congress should be over. The prize awarded to a furious piece of propaganda. Everybody upset, everybody intriguing, general unease. The Government, through Von Pekar, was to see to it that the Congress showed Hungary to the world as a martyred nation demanding its rights, an aristocratic and grand nation unjustly oppressed by losing its power over the inferior races in Czechoslovakia, Roumania, etc., etc. That is a brief account of *the particular* Hungarian atmosphere in which the PEN Congress began. Hardly were we in Budapest before we were plunged into it: young, indignant Hungarian writers buttonholed us and told us all about it. (2) The *general* atmosphere was the same thing written larger: the same Government that received us so grandly in the Prime Minister's Palace and the Royal Palace has the great mass of the people cowed, unless they are content to be fed on daily hate of other nations around them, and enthusiastic for the secret military designs of the country. Shortly before we came, a tailor (I think a tailor), suspected of giving out Socialist pamphlets, was bound hand and foot, hung upside down in his house on a bar between two chairs, and bastinadoed on the soles till he was unconscious: when he came to he was beaten again and, finally, he jumped out of his window, bound as he was, and broke both his ankles. His wife, who was pregnant, was forced to witness his bastinadoing, and when she heard her husband land with a thud in the courtyard below she thought he was killed, and she died herself of shock. Ernst Toller went to see this man in hospital on the day we were received by Horthy: Toller was taken there secretly by the wife of the doctor who was attending the poor creature, and Toller told us about it: his description of the state that the man's feet were in does not bear repeating. Another man, a country gentleman this time, was hanged on a tree before his own door, while his wife was away pleading for him to Horthy. And so forth and so forth. Conscription is in force, although secretly: every page boy in the hotels has to put in his military service at certain times, in his local organisation: if he does not turn up the hotel is fined and he is sacked. In every tram-car there is a prayer, running something like this: 'One is God, One is the heart of a nation, One is the harvest, One may be again the empire of Hungary, Amen.' And all the children in the schools pray this daily. The slogan of the nation is 'nem nem shoka' meaning *no, no, never*—that is to say never will we submit to the present frontier of Hungary; we insist on the old frontiers. This slogan is put up outside the houses, by the doors. In short, the general atmosphere is filled with hatred, revenge, and cruelty. Perhaps this should not have depressed us, but it did; and I spent Thursday afternoon of Congress week in roaring and greeting in my bedroom over the state of Central Europe!

In the Congress itself, of course, this political tension, although apparent, was subordinated to literary ideals. And one small result of the Congress may show you both the extent of the tension and the value that arises even from a miscellaneous assortment of writers paying at least lip-service to ideals of freedom in literature. The resolution passed by the Congress protesting against interference with the freedom of literature, and arranging for representations to be made, by nations concerned, to the Executive when any such interference occurs, was welcomed with the wildest delight by the Budapest papers, even by papers that were not socialist. For fourteen years, they said, we have wanted to say this and we did not dare: it takes foreigners to come here and say these things freely, and we are grateful!

(3) Our personal difficulties as Scottish delegates must be added to this. From the very start we were treated as members of the English delegation, not as independent representatives. On the list of delegates we were described as 'angol', English, and we had to go to the Central Bureau and protest before we were allowed free quarters in our hotel. In fact, we had to assert ourselves continuously

as being at least on the same independent footing as the delegates from Esthonia (!). The climax came in the Royal Palace, when the official reception by Horthy was arranged: the nations were arranged in a semi-circle, the head of their delegations in front and the others behind, and there was no separate provision made for Scotland: we were to be lumped together in one crowd with the English. Of course we protested: we had the satisfaction of making old Pekar hastily scribble us in in pencil on the typed list, and although we stood beside the English we did so with a little gap between us, and Edwin, as the Head of the Delegation (wha!!!! that was a story!) was separately presented to Horthy. All this made Edwin so nervous that he forgot to present me, I might say: and I had the dubious distinction of being the only person in the room who did not grab Horthy's hand. (Horthy himself is a pleasant-looking, unaffected man, very like an English naval officer: they say he is merely a figurehead and that the real power is in Bethlen's hands.) But you can imagine how this need to protest upset us, for we are not naturally protesting people. I like to have my status taken for granted, and Edwin is by no means assertive. It was for the sake of Scotland that we stuck out: it would have let down the whole Scottish PEN if we had not done so. I should think that by this time the Hungarian Secretary, Dr Mohácsi, simply hates the sight of us! I do not think it would have happened in France, but it *might* have happened elsewhere. Next year in Ragusa it will *not* happen, for we drummed it into Stefanovič and Čurčin, both of them exceedingly pleasant men, and they know anyway about the Scottish Women's Hospital in Serbia, etc., and have some notion of how Scotland stands up to England: Stefanovič is the Jugoslav PEN President, and Čurčin is one of the most delightful men I have ever met. You will like them both, and I think you will have none of these difficulties. Herman Ould says that constitutionally, of course, the Scottish PEN is established as an independent centre. But the Hungarian PEN is apparently unaware even of its own constitution.

From all this I would add that a Congress in Scotland will be the best and most immediate method of driving the fact home to the smaller nations of Europe. The Congress invitation was given in the name of *Scotland*, and a thoroughly Scottish Congress in 1934 would educate a vast mass of opinion throughout Europe. Of course, we cannot both eat our cake and have it: as an independent Scotland we must rank with the smaller nations, and cannot have the prestige of England or France or Germany. But it will be our own prestige, and we must establish it. . . .

Much love
Willa

35: TO HERMANN BROCH

Crowborough
2 June, 1932

My dear Herr Broch,

I too must thank you for all your great kindness to us in Vienna, and for the pleasure of meeting one who, without knowing it, had done so much for us. I hope that, in trying to convey some of our gratitude, we did not tire or disturb you: human understanding is difficult as it is, but when the barrier of another language is added, the difficulty is unfairly intensified. I was sorry all the time I was in Vienna for my faltering German—we both used to speak it far better, indeed fairly well, years ago, when we stayed in Austria and Germany—and it was most unfortunate that it should fail us just when we particularly wanted to summon it.

I have been reading your *Pasenow* again, also part of *Esch*, for the essay I wish to write about you. I had been so immersed in your book for so long—during our translation of it—that I had begun to fear that I could no longer hope to feel and indicate what was unique in it, and so fail completely with what I wanted to say about it. But to my delight the re-reading of *Pasenow* and *Esch* brought all my first surprise back, all the first joy of discovery of something undreamed of. No, in spite of what you said in Vienna, I cannot think that your book will ever be forgotten; at any rate it will not be forgotten by me, for I really think it has given me the deepest experience I have ever had from an imaginative work, since the time, in my 'teens, when I discovered poetry. You have done something decisive for my generation—lost though it may be: so I can't help again expressing my thanks to you, even if they may seem importunate, though they are not intended to be.

I wonder if you would care to have T. S. Eliot's poems. I should

---

35 Pasenow *is the first part of* The Sleepwalkers, *and* Esch *the second. Muir's essay on Broch appeared in* The Modern Scot *in August and in the American* Bookman *in November. His* Six Poems *was published in a fine limited edition by the Samson Press in 1932.*

be glad to send you the book—it isn't expensive. Eliot is accounted a difficult poet, his poetry is probably more difficult than these six poems of mine, though I find it impossible to decide on that; but he is probably our best poet in England, and I think you would not find him so impossible, and probably find him interesting. Please give my kindest regards to Fräulein Herzog, and please take to yourself all my gratitude and good wishes.

Yours
Edwin Muir

36: TO WILLIAM JOHNSTONE

Crowborough
19 July, 1932

Dear Mr Johnstone,

... I want to say how much I admire your design for the wrapper for *Poor Tom*, which arrived this morning. It is a brilliant piece of work, full of imagination and power, and extraordinarily ingenious in its use of the various motives in the book, of which you make something quite original. I don't follow all the elaborations of your design; but that doesn't worry me in the least; perhaps you'll explain them to me some time. I'm not in London very often, unfortunately, but my wife and I will be going there tomorrow week (Wednesday, the 27th), and perhaps we could have lunch together somewhere. If you could let me know whether you're free, I could fix up place and time.

Yes, F. G. Scott has often mentioned your name to me; but F.G. is a very bad correspondent, much worse even than myself, and I don't think I've had more than two letters from him in the last four years. One of them, strangely enough, came only a few weeks ago. He is in the middle of a new productive period and is doing very wonderful work. I know this, for we were both up in Scotland

---

36 Poor Tom: *having been refused by Heinemann, had been accepted by Dent. Mr Johnstone writes to me: 'The book jacket ... was quite a change in style from modern abstract art to work of a more representational and imaginative expression. At that time I was friendly with Mr and Mrs Richard Church.... Richard Church was appointed Poetry Editor to J. M. Dent and I was instrumental in bringing Edwin Muir's book to Richard's notice, who asked me to do the book jacket. Unfortunately the book was a failure, only some eighty copies being sold....'*

last Whitsun and heard a great many of his new songs. *The Modern Scot* is publishing one of the best of them in its forthcoming number, and if you like music I think you would be excited by it.

I hope we'll be able to meet on Wednesday week. And my congratulations again.

Yours sincerely
Edwin Muir

37: TO MR AND MRS THORBURN

Crowborough
29 September, 1932

Dear Lizzie and George,

Forgive me for being so long in writing. Here is my latest effort: I hope Lizzie won't look for any living model (or dead one either) for any of the characters: that would be completely wrong, for they are all synthetic, made up of scraps taken from all sorts of nooks and corners, and mostly pure imagination, like the main situation. The book is unfortunately a very lugubrious one; but I had to get it out of my system; and I look upon it only as the first third of a whole, the second of which I look upon as noisily comic—if I can bring it off. Meantime I hope that this instalment won't give the whole of you the blues—probably George, being the man of the house, should try it first.

I often intended to write you all about Budapest, but one thing and another came; we've been looking for a house in London all summer; we've found one now and are 'flitting' in a week's time: after that our address will be 7 Downshire Hill, Hampstead, N.W.3. We'll be glad to get back into human society again, after almost six years of living among English grass and clay. The street we're in—and we were lucky to get in it—is just beside Keats' Walk, very quiet and old fashioned and near the Heath. . . .

And on our way back through Vienna we had Broch's company for three days, which was worth the infernal torments of Budapest. He's the greatest man there is, I think, and so intensely sensitive, so shy, so easy to hurt, that life must be a torture to him—though he loves gaiety and simple kindness, almost intensely. When

---

37 latest effort: Poor Tom. *While accepting that it is a novel one cannot deny that there is a large autobiographical element in it.*

the book appears you'll have a copy of it: it's a very astonishing work.

All good wishes to you all. Is there really a revival of Scottish feeling? Or is the wish father to the thought? I've read what people have written in the Scottish papers, but I have given up having any belief in papers.

Love to you all from us both.

Edwin

38: TO GEORGE THORBURN

7 Downshire Hill
N.W.3
11 March, 1933

Dear George,

Forgive me for being so late in writing. It's a dreadful world that we're living in just now: like the Dark Ages, when one civilisation was breaking up and another forming with painful fragmentary slowness. But that seems to be how great changes take place; we're in the trough now, but something eventually is bound to come, some new form of society; the present misery convinces me far more of that than I was ever convinced during my early idealistic socialism. And it is all bound up in some way, those early dreams, and this going through the mill of change. I don't like it, nobody can like it; but it seems the necessary way in which things happen, and a new society will sometime be born out of it: for societies are born, and very painfully, it seems, and not made. We're suffering just now the pains both of death and birth: the only thing we can do is to think of the birth instead of the death. This may be fanciful: but London gives one a very strong feeling of it, and lots of friends of mine feel that something like this is happening. We're in the trough between something that has been great and something that will be great: an extraordinary, even if painful, time to be living on the earth.

We've had a funny time since coming to London. Immediately after we took the house I lost my job with Secker, on which we were depending for a livelihood. (They couldn't afford to keep me on any

38 Secker: Muir had been acting as a reader for Secker. Now he undertook reading for Gollancz, and also to translate Sholem Asch's Three Cities. *Orage had recently come back from U.S.A., and was editor of* The New English Weekly, *to which Muir contributed.*

longer.) At Christmas we were down to £1. 10. 0, with no job in prospect, the rent due, myself down with the flu'. In the first week of the year I got a job from Gollancz, also a huge book to translate; and the same week *The Listener*, quite out of the blue, offered me the job of reviewing novels for them. So that out of hopelessness we were raised in a few days to comparative comfort. I've hardly ever felt more thankful in my life. I'm sending £4 for you and Lizzie as a thanks-offering, and hoping that it will be of some little use. We're all right for several months to come at least, and can quite well afford it.

What does this means test come to? If you have saved anything, does it mean that they will penalise you for it? That would be too damnable, and I would get round it some way if I were you. It must be dreary beyond words, this waiting for work, a perpetual empty Sunday. Have you ever thought, in your spare time, of writing down your experiences and thoughts, telling what your life has been? If you felt it difficult I would give you a hand with it; but it may not appeal to you at all. I'm translating; Willa is finishing her second novel; I'm thinking of another; also writing some poetry, inspired by this present world we find ourselves in. We like being in London after the deadness of the country: I find the people we meet are more human than I had expected. I've seen Orage a few times: he's rather a pathetic figure now, I think, without knowing it; still leading an advanced army that has long since fallen into the rear; I don't think he feels quite at home. But he's a nice man.

I don't know how Scottish nationalism is to survive in the general revolution that seems to be sweeping over all civilisation. It seems to be a counter-movement, but it may be simply another form of the general process. I'm all for it, in any case.

We would like to see you all again, but I doubt whether I shall be in Scotland for some time. All our love to you all, and all good luck.

Yours,
Edwin

39: TO HERMANN BROCH

Downshire Hill
20 November, 1933

Dear Hermann Broch,

I hope you will forgive us both for our long silence. It is not ingratitude, or due to any lessening of our warm affection for you. Willa has had a nervous break-down; I have been worried and overworked; and the boy too has been ill. We have often wondered how you were; and now, having got Fischer's autumn list with the announcement of your new book, and a note saying that a copy was being sent to me, I am forced to write to you and ask.

For the book, for some reason or other, has not arrived. Nor has the copy which Fischers said they were sending to Secker. Neither of the two has come, and it is about a fortnight since Fischer's letter reached me. So I wonder if you could have a copy sent to us from Austria; I despair of getting it otherwise. Secker is most anxious to have our report on it, and, over and above that, we are most eager to read it.

A quarterly here, *The Modern Scot*, is anxious to have one of your short stories for publication in January, and we have promised to translate it within a month. Is that according to your wishes? *The Modern Scot* pays, and pays quite well, and the payment will go to you. I think I may manage to place another with *The Criterion*. I am sorry to say we have made no headway as yet with your play. Willa translated it many months ago, and has tried it on several theatre managers, but as yet with no result. The theatre world in London is fantastically commercial and fantastically ignorant and stupid: probably cause and effect. We are trying another man at present, an intelligent actor with connections. But nothing—nothing at all, has been achieved yet. I can't say how disappointed we are.

You said in your last letter that we might expect to see you

39 Gavin had been run over by a petrol lorry in July and his leg broken, at a time when Mrs Muir was feverishly busy finishing a translation of Sholem Asch's Three Cities, *published in October. In August they went for a holiday in Orkney. Broch's new book was* Die Unbekannte Grösse (1933), *published by Secker in the Muir's translation as* The Unknown Quantity *(1935). His short story mentioned was 'The Passing Cloud'. Robert Neumann: (1897–00), Austrian poet and novelist, some of whose novels the Muirs translated.*

81

sometime soon—I do hope the news is not too good to be true. You know how warmly we look forward to that, and how anxious we are that things should go well with you. We shall welcome you here at any time and at no matter how short a notice. I hope you will remember that.

Willa was really very run down, and at last reached the stage where she was allowed neither to speak nor to read. If she did not take an immediate rest she was told that she would have to rest later for six months. It was partly the worry about our little boy, and partly over-work. She is now much better, but not yet back to what she should be. I hope she will be by the end of the year.

Things are not cheerful in this country, exactly; but when I think of other ones I fancy it is almost a paradise in comparison. I met Robert Neumann the other day for a few minutes and spoke about you; he said he was one of your oldest friends.

We're immersed in work as usual,—I do my best to keep Willa off it, but generally without success. It's strange how the ordinary routine of life goes on in London as if nothing were wrong: it is very strong, one sometimes feels there can be nothing stronger. And 'cheerfulness keeps breaking in', thank goodness, however incongruously.

Love from us both, in spite of all apparent signs to the contrary.

Yours
Edwin Muir

40: TO STEPHEN SPENDER

Downshire Hill
4 May, 1935

Dear Stephen,

... I liked your poem very much, and certain verses in particular, which seemed to me very lovely; the second verse with the men like

---

40 *your poem: I think he must be referring to 'Exiles from their Land, History their Domicile'. your book:* The Destructive Element, *reviewed by Muir in* Spectator *10 May 1935. four poems: It is possible that these are the 'Four Poems' published together in* The London Mercury *in March 1936 —I later called 'The Private Place', II later 'The Law', III later 'The Sufficient Place', IV 'No more of this trapped gazing', not reprinted; but 'The Sufficient Place' does not fit well with what is said about the third poem in the P.S. Spender was at this time in Vienna.*

flags, the first four lines of the third verse, most of the fifth verse and especially the last four lines, and almost all the sixth. The opening two lines, and the movement of the whole flowing from them are very fine, I think. I like very much the freedom and naturalness and inventiveness of your use of language: inventiveness is rarely united with the other two qualities in modern poetry, though ideally it should go with them. I have naturalness in my own poetry, but I'm afraid I often lack freedom and inventiveness, which are qualities that can't be picked up and put in, and so I shall have to do without them. But I admire very greatly the union of these things in your poetry, and I think they are bound to carry you much further and into a larger kind of poetry than the virtuosity and forced 'newness'. I think we are all far too much moved by a spirit of emulation, and and when something 'new' appears feel almost in conscience bound to produce something new, whereas if we wrote from the solidest basis within ourselves we should produce something that is new. I know that in my own experience I have generally to burst through to that solid foundation (at least it always feels like that) and only rarely touch it: for to me it is the most difficult thing in the world to reach. I am very rarely on it, most of my life is somewhere else. I have the feeling from reading your work that you are much more normally on it, and the poetry you write therefore gives me a real feeling of freedom—I can't feel that it is a rationalisation of the fact that you can't write in a freer style. I think that probably before every poet there hangs an idea of a freer style than he can ever reach, or that he only reaches in moments of supreme inspiration, or in isolated lines given by grace. I can't say: I am not so conscious of these things as you are. I can feel what you say about a spiral development, and can see that that would break through something and give greater freedom, and I feel sure that if you feel as you do about it you should attempt it.

    I have been reading your book, which I should have thanked you for before this late stage in the letter, and admire it more than I can say. *The Spectator* has sent it to me for review, so I shall say what I think of it there, or try to, in the 800 words I am allowed. I am not such an admirer of James as you are, but you show such an intimate understanding of him that I am prepared to believe that you are more right than I am, for my understanding of him is much more casual. I liked very much your two essays on Eliot and also your essay on Yeats. But I shan't say anything more about the book now.

I am enclosing four poems, three of which I am doubtful about: they will all fit eventually into the rough scheme of a sequence I have in mind. I am getting away from my obsession with Time (a static obsession) and these poems are stages, some losing, some winning, in the battle. I have been coming more and more towards a socialist or communist view of things for some time (I was in the Socialist movement in Glasgow before the War, but the War put an end to that for a long time). I think the *hin und her* of that development might be as good a theme for a sequence of poems as the expression of a communist attitude without the doubts and fears. (You express the doubts and fears yourself, but there are not many others who do.) At any rate I feel that I may put all this into poetry, if I have the luck.

I hope you have seen Broch and that you like him. He's a very extraordinary person, very strange and with an almost unearthly sensitiveness. I'm so glad you think so much of *The Sleepwalkers*; I hoped you would.

Yours ever
Edwin Muir

The first poem is elaborated from a nightmare I had one night in Orkney. I showed it to a friend and he objected that the rhythms were all broken, but I think they should be, and I wish they were more so. But I'm doubtful of this poem, as of the pretty one that follows it as a sort of relief: an attempt to write of quite deep things simply and lightly, which I'm afraid fails. The third poem I like very much myself, except for the last verse. The fourth I like only for one or two lines, and may give it up altogether. Please don't trouble to write much about them unless you should chance to like them.

41: TO STEPHEN SPENDER

Castlelea
The Scores
St Andrews
Fife
4 September, 1935

Dear Stephen,

... As for our contract with Heinemann ... If you feel we should give up our agreement, I would be glad to do so. ...

I agree with a great deal of what you say about my last poem, and I have amended a few things. The theme of the poem, especially of the second part of it ('if there is none else to ask or reply', etc.), was, as I consciously saw it, the modern historical view of the world, in which there is no reality except the development of humanity—humanity being in that case merely an I and not I, a sort of long and interminable monologue of many. This view of the world has always repelled me very deeply and even horrified me—though I have only recently been able to explain partially to myself why. The question I ask myself in the poem is whether there is not some reality outside this I and not I (that is humanity in its historical development). My own deepest feeling is that there is, and I think it is a feeling that you get in all the greatest poetry and music, in Beethoven for instance, but just as clearly in another way in Mozart. That is not the strongest argument for it, nor the real argument, but it is a sort of corroboration. To ask this question at all is nevertheless a terribly difficult thing at present, and that is why one is in such a danger of falling into the pathetic, as you said. It is difficult because we all tend more and more to see life historically and temporally; for instance the whole impetus of Communism on one side (and the

---

41 *Muir and Spender had undertaken to translate Hölderlin's poems for Heinemann. Difficulties about the date of payment of the advance as well as the authors' doubts led to the abandonment of the project which was a relief as well as a disappointment to Muir. He wrote to Spender on 16 October:* 'The more I have looked into Hölderlin and attempted to render his quality of imagination, the more convinced I have become of my incapacity to do so. I have read the prophetic poems again and again for the last twelve years and I have got used to them in German, but when I try to catch them in English they seem to melt away.' *my last poem:* 'The Solitary Place,' *originally called* 'I and not I.'

really important side at present) comes from a purely historical view of the world. Communism has another side, too, since the final end that Marx saw was the abolition of the state, and a condition of general freedom: he actually had a little of Hölderlin in him. But I can see no possibility of equating these two communisms or of getting to one through the other. Indeed it seems to me the most transparent error. There is no bridge in Marxianism, except a mechanical one, between communism as a historical phase and communism as an ideal; you said yourself in *The Destructive Element* that the technique of communism tended to become the content of communism, or something to that effect: these weren't your words. My own feeling is that in allowing ourselves to adopt a purely historical view of human life we are losing half of it; for history too is a sort of substitution of the technique of existence for the content; there are ever so many things about which it can tell us nothing, otherwise why should there be poetry and music? This is a long rigmarole to set down in explanation of my poem; but the poem is only part of an argument that I hope to carry on, if I have good luck. I don't think my point of view essentially conflicts with yours; I know that we live in a terribly dangerous time; but we're surely bound to add to the danger if we ignore all of one side of life. I have not made myself clear at all, I am afraid, but perhaps we'll be able to have a talk sometime again. Willa and I would be glad to have you here at any time; we have a spare bedroom; and this is really a lovely place and a lovely house: it looks straight out to sea....

Yours ever
Edwin Muir

42: TO GEORGE BARKER

St. Andrews
14 February, 1936

Dear George,

It was so nice to hear from you again. I've been unwell for some time, but I'm getting better again. I like this place very much, and am glad to be out of London, which still seems a kind of Hell to me, though sweetened by visits of kind angels. Here the angels are more Presbyterian, but the surroundings as near as possible the opposite of hellish; I doubt if even Plush Piddletrenthide (I mention it for the mere wanton pleasure of typing such a succession of syllables) can beat it. We look straight out to sea over a medieval castle, and there are the loveliest grassy cliffs a little distance along the shore. You must both come and see us and stay with us sometime.

I liked very much your poem (or fragment of a poem) in the *Mercury*. I think you are showing more freedom and inventiveness in your employment of poetry every month, and the only feeling I have about you is that you have only to go on. I think the radiance and easy graceful unforced movement of this latest poem give it a most lovely quality. I have no other comment to make upon it: why should I? You are developing as a poet should, a very rare thing to happen; you're the white blackbird, the nonpareil. I'm the round peg in a square hole, or rather, being an angular Scotsman, the square peg in a round hole; I've spent half my life rubbing off my corners instead of sharpening them, like the rest of my countrymen, and I don't know whether even now I fit the beautiful perfect O of poetry very comfortably. But I've been writing some poems, a few of them will appear in the *Mercury* next month or the month after

---

42 George Barker (1913–) attracted Muir's attention by his first book Alanna Autumnal *(reviewed by Muir in* The Listener *8 November 1933). For his account of visits to the Muirs in Hampstead see* London Magazine *June 1956. Plush Piddletrenthide: village in Dorset. Barker's address was The Butts, Plush, Folly, Piddletrenthide. His poem in the* London Mercury *(February 1924) was 'The Shades.' Muir published a poem 'It might be the day after the last day' in* The Spectator *the following March, but did not reprint it. Better use was made of the idea in 'The Dreamt-of Place.' Barker's projected volume of criticism,* Essays on the Theory of Poetry, *got lost.*

that, and I have since got a very good first line, I think, which I have been boasting about:

> I think the day after the Last Day
> Will be like this

But the ones that follow do not come up to the sample, I'm afraid, though I've managed to strike out one or two tolerable ones.

I think we shall both be able to get far more of our own work done here. It's very nice of you to think of dedicating your book of criticism to me; thanks more than I can say, and the news is as welcome as an undeserved compliment. I am so glad your relations with Eliot are so good; nothing better could be wished for; and he's a very fine fellow. If you can manage it at any time, please believe that the above invitation is sincerely meant. This place is very lovely in spring....

Yours ever
Edwin

43: TO WILLIAM MONTGOMERIE

St. Andrews
5 April, 1936

Dear Montgomerie,

Your experiment with alliteration and assonance is very interesting, and shows how curiously full the poem you deal with is of both these things, beyond, that is, the immediate witness of the eye and ear. I don't know whether much work of this close kind has been done; if it has, then I have not followed it. I think it has not been done, because if it were it would be, literally, endless, and lead to no result except that poetry is poetry. As to whether the alliteration and assonance in the poem you quote were unconscious or conscious, only yourself can tell that; but it depends, I should say, on whether you are a very conscious poet or a more or less spontaneous one. Both elements probably enter. I am convinced, for instance, that any line which sings in one's mind before being actually set down in writing possesses naturally the consonant and vowel correspondences you point out. On the other hand there are clearly lines in

43 Montgomerie (1904–), poet, lecturer, expert on ballads. George: Stefan (1868–1933), German poet.

poetry, and very good ones too, which express the poet's conscious delight and mastery in such devices, for instance

> When to the sessions of sweet silent thought,

where one can hear Shakespeare listening to the chime of the esses, or

> In wanton Arethusa's azure arms,

which takes its wantonness from the flagrantly open vowel alliteration, or Chapman's

> She lay outstretched like an immortal soul
> At endless rest in blest Elysium,

where the open vowel beginnings in the first line give the feeling of largeness, and the chiming of the esses in the second the effect of sweetness. I don't think that in such matters any new discovery has been made in poetry since the Elizabethans; some poets are peculiarly sensitive to the life of words, and to their sound; Hopkins, for example, had an immense feeling for consonants, as Keats had for vowels. Consonants seem to me to get their effects by a more or less subtle and sometimes disguised repetition, and vowels by an infinitely skilful variation, though there too repetition is sometimes extraordinarily effective. The poetic state, the state in which poetry is produced, is a state balanced more or less exactly between the conscious and the unconscious, between inspiration and formulation; something is happening to the poet, and at the same moment he is shaping it towards an end in his mind. This makes the deliberate use of alliteration and assonance a very delicate matter, a matter of the most subtle intuition and not of rule. I don't know whether I have touched on the sort of thing that is concerning you or not, although I think these questions are always in the mind of people who write poetry. About poetry that is interesting technically, German or other, I can't say very much. All poetry is interesting technically, or rather the technical interest is one interest. I should say Rilke and George, in their different ways, would be called technically interesting, the former particularly. Hofmannsthal I have a great love and admiration for, and I don't think that for sheer perfection there is any other German poet to touch him; but that is a private preference: I suppose, however, you know all these three poets. Trakl is also a very fine poet. But I shall have to stop; about problems like these one could go on writing for ever. I think you are probably right in saying that in London they are dealt with in conversation.

Yours sincerely,
Edwin Muir

Kindest regards to your wife.

44: TO DAVID PEAT

St. Andrews
19 August, 1936

Dear David,

Forgive me for being so long in writing, but Willa and I have been away for a holiday, the first we have had for two years. We went up to the Western Highlands, which is entirely Free Kirk and Sabbatarian, and reminded me of the atmosphere in which you were brought up. I did not know that such things still lingered on; but they do; and ministers up there boast that 'not a wheel turns on the Sunday'. Willa suggested that God's wheel still did, but it is doubtful whether Western Highlanders quite approve of such activity on a Sabbath. Yet they are fine people all the other six days of the week, the best people one can find in Scotland, I think.

I have been reading all you sent me, David, and I am inclined to agree with your other advisers that you should try if you can to write, at your leisure, and whenever you feel fit to do it, a detailed autobiography. I feel it should be quite frank to be of the use you want it to be. Much the best part of what you have written thus far seems to me to be your account of your time in the Mental Home and your description of your dreams. These are so good because they are exact and detailed... I'm sorry I am so far from you, and I am glad you have found sympathetic friends. The world is a terribly unsympathetic place at the moment, with poor Spain torn in two, and Italy and Germany preparing to batten on it. Any gesture that would waken human sympathy now would be of value. I

44 David Peat, close friend of Muir's during his time at Gourock in 1912–14, having struggled bravely against nervous illness and become for a time quite a successful journalist, had recently spent much time in mental homes. His The Autobiography of David, *was published anonymously in 1946, edited by Ernest Raymond, and contains (pp. 73–5) a picture of Muir in the Gourock days.*

feel you have gone through far greater sufferings than the Spaniards dying of wounds or executions; and that you have kept your faith in life is an achievement greater than any other I know of in the life of any of my friends. I feel I would be quite incapable of it myself.

Do you think the writing down of your life would do you good? That is the chief thing, though it might seem selfish. One does oneself good by doing good to others; I know this is true, though I do not live up to it. I feel that there is nothing truer than the saying that one can only realise one's self by losing it; and one way of losing it would be to give it away to whoever likes to have it in the form of an honest and faithful account of it. You need have nothing to fear. But I can't give you advice, for I have no right to do so. I do think that if you can write your life, you will write something which will be very good in every sense, something unique and yet of deep human interest.

We are living quietly here. Gavin is turning out to be a very nice though peculiar boy, musical (he composes on the piano for hours on end), but unspoilt. He has made me realise what a struggle children have to understand the world and act sensibly (or is it sensibly?) in it. Willa is in much better health than she was in London. The Scottish Nationalists have been trying to get hold of me, but quite without success, for there seems to be only one side one can take now, and it is not Nationalism. Do you remember the Local Parliament in Gourock? How far away it seems now, with the Prime Minister bringing out his 'for to's.' I had a sail down the Clyde this summer; I never realised before how lovely it was. I think my time in the bone factory clouded all my stay in Gourock, in spite of your friendship, which was the only bright spot in it. All good luck and good guidance, old man. And love from us both.

Yours ever,
Edwin

45: TO STEPHEN SPENDER

[*St. Andrews*]
[*July–November, 1936*]

Dear Stephen,

I am enclosing a poem, which I would like you to see, for you are more interested in the subject of it than anyone else I know. The poem is by no means perfect, and it is a purely imaginary and I am afraid personal description of Hölderlin's real journey, which has haunted me ever since I first read about it, why, I don't know enough about myself to say. I hope you will like some verses of the poem. I don't know if it has much relevance to the present world. I hope it has, but if it hasn't I can't help it; for I find that while consciously I am a Socialist, and would like to write poetry that would in some way express that fact, when I actually start to write, something else comes up which seems to have nothing to do with Socialism, or is connected with it in some way too obscure for me to detect. I expect that any feeling of pure humanity must in the end make for Socialism, for Capitalism prevents us all from being human. The end of poetry, in a Socialist society, would be thro pure humanity, without inflection: I feel that is the only thing it could be. I don't pretend to have achieved it in my poetry, even in a single line; but it is something resembling it that excites me and makes me happy whenever I succeed in writing poetry at all. I feel all this far more definitely in your poetry than in mine; I doubt whether many people would feel it in mine at all.

... I have an idea for a poem which *might* be socialist: that is of the first road, straight and simple, in Eden, and all the roads branching off from it and crossing one another, the mark appearing on Cain's brow, the wound in Christ's side as if by magic, making, both the roads and the marks on the human body, towards some form. I have only caught the tail of this theme yet, and do not know whether I shall capture it, or how I shall treat it if I do.

Love from us both and all good fortune to you. I wonder if there is any hope of beating off the Fascists in Spain, with Italy and Germany and Portugal for them and apparently nobody against them but the Spanish people. If one could only foresee the next few months!

Yours Edwin

45 *undated, but presumably written between the opening of the Spanish Civil War (July) and the letter to Spender of 19 November.*

46: TO STEPHEN SPENDER

St. Andrews
19 November, 1936

Dear Stephen,

I would like to send you a poem, but I haven't written anything that I feel would be suitable. I have written one poem inspired by the situation in Spain and generally, but I feel for the present that I had better keep it to myself, it is so hopeless. I have also written another, but it is more or less in the vein of the Hölderlin poem, and though I like it better, it would not be suitable either. But if I write one that is suitable I shall send it to you. . . .

I am glad you liked the Hölderlin, which was not, of course, in the least like Hölderlin: but that journey has always appealed to my imagination. I have an idea for a story about the present state of things in Germany dealt with in the style of Kafka, with elaborate investigations and arguments. I think it is not a bad way of approaching the subject. We are translating Kafka's second book, *The Trial*, which should appear in Spring. I admire him more and more: his fascination is simply endless: and a feeling of greatness comes to me in every sentence. We have become members of a Left Club here, drawn from various sections, academic, trade-union and so on, which should sometime become of some use. All good luck to your play. I can see that it is right you should care more for public things than for personal things, and that public things should rouse in you an emotion as spontaneous as a personal emotion. I see that, but I can't bring about the necessary transformation in myself, perhaps because I was born in a different age, and on the top of that in a different world; for the Orkney Islands where I passed my childhood was at that time the same as they had been for two hundred years before; untouched still by Industrialism, and still bound to an old co-operative life which preceded that: the very idea of competition, for instance, was unknown. That really means that I was born over two hundred years ago, or perhaps more, so no wonder if my poetry is an acquired taste, and no wonder if I find difficult what is not easy even to your generation. I don't suppose you can have any idea how completely cut off Orkney was at that time: anyone

46 Spender had asked for a poem for The Left Review. *your play:* Trial of a Judge.

who went down to Leith for a visit came back with news of a strange world. To have come from such a distant place into this one should actually give me an advantage in some way, but what that way is is a different matter, and very hard to discover.

Willa sends her love,

Yours
Edwin

47: TO GEORGE BARKER

St. Andrews
31 March, 1937

Dear George,

Forgive me for being so long in replying, but I have just been finishing at great speed a piece of translation which should have been finished long ago. I am now enjoying a comparative rest.

I was immensely interested by your essay on psychology and poetry. You bring up an essential point which is universally ignored, and to me you seem to deal with it clearly and admirably. I feel you might have dealt more at length with the distinction you make between poems and poetry, so as to bring out more vigorously the ungetatability of poetry, except through its destruction as poetry.

I think your posing of the choice as a moral choice is very fine. I think I begin to disagree with you when you compare poetry with religion and assume that because the one can be 'destroyed' the other can be too. I feel your parallel between religion and literature should be worked out more, with a clear indication of where they resemble each other and where they differ. In a way it may be argued that religion has been destroyed by being turned into poetry; the old absolute belief has been weakened, and a contingent belief, or suspension of belief, has taken its place. There does seem to me a decisive difference between the kind of belief on which religion is founded, and the kind of imaginative assent we give to poetry. One can think of countless legends of a man born of a virgin, and can hear them being told by many a fireside to listeners who accepted them purely as legend, simply because there is always a kind of truth in story-telling, due to the fact that we live in time. But you

47 your essay: part of the collection, Essays on the Theory of Poetry, *which was lost.*

know as well as I do the difference between this acceptance of legend and a real belief that Christ was born of the Virgin Mary. It has sometimes been argued that it does not matter whether Christ was an actual historical figure or not; but I think the difference between religion and poetry lies simply in that, or at least lies in that. For poetry the actual Christ is not necessary, but for religion he is. The religious Christ, theoretically at any rate, can be taken away, by historical research, science, etc.; or if not taken away can at any rate be modified. But it is hard to see what can be done with the imaginative Christ, since he is quite inside the mind. Psychology can tell us what he stands for, perhaps, but I think it would be more true to say that psychology can only discover the literally numberless things he stands for; I cannot see it pinning him down to any one thing. But I have got away from what I had to say. I think the difference between religion and poetry might have been brought out more: I admit the dangers of psychology; I wouldn't wonder if it has been partly responsible for the debility of poetry, as you say. Do you go into that in any of your other essays? I think it would be interesting to examine some more modern imagery, as you have done in this essay.

Please do not think I am carping. I think your essay is intensely interesting and very timely: it is at the opposite pole from most writing about modern poetry, for it deals with a fundamental problem.

Thanks for what you said about the poem I sent you. You were quite right about 'age' for 'aeon'. I have improved some of the other verses too. I think Dents are to bring out a collection of 25 poems this spring, and I shall send you a copy. They are mixed, but I like some of them very much. It is lovely here now, with the spring in the air (as people say), and the sea quite changed. I have an idea for a much longer poem than I have been writing, but whether it comes to anything I don't know. All good from us both

Yours
Edwin M.

48: TO GEORGE BARKER

St. Andrews
5 June, 1937

My dear George,

I did not get your poem for review, and I did not know the date of its appearance soon enough to send to any paper and ask for it. I bought it about a week ago, or rather got Willa to buy it for me for my birthday, along with the *Upanishads*. I wish I had got it for review, for I read it with more excitement than any other modern poem has given me at a first reading; and I was dismayed by the reviews I happened to see, particularly the crass, complacent, infinitely stupid review in the *Times Lit*. The poem impressed me immensely, and what is more to the point, carried me away with it, on a tide of almost continuous poetic excitement. I can't understand a reviewer of even moderate sensibility and intelligence not recognising the genius that pours through the poem, except on the hypothesis that he was looking for something else, a recognisable sequence of political catchwords to tell him that this was in the latest mode. This poem seems to me by far the best thing you have done, as well as one of the most striking pieces of sheer utterance written in our time. I think, but I judge from a first reading, that the poem, as a tumultuous outpouring of secrets, visions, terrors, corresponding images, slackens off somewhat towards the middle, loses something of its magnificent energy, perhaps by undue repetition. I feel that book six, for example, shows a definite sudden descent, though it contains wonderful things; I could have believed from books one and two that you had seen Blake, but I felt that, as for himself, you presented him too ingeniously. I may be wrong, and I feel that I have no right to criticise such a performance as this poem, for I could never hope to approach it. The first two books I thought extremely powerful in the way in which they conveyed a sense of terror. The objection of some of the critics to your abdominal imagery seems to me pure stupidity, for that is one of the things which heighten the terror most. On the other hand, I do feel that there is too much abdominal imagery in the second half; it gave me the impression that after getting rid of this pressure of terror

48 your poem: Calamiterror, *reviewed in* T.L.S. *on 22 May and in the June number of* The London Mercury.

you were still returning to it. My own experience in reading the poem was that I was carried forward irresistibly to the end of book five from the beginning, that in book six I felt a diminution of the impulsive force (this was not due to the mere appearance of Blake, but, I really think, to a slackening of force). Book seven, I thought, was very beautiful. Book eight I had read before and liked very much, and the two remaining books I also liked very much. The continuous rush of the imagery is superb, until it is slowed down somewhat, made easier, in other words, by repetition. I agree that repetition is justifiable, even effective, but I feel that you overdid it. This sounds cold, and has little to do with the actual effect of the poem, which is terrific, really terrifying, and in some way astonishing. I can see no explanation whatever for the reception the poem found, except that the critics are too mediocre to recognise its immense superiority to the poetry which they normally praise, and the fact that it is very unlike any other poetry that is being written at present. I am very sorry; I hope you will not be discouraged; this should have brought you either recognition or execration. I haven't seen this month's *Mercury* yet, but I am going to get it, and will see your portrait and read Michael Roberts's review; I am glad he praised you. The poem will stand all that these time-serving fools say about it, and survive them. I shall probably write to you again when I have read the poem a second time.

Yours
Edwin M.

49: TO STEPHEN SPENDER

St. Andrews
6 October, 1937

Dear Stephen,

... I am delighted, and thankful as well, that you like my poems so much: thankful, for I never expect them to be liked, and your way of looking at life, I feel, is so different from mine, though I think they must be similar somewhere. Your review I liked very much, and I feel your point about the argument existing outside the poem is a very true and a very fine one, crystallising something which I have dimly felt myself, and of which I have been growing more and

---

49 *your review: of* Journeys and Places.

more conscious. The remedy, if any, I think, is for me to get more outside myself, and I think I have been able to do this a little more recently: I think it may happen yet, though it should have happened before.

Yes, I had already heard the news you sent me and I should have wished you happiness long before this in your marriage. I do hope we shall meet you both sometime. I am sorry that you have had trouble with the Communist Party since joining it. I meet many communists here, chiefly Dundee ones, for Dundee is only half an hour away, and I like and respect them; but I feel I shall never join the Party, indeed I could not. I agree with the ends of Communism completely, but the philosophy, the historical machinery, deeply repels me: I cannot think of it except as a coffin of human freedom. The whole impulse of Left literature, which is an impulse of pure humanity, (I shall have to define that, perhaps circumscribe it, but I stick to it all the same) seems to me in danger of being dehumanised, formalised, throttled by an automatic ideology, which denies humanity except in a great bulk, so huge that it has no immediate relation to our lives: the 'masses', for instance, not as a collection of men and women, but as an instrument, dehumanised as an army, a single objective mass possessing the attribute of force, and able to act only as a force. And human life as a historical process marked by ages, and the changes of ages, not the changes of an ordinary human life which make us know each other and force on us such feelings as understanding, love and pity, force us to seek for something better than the life we endure—all that, too, seems dehumanising to me, cold and without real human feeling. I have come to the conclusion that the whole Marxian apparatus is a terrible dead weight on the hope of Socialism, a terrible perversion of it into something else altogether, whose roots are partly in Capitalism and partly in the Old Testament. Perhaps in thinking this I am suffering from an extreme reaction; I don't know. Though I do not go the whole way with Huxley, I feel that there is some truth in what he says: a truth to some extent applicable to the

[The rest of this letter has been lost.]

50: TO SYDNEY SCHIFF

St. Andrews
17 May, 1938

My dear Sydney,

It makes me sad to think that we have so completely lost touch with each other, but it is at least a good reason that brings me to write to you again now. I have heard from Anja Herzog, Hermann Broch's friend, that you have kindly offered to help him, and I should like to thank you personally for your generosity.

Miss Herzog wrote to us some time ago from Paris, telling us all about Broch's position. We therefore wrote a harmless letter to him to stay with us; in fact he has had this invitation for a long time, for we were afraid of something happening such as did happen. We found out later through Anja that the difficulty is to get an English visa, for men in Broch's position cannot get a return visa to Austria (or rather Germany, for that's what it is now), so that to ask for an English visa is virtually to ask leave to stay in this country and settle there. So it is very difficult to get an English visa. The Home Office asks first of all whether the man who asks to be admitted can keep himself here, without falling on the hands of charitable institutions, etc. We should be glad to keep Broch indefinitely, means or no means; but that will not help him, unluckily, to get an English visa. I don't know anything about his private means, or whether he can get the benefit of them outside Germany, if he has them. I know that he has almost finished another long novel, for the MS. is safely here.

After hearing about the visa from Anja, I wrote to a friend of mine in London who is in the Civil Service. He told me that what should be done was to write to the Under Secretary of State, Aliens Department, Home Office. I have done this, saying that I am prepared to keep Broch here, that he is a man of irreproachable character, without political affiliations, and a distinguished writer, in fact a person eminently suitable to be admitted. I have also written to Aldous Huxley and Herbert Read, both of whom, I know, admire Broch's work, asking them to write also to the Home Office. Anja

50 another . . . novel: The Death of Virgil. *This was finished in 1940. Broch hoped the Muirs would translate it, but they did not like it so much as his earlier work, and felt unable to undertake it. Mrs Muir was writing a novel based upon their life in London, which has never been published.*

has just written to say that you would like to help, and that it appears, is the right thing to do: I mean to write to the Home Office.

I suppose you know most of what has happened to Broch, that he was in prison for a few weeks after the Hitler invasion, and is now out again, but very anxious to leave Austria. He is such an extraordinarily sensitive creature, that it makes my heart sore to think of his position. It is terrible to think that men like Hitler have power over such men as Broch. We both met Broch in Vienna several years ago, and in a few days came to love him.

The world seems to be showing its shape more and more clearly every year, almost every month, and warning us more and more that it will have to be changed. It isn't even the same world in which I met you last; or perhaps it is the same world, only I did not know it then.

I hope Violet and you are both well; our private lives go on, whatever happens, and I can't imagine them not being important to us: they must be important to ordinary people even in Germany, little as they have left of them. We often think of you both, with affection and gratitude. We are still translating, with intervals of our own work: up here, where it is cheaper than London, we hope to get more of our own work done, and less translation. Willa is writing a novel, and I am taking notes for something like a description of myself, done in general outline, not in detail, not as a story, but as an attempt to find out what a human being is in this extraordinary age which depersonalises everything. Whether it will be a success or a failure, I can't say; it may be that I have found at last a form that suits me; it may be that I haven't found a form at all, but merely a collection of fragments. I have begun to note myself, anyway, and I find that in doing that I am noting other people too, and the world around me. That is bound to have some value: the problem is to discover what you are, and then what your relation is to other people: I am starting from that and it takes me in ever so many directions, inwards and outwards, backwards and forwards: into dreams on the one hand, and social observation on the other; into the past by a single line, and over the present by countless lines. At any rate I am learning in the process, whatever the artistic result may be.

I don't suppose there is much chance of our meeting for some time, but if ever you come to this inhospitable country, you will receive a hospitable welcome here, at least. With love to you both from us both. (Gavin is turning into a nice, good-looking boy, almost disconcertingly intelligent.)

Yours ever,
Edwin.

51: TO SYDNEY SCHIFF

St. Andrews
28 May, 1938

My dear Sydney,

... I am so glad you are interested in my projected book; I am still taking notes for it. When I doubted whether it would be a success, I was not thinking of money success (though that would be welcome enough, but unlikely), but of the possibility of giving artistic unity to what I have to say: in fact, I don't know whether I want artistic unity; I would like to avoid all make-believe; the arranged patterns of modern novels give me such a stale, second-hand, false and tired feeling. And I have no wish to confess either, for the sake of confession: I am too old for that: I want some knowledge; it really comes to that. But will I achieve it? A little perhaps, and even a little is of some use.

I am so glad that you are both well, and I cannot believe that you are feeling your age mentally. As for physically, I am feeling my age on that level, too. I'm 51 now, though I still look ten years younger, or so people say: none of my family has ever looked his age; whether this is a good or bad sign I find it very difficult to say. Gavin is ten and a half now. He is extraordinarily gifted in music, or so people who know about it say, composes extensively, and has a terrific passion for Mozart and Bach, and even for parts of Beethoven. His other gift is for mathematics. We have managed at last to get a very good piano teacher for him, which is providential in this remote place. He is learning the violin as well. He is really more than we had expected, in every way. Of course, all this may vanish with puberty, and he may become an ordinary boy.

I don't know when either of us will be in London again, but if I am during this year I should like to see you both again, and I shall certainly let you know.

With our best love to you both,

Yours, Edwin.

52: TO ALEC AITKEN

St. Andrews
July 1938

My dear Aitken,

We were so glad to get your letter, for we both felt at once an affinity with you, which probably goes deeper than any of us knows yet, and I assure you that such spontaneous friendship is rare to us, as to you. I want it to continue, and I'll do anything I can to make it continue. I feel that in some ways our experience coincides, though I feel that yours, in the things you mention, has gone farther than mine and is more exact. The sycamore leaves and the wasp-wings opening and shutting in slow motion gave me an extraordinary feeling of beauty: I can faintly visualise it, and when I do, for some reason I have a picture of brilliant light, more intense than actual light. I can't conceive with my mind at all the sonata of Beethoven heard in an instant; it is too much for me; you must try to describe it some time. The most strange and the most beautiful experience I have ever had was a waking trance, a long, very rapid series of vivid pictures, which may have actually occupied a very short space of time: including a fight with a curious heraldic monster, and ending up in the shoulder of God, a huge figure sitting on a throne, with rings of the blessed round Him. I must tell you about it when we next meet. I am making notes at present for a book, into which I want to put a number of these things.

We are often bothered pretty deeply about Gavin, as Willa says. The slightest psychical stimulus produces almost immediately such a strong physical response, driving the blood from his face, often actually hollowing his cheeks. Excitement can turn him green. I don't know what is to be done with a sensibility like that. On the one hand it is a strength, and goes with his enjoyment of music: on the other, it is sometimes almost paralysing to him. We have never encouraged him consciously in following out the intellectual and musical drive within him; for I can only think of it as a drive. Actually we have discouraged him sometimes, put on the brake, not directly, but by drawing his attention to other things. I don't know whether he is feeling the reflection of a breakdown of my own. I did

52 Aitken (*1895–1967*) was then Reader, later Professor of Mathematics at Edinburgh University; a brilliant mathematician he was also keenly interested in music and poetry.

have a severe breakdown in my youth, caused by the death of four of my family, my father and mother, and two brothers, in the space of two years. I have not got over that yet, in spite of the time between. And I had a breakdown of some obscure kind when I was six, which I feel has altered all my life: not absolutely, of course, and even 'altered' is a questionable word: one's life is what it is. I merely mean that there was a profound change at that time, a sort of convulsion which I can't entirely put down to growth; perhaps the first intimation of guilt; but that is conjecture. I'm very attached to Gavin and very moved by him in all sorts of ways, powerfully and happily. The enormous feat of intellectual digestion made by a child in the first few years of his life, thrown into a world he knows nothing about, is extraordinarily moving. To see him seizing upon these foreign things, grappling with experience before he knows it is experience, distinguishing and reasoning about the objects which make up the world, gives me a better opinion of mankind, and of myself.

But this is a letter all I, I, I. And now I'll go on again to thank you for what you say about the *Variations*. Willa is perfectly true when she says that we expect nobody who comes to the house to have any knowledge of my poetry, and so we assume the opposite. What you say about the poem warms my heart. But when you came I was too moved by some of the things you said to consider that I was a poet, or to care about it, except essentially, in recognising that the world you spoke about was the world from which what I like best in my poetry was drawn, largely unconsciously. But I am rushing on: I must put a brake upon myself. Do come for a long week end before the summer turns into autumn. We must see each other as much as we can. All good to you.

Yours ever
Edwin Muir

53: TO ALEC AITKEN

20 Queen's Gardens
St Andrews
Fife
23 July, 1938

My dear Aitken,

Thanks more than I can say, for your letters, and what is in them, and for the Eddington. I'm ashamed to say I have never read Eddington: I did read half-way through Jeans's *The Univers around us*, once, but it seemed too much like a fairy-tale, that is, not a genuine fairy-tale, but a synthetic one, and I put it down again. I was

> *53 enclosed volume:* Journeys and Places.
> *Aitken wrote in a notebook: 'July 27, 1938. Under Harestone Hill, in the Lammermuirs, east of Lammerlaw. I had delayed in the Hopes Glen, in the curious and quite irrational conviction that someone was going to break in on my solitariness, to deflect me in some interesting way from my purpose, which had been to climb to Meikle Says Law, the highest point (1,750 feet) of the Lammermuirs. But in the sun-flooded trees, the stream running clear below, I had lingered, stopped, and begun to read Edwin Muir's* Journeys and Places, *which he had sent to me after the Colloquium and Gregory Tercentenary at St Andrews, where I had met him for the first time.*
>
> > There is a road that turning always
> > Cuts off the country of Again.
>
> *As I read these lines, the stream below became Heraclitean; then I turned to "Hölderlin's Journey", to me, still the most characteristic of all Edwin's poems:*
>
> > 'And watched beside a mouldering gate
> > . . .
> > From the cold and the living head.
>
> *This "mouldering gate" I felt to be nearby, somewhere in the side-roads up from Gifford, as if at Linplum; perhaps somewhere else, as in my own life.*
> *Poetry of such still, deep musing does not help one to climb hills. I dallied on in the glen, but at length held myself to a resolve, struck across the shaws and followed the curves of least effort that the sheep have traced in their non-Euclidean mountain-space.'*
> *letter on the War: I have found no trace of this, but Aitken wrote an honest and sensitive account of his war experiences in* From Gallipoli to the Somme *(written 1917, revised in the 30s, and again before publication in 1963).*

conscious, very soon after I met you, that mathematics, as you know it, is the pathway into a strange world which can be reached by other means, by music and poetry: and though the mathematical way is closed to me, or at any rate obstructed by endless things which I do not know, I think we meet in the place, or at least have sometimes, by different routes, found the same place. I am going to read Eddington straight away, which may mean slowly, I'm afraid. And will you accept the enclosed volume, which I hope you haven't read yet. When I look through it, I really seem to see a faint glimmering of mathematics somewhere in it.

Willa swears she had no disapproval at all when you mentioned the War. I was not in it myself, not from conscientious scruples, though I never thought of it idealistically. I went up to enlist, but I was turned down, and to understand that one has to understand the sort of youth I struggled through. I began working in an office in Glasgow when I was 14. At 16 I had to have a growth, a rotten gland or something, removed from my neck: the scar is still there. At 18, after the deaths in the family, I had to fend for myself as a clerk on 14/- a week. There followed another physical break-down, but I had to work on through it, using a stomach pump every night. During the War, after this training of undernourishment and psychological distress of various kinds, I was in doctors' hands most of the time. My tough maternal stock, Willa's endless help and understanding, and freedom from the grind of routine and poverty, have made me now a comparatively healthy man, as you can see. It astonishes me whenever I think of it. This, I think, will explain the feeling of discouragement you divined in me. I hope you won't think this short account of my early life a complaint. It isn't; but merely a partial explanation. As for my poetry, it has never 'taken on', except for Willa, a few friends, a few poets like Walter de la Mare, and that is naturally discouraging, but would never make me give up the writing of it, when the impulse comes. But encouragement, on the other hand, strengthens the impulse. I feel certain that nothing is better than encouragement. I've acquired a certain reputation, not a big one, by going on writing poetry; but that is almost worthless, for it is not a matter of understanding, and understanding is the only thing of any use to a man who is saying what he thinks, in poetry, mathematics, or any other form of utterance. So I feel thankful to you again for what you say about my poetry, and I know that such things have an effect. I only wish I could help you in the same way, and perhaps I shall in some fashion or other: I sincerely hope so.

I was much moved by your letter on the War, which should be published in some form or another. Could you not recast it for the general public? You say so many things which I feel to be profoundly true, and say them with such eloquence.

(I have had to break off to take Gavin to a party in Cupar, and other things have turned up; and now I must write a review, a long one, which must catch the Sunday afternoon post.)

Do come for a *day* then, if you can't for a week-end. There are a host of things we have to talk about, which can't be discussed satisfactorily in a letter.

Love from us both.

Yours
Edwin Muir

54: TO SYDNEY SCHIFF

St. Andrews
9 December, 1938

My dear Sydney,

We have been troubled about Broch too. We have had two postcards, the last of them about five weeks ago, which said that he was 'working wildly'. He has sent no address except that of the American Express Agency. It isn't like him, and I only hope that he is not ill. I know from his stay here how scrupulous he is about answering letters; he spent the first three weeks doing nothing else, for he was always receiving letters from unhappy people in Vienna who thought he might be able to help them; and he was tireless in replying to them. I don't know exactly what can be done; Willa has written again to him at the American Express. But I hope nothing has gone wrong. He is in any case a man of scrupulous honour and there must be some explanation for his silence.

We are working hard and struggling along. The general situation, as you say, is past speech. My book on contemporary literature (the last volume in a series on English literature edited by Bonamy

---

54 *After getting out of Austria, Broch had stayed with the Muirs for over a month, then with the Schiffs, and had then gone to U.S.A., where he eventually settled at Princeton. Muir's book on contemporary literature was* The Present Age *(1939).*

Dobrée) will be out in spring; I shall send you a copy if I may. I am writing a sort of autobiography: that suiting my style better, I think, than an autobiographical novel. I hope you are both keeping well, and I wish we could see you sometime again. With much love to you both.

Yours ever,
Edwin

55: TO SYDNEY SCHIFF

St. Andrews
16 January, 1939

Dear Sydney,

Forgive me for not replying sooner. But Willa has been unwell; she has been ordered by the doctor to lie on her back and rest; her heart is weakened and missing its beat; and after her rest she must have a minor internal operation. I have been unwell too, and have had to have out all my remaining teeth but two; after this I shall be all right again. In the middle of all this, Gavin has had chickenpox; but that is a minor matter, and he is almost well again. But it has been a troubled time, and as far as Willa is concerned, still is. She has been overstraining her strength, it seems, for months.

Thanks for Broch's letter; Broch is a great man and a very good man. I don't know whether I agree or not with your opinion: that the only hope of the world lies in the gospel of Christ. As you know, I have believed for many years in the immortality of the soul; all my poetry springs from that in one form or another; and belief of that kind means belief in God, though my God is not that of the churches: and I can reconcile myself to no church. I have as little use for the materialist doctrines of Communism as you have, and Fascism seems to me definitely evil. I look upon myself as an anti-Marx socialist; a man who believes that people are immortal souls and that they should bring about on this earth a society fit for immortal souls. Immortality, unfortunately, does not make them good, and hardly any of them are conscious of immortality; they act for immediate and generally private and petty ends. Most of them no doubt have to do so for reasons of necessity: that should not be. I am quite clear in my mind that society must change, that Capitalism must be transcended; but if the change comes through the terrible Marxist machine of Materialist Determination, it will be a major calamity, for it denies the soul, and there cannot be a more fundamental denial than that. But everything is dark, and is getting darker: the horrible persecution of the Jews is the most obvious symptom of the madness which tinges all the new movement in Europe, but the movement itself threatens us all, and threatens everything that we not merely hold dear, but everything necessary for a real living life as apart from an ostensible one. There is a real denial of humanity here, as Broch says; there is more, a contempt for humanity, hatred of anyone with a separate, unique life of his own. The capacity to recognise immaterial realities is almost dead, it seems to me; is quite dead in the sphere of action at any rate, the sphere in which Hitler, Mussolini and Chamberlain move. And in the last resort we live by immaterial realities; that is our real life; the rest is more or less machinery. We are moved about, caught, wedged, clamped in this machinery; and that is what is called history.

I wish you both well and think often of you. I don't know when I shall see you again. I am as sick, I think, as you can be, over the dreadful things that are being done to the Jews, and the darkness that has fallen over them. I am ashamed, as every citizen in this country should be, of the part England has played. And I share, with everyone else, part of the responsibility for it; for we have all been too easy-going and thoughtless and hopeful.

My love to you both,

Edwin.

56: TO GEORGE BARKER

St. Andrews
21 May, 1939

My dear George,

Forgive me for not replying sooner to your letter and particularly your poem. I have been suffering torments with neuralgia, the result of temporary over-work and anxiety: Willa has been ill and had an operation, and is only getting better now. So forgive my silence. I was very much moved, astonished (in the fundamental sense, as one is astonished by some beautiful natural spectacle), and

56 your poem: '*Elegy on Spain (Dedication to the photograph of a child killed in an air-raid on Barcelona).*' *chorus:* '*The Refugees*', *published in* New Alliance *I (Autumn 1939); only about the last third of this has been reprinted.*

impressed by your poem. It seems to me by far the best thing you have done, and gives the impression also that there is a great deal of the same inspiration behind it. The music and sweep are splendid: the measure and spontaneity in them following the feeling and yet creating this sense of astonishment. What can I say about the poem except to congratulate you? I always knew you had extraordinary powers in you; if I am astonished, it is not by you but by the poem itself. Your power of expression must have matured enormously in the last few years; you had always lots to express, and now you are expressing it. Merely as a recitation the poem must be very moving. My mind is too tired at the moment to say much more.

 I have been turning over for some time too a sort of recitation, a chorus on the subject of the Refugees, but have been too tired to get anything worth while done, though the theme keeps coming back to me. I think it is a wonderful theme, but do not feel wonderful. A lot of my energy is wasted in trying to ignore this mad, comic-opera world, which other people have made and other people will unmake, and unmake other things more worth while at the same time. Forgive me for being so morose. I still hang on to my belief in immortality (on which we had long arguments in Downshire Hill); but it is awful nevertheless to have a world like the present one, and be so powerless to do anything to alter it. I've been reading Rilke recently too, the *Duino Elegies*: if you haven't a copy I'll be glad to send you one, for by chance I shall have two in my hands. It's a marvellous poem, but curiously enough, has false and prosy bits.

 This is a dry letter. If you can come and see us sometime this summer, do. It will be like an angelic apparition in a Calvinist Kirk. I'm beginning to feel better. Much love to you both

Yours ever

Edwin

The photograph of the dead child is wonderfully beautiful and horrible and I don't know what besides. I wonder where you got it.

57: TO ALEC AITKEN

St. Andrews
1 July, 1939

My dear Alec,

I find that my broadcast is not on the 4th after all, but on the 10th—I mixed up the day with Gavin's school sports. So we may manage to meet after all, if you are free on that day. What you say about that house makes me very anxious to see it. I happened to find myself one summer morning early in an old English house (or rather the grounds of it). I forget its name now; but it had a moat with weeds growing in it; there was a lake completely covered with green slime; and in a forlorn garden two white peacocks were screaming: a complete picture of desolation, yet very beautiful. These are merely rude palpable[?] notes, which do not give any idea of the enchantment of the place—the early morning stillness, and the freshness of the surrounding woods added greatly to it. I do hope we shall be able to see this house, or place, of yours; it depends entirely on whether you are free. I do hope so.

I agree that de la Mare's anthology is too inclusive—I should have been inclined myself to include passages only which had a dream atmosphere. But his inclusiveness does, I think, show one thing: how deeply the things he chooses are involved with all English imagination, poetry in particular. The anthology really gives as complete a criticism of life (in Arnold's sense) as one could get from an anthology planned on the broadest basis. Another interesting thing, I think, is that the dream is much more organically knit into the older English literature (seventeenth century in particular) than into the later; in Sir Thomas Browne and Bunyan and Traherne it is as a part of *waking* life; in De Quincey and Coleridge it is a specific, separate thing. Or so it seems to me, fond as I am of De Quincey and Coleridge. I'm so looking forward to seeing you.

Yours ever Edwin Muir

57 that house: Cammo near Barnton, just outside Edinburgh. Aitken had been deeply impressed by its grounds—melancholy, decaying, strangely beautiful—when he had walked there several years before and accidentally encountered its eccentric owner, Mrs Maitland Tennant. Muir's own experience in the grounds of an old English house was used in his The Three Brothers, *pp. 61–4. anthology:* Behold this Dreamer *(1939) which contains two poems and two prose extracts by Muir.*

58: TO HERBERT READ

St Andrews
25 October, 1939

Dear Herbert,

... I only know the first volume (1,000 pages) of *Der Mann ohne Eigenschaften*. I think it is a very problematic venture, as you say, though perhaps not quite so problematic as Broch: the style is much easier and much more straightforward. I found it very amusing and witty; what would hold up the ordinary reader, I think, is its lack of ordinary progression, its methodical meandering. It is certainly a remarkable book; Broch has a great admiration for it. But I have no idea how it would go here at all; it could not in any case sell well, I am afraid. It is wittier and less metaphysical than Broch, and it does not contain these enormous labyrinthine sentences. Broch was here for a few months, but went to America last September. He was very pleased at having written one day the longest sentence 'in the world' as he called it: four pages of closely typed foolscap: followed by a sentence of three words....

Yours ever
Edwin Muir

59: TO ALEC AITKEN

St. Andrews
4 January, 1940

My dear Alec,

Forgive me for not replying sooner, but I've been working day and night to finish my autobiography before the end of the year: I simply could not bear to have it dragging on into 1940. I managed it, and the book left for the publishers in 1939. I think you will like it, or at least be very interested in parts of it: I have stolen one image from you in it—I wonder if you will recognise it when you come to it. I find with some dismay, after going over my life, that I have no philosophy—here am I, a middle-aged man and a professional writer,

---

58 Read *(1893–1968)* was then a director of Routledge and Kegan Paul, and must have consulted Muir, whom he had known since at least 1931, about the possibility of publishing a translation of Robert Musil's *(1860–1942)* great unfinished novel. No English translation was published until much later *(*The Man without Qualities, *3 vols, Secker, 1953–60).*

and I have no philosophy. I had a philosophy when I was 27, but it was not my philosophy. I have no philosophy now—that is no rational scheme for accounting for all the time I have lived in the world, or comprehensively for life itself. And this lack—which I must share with several million people—really does dismay me in some part of me, and gives me a troubling sense of insecurity. I believe that I am immortal, certainly, but that in a way makes it more difficult to interpret *this* life (in another way it makes it easier: I would be the last to deny that: if life were *only* this life, I would find it virtually impossible to find a meaning in it—moral or aesthetic). If we're moving towards a society which compared to this will be a sort of heaven on earth (and I doubt it), how can that society, a mere point in history, justify all the grinding cycles of suffering and cruelty and mere grey living that were necessary to lead up to it? I think Ivan Karamazoff was quite right in saying that if that was how things were he would hand back his ticket. I suppose what I mean when I say I have no philosophy is that I have no explanation, none whatever, of Time except as an unofficial part of Eternity —no historical explanation of human life, for the problem of evil seems insoluble to me: I can only accept it as a mystery, and what a mystery is I do not know. All these thoughts have been roused (and clarified a little in my mind) by writing my life: there is very little in the book itself about them. All I can say I have, confronted by these things, is faith, and I think that perhaps my faith is a little too easy, considering the enormity of these things. But faith can produce a sentence like: 'I am the resurrection and the life'. (It seems to me the most sublime sentence ever uttered, especially the order of the terms, the resurrection preceding the life, as if a real life only began with a resurrection, even in this world (and I believe this).) So that there may be something more in faith than we can account for, a source of energy and reconciliation which philosophy cannot reach. I do not know: I wish my mind were more single and clear.

I agree with you completely about 'The Refugees', which I'm glad I have written, on the one hand, and not particularly excited by myself, on the other. It was inspired by quite sincere feeling, but never *rose* to the right height, the pity and indignation never transmitting themselves, except in one or two lines in the last part. Now that my life is off my hands, I hope that some poetry will come to me again: I've already had some premonitory symptoms, but they have come to nothing. You must have these experiences in your mathematics too, or whenever these symptoms come to you, do they produce something?

It is a sad and threatening time: will we ever see a likeable look on the world's face again—not a smile, necessarily, that's too much to ask for, but a slow, peaceable expression. It would mean a great deal for everybody. There is less hatred blowing about than I had expected. But I have felt the invisible power of war which tries to reduce us all to a dead level, and regards your work and mine as trimmings, as luxuries, when the work of destruction, on so many fronts, has grown so important. I don't mind a more or less egalitarian level at all when it is a living level; but the dead level reached by denying all that you value in yourself is horrible. And whenever a modern war breaks out, there it is in the offing. But I'm not going to be levelled, if I can help it. It seems to me that this is a time when anyone who serves the intellect and the imagination must stick to his work as hard as he can: civilisation (a poor word for what we all want in our hearts) is necessary. So here's a good new year to you all. We're fairly well: how long we shall be I do not know: but all the world is on the knees of chance. I wish we could see you again. I've often had the ambition of living in a manse. I'm glad you are having comparative peace. Love to you all

Yours always
Edwin Muir

60: TO HERBERT READ

St Andrews
26 January, 1940

Dear Herbert,

You wrote some time ago very kindly suggesting that I might elaborate the ideas in my essay on Calvinism and Communism. Since then some more ideas about the subject have been occurring to me: particularly the realisation that both creeds are creeds of Wrath, for the theory of the Class Struggle as the chosen principle of progress seems to me to rest on a view of history as wrath and nothing else, with an unexplained hiatus, at the end, filled with the perfect communist society, which really corresponds to the Biblical

---

60 *Nothing came of either of the projects mentioned in this letter.*

vision of the Millennium. I suppose history is really mainly wrath, just as human life, for the vast majority of people, is mainly reprobation; and this fact gives both creeds a strong realistic effectiveness, as interpretations of the present actual state of man or of society. But where I disagree violently with them both is in their seeing a divine principle in wrath, like the Calvinist, and the only liberating human principle in wrath, like the Communist. I think both theories are extraordinarily alike here, alike, that is, in elevating the form of most human activity (which I suppose is struggle and anger) into the principle of human activity, and beyond that, into the principle of good, at least of advancement. There is obviously a good deal of Darwinism behind the Marxian theory. As for where advancement (so far as there has been any) has come from, I suppose you would agree with me that before it could prevail it had to pass through the phase of anger, that it had to meet opposition and enmity and fight against them; but I feel pretty certain, on the other hand, that the spring of advancement, the thing that has always had to be fought for, did not come out of opposition or anger at all, though when it enters the world of action it rouses anger, until, when the anger has burned itself out, it emerges in a somewhat defaced but still positive and workable form. I think there is a possible middle position between the pure pacifism of Huxley, which assumes that anger can destroy everything, and the catastrophic view of the Marxians, who, after assuming that wrath is the principle of advancement, suddenly arrive at a society in which there is no anger at all. I think that Russia's latest exploits in Finland must have shaken some even of the Marxians, though I haven't met one yet who admits it. But they seem to have lost all capacity for thought, so far as thought means judgment.

... I have no idea of the length or nature of the book you had vaguely in mind. On the other hand, I think this is probably a good time for a candid examination of Communism on these or similar lines. If I were to write one, it would not be very long, I think; probably about fifty thousand words or so. And there is another difficulty. We aren't very well off, and this war is bound to make us less so, unless we can make some money. I have no idea how a book such as this would repay the time I should have to spend on it. Willa and I have actually been thinking of starting on a detective story, which we have been making up in our minds for several months now for our own entertainment; but I don't know, either, whether detective stories are profitable. I wonder whether you could give me some idea about that: our story would be quite an amusing one. I have actually been dreaming about it, and woke one morning with a first-rate bogus character in my mind, name and qualities complete. Perhaps if things were really favourable, I could undertake the Communist book and the detective story together, and make one repay me for the other....

Yours ever,
Edwin Muir

61: TO WILLIAM SOUTAR

St Andrews
3 February, 1940

Dear William Soutar,

Forgive me for not replying sooner to your note and particularly to your poems, which ask for a much more eloquent answer than I can give: Poetry is the only answer to poetry. I should have replied sooner, but I have been writing my life, and have managed to finish it at last (at least up to 1922)—a curious labour, almost as difficult as living itself, but interesting at least. The difficulty that strikes me about life is not that it is uninteresting (as so many uninteresting people call it) but that it is interesting in too many different ways, that is, confusing; so that it takes a genius, and a very great genius at that, to pierce through its countless meanings to the one that illumines them all. I suppose the importance and necessity of religion lies in that; for the great religious figures have this particular gift *in excelsis*, and they can give it out to others so long as there is a faith and a religious community. I have been struggling with such questions in my book; the difficulty with me is that I have the faith, but that I cannot belong to any one Christian community. I believe in God, in the immortality of the soul, and that Christ is the greatest figure who ever appeared in the history of mankind. I believe in the Fall too, and the need for salvation. But the theological dogmas do not help me; I can't digest them for my good; they're an obstacle to

61 William Soutar (1898–1943) had been ill since his early twenties and had been confined to bed in his home in Perth since 1930. your poems: In the Time of Tyrants, *issued in a small limited edition in December 1939, with an introductory note 'On Pacifist Faith and Necessity'. The friend who left Muir a Dante was John Holms.*

me (perhaps they shouldn't be, but they are); and so I'm a sort of illicit Christian, a gate-crasher, hoping in my own way to slip in

> At David's hip yet.

I was greatly moved by the integrity and the high temper of your poems, and of the introduction as well: they hang together absolutely, as things from one integral centre do. You have given these questions of Pacifism and Marxism and Christianity and their relation to one another more thought than I have: I have been troubled more, and perhaps too exclusively, by personal things—the hope of finding a meaning in life and in my own life. I feel the need to see life timelessly: the only way in which it can be seen as a whole. Religion sees it timelessly, but Marxism sees it historically, and like religion, sees history mainly as Wrath, but unlike religion, sees nothing else but wrath. The theory of the class struggle is based on a vision of history as wrath. Wrath may be the form of most of history, but Marx makes wrath the very principle of good, or at least of advancement, and that is because his good and his advancement are purely historical. Good things have certainly to be fought for, because they raise enmity to them in the world; they have all to pass through the phase of wrath before they emerge, damaged, diminished, but still with some virtue in them; but the spring of good itself has nothing to do with wrath, and could never rise if wrath were everywhere. This may seem to you an unjust interpretation of Marxism; it must, since you hold both to it and to Pacifism. But I can't get away from the thought that the Marxist conception of life is a conception where there is no God, no divine Spirit, either immanent or transcendent; and if God does exist, that must be the most important truth of all, taking precedence of all other truths; and any interpretation of history which leaves it out must be mutilated, a monstrosity. I am not too clear in my own mind about all this; I want a rounded conception of existence, and all I can see is a flash here and there, which tells me that such a conception exists, perhaps outside of Time, I don't know. I feel I am being ungenerous to you in taking up these objections, but sincerity has the power to waken sincerity, and if I had not liked and respected your poetry so much I should not have said what I have said. (And what I have said does not affect the poetry, which stands on its own feet.) I should like to come and see you again sometime when the light and the weather are better; I enjoyed so much seeing you last time; it was one of the most delightful days Willa and I have had since we came up here, and we often talk of it.

I hope you did not have a Temple Dante already. The one I sent you belonged to me, but a dear friend of mine left me another at his death a few years ago, with his name and markings in it, and I have used it ever since. I have got so much enjoyment out of Dante, with only a slight smattering of Italian to help me, that I thought you might get the same pleasure, or perhaps even a greater one. I suppose there's no one to equal him, except Shakespeare, and they are very different. We both send our warmest regards to you and your father and mother and sister, who were so kind to us. I hope you are still writing poetry in this dreadful time.

Yours ever
Edwin Muir

62: TO DAVID PEAT

St. Andrews
28 February, 1940

Dear David,

I am sorry to be so long in writing to you, and I am not writing now merely because of the enclosed passage from my autobiography. I have been thinking a good deal about my own life recently, and feeling more and more that it is not what it should be, and I feel guilty that I have let our old friendship drop so much, without giving it anything on which it could nourish itself. You were a very dear friend of mine at a time when I very much needed friendship; I know I helped you too, as you helped me, and I am very glad of it now; though that was not the cause of our friendship, but merely its outcome; for the friendship itself came from liking and fondness, which is a justification in itself and a good in itself. We drifted apart, both geographically and in other ways; my last two meetings with you made me feel that I could not reach you; I did not blame you for this, but on the other hand I did not blame myself enough; I should have had more instinctive wisdom, more wisdom of the heart, and I should have been able to help you in some way. At any

62 enclosed passage: The Story and the Fable, *pp. 167–70 (*An Autobiography, *pp. 141–3). Generously Peat asked Muir to omit all criticism of his father, whose severity Muir had been inclined to think partly responsible for Peat's neurosis.*

rate, I should have written to you oftener. Forgive me for not doing it: it is not that I have less affection for you, but that I am prone to spiritual laziness and sloth, and that the world is too much with me, late and soon: when Wordsworth wrote 'late and soon', he wrote something which touches me painfully. The world is in a bad state (the world that is too much with us, late and soon), and friendship is a thing so far above it, that I feel we may carry it into the next life; at any rate we should guard it in this. I am not writing to you because I am lonely; actually I am happier than I have been, in spite of the state of the world, for I have had something like a sense of the presence of God, a sense which I have never consciously been aware of before, though I am now 52; it is too new and strange for me to write about it, and so inexperienced that I am afraid of writing about it. I have believed for a long time in the immortality of the soul, but this is something different: I tremble to lose it again by my own fault. Perhaps I should not have written about it at all, for I cannot tell anything about it, but only so far feel it at times.

    I have enclosed the passage about you, wondering whether you would want anything in it altered, or whether you would rather I left anything out. I hope nothing in what I say will wound you or embarrass you; and if this is so I shall leave it out. I've found all through the autobiography a great difficulty in writing about the friends I have known: about myself I can tell anything I like, for it can offend nobody but myself. Please tell me, old man, what you think of the passage and if you would like anything in it corrected or left out.

    I hope this war will end sometime soon, without further suffering and bloodshed, and that mankind will return to some charity and good sense. I hope things are going better with you. We are struggling on, and hope to weather the storm with what faith we have. Much love to you and Evelyn.

Yours
Edwin

63: TO HERBERT READ

St Andrews
29 February, 1940

Dear Herbert,

... You suggested I might mention a theme for a biography, and there are two figures in whom I am really interested: James Connolly and Cunninghame Graham, but whether either would come near enough to the idea of the series I do not know. The first was, I think, one of the greatest men of his time and one of the most interesting and moving; a genuine thinker as well as a great leader. The second fascinates my curiosity, and I also have a baffled admiration for him (I met him once or twice): I think he never went very far in politics because he had a clear perception of human corruption and no ambition at all; it was probably lack of ambition combined with pride that made him such a riddle. But Connolly is much more to my taste. A possible biography would be John Burns, but I feel an Englishman would deal with him much better. I don't know whether these suggestions will be of any use to you....

Yours
Edwin Muir

64: TO HERBERT READ

St Andrews
12 May, 1940

Dear Herbert,

Thank you so much for all the kind things you say about my book. I had no idea that our lives showed such a close parallel; in reading, it must have moved you in quite a special way. I had a lot of difficulty in writing the book, especially in the Glasgow chapter,

---

63 James Connolly: (1870–1916) Irish socialist, labour leader and writer. Cunninghame Graham: (1852–1936) Scottish writer, radical, nationalist, aristocrat. Nothing came of these suggestions.

64 Read's early life especially had been parallel to Muir's—happy rural childhood on a farm, early death of father, unhappy later boyhood away from early environment, period of clerking (much shorter than Muir's) in big city (Leeds), influence of Nietzsche, temporary conversion to Guild Socialism, writing for The New Age. The Green Child *(1935) is a philosophic romance by Read.*

where all the calamities came upon the Muir family. I feel I probably have a sort of obsession about Time, and I wish I could look at it more objectively. Instead of seeing Time as the dimension of growth, I see everything passing away—the other pole, and I expect there is some perversity in my attitude, though on the other hand it is what stimulates my particular kind of imagination. I was very much struck by *The Green Child*; I think it is a very beautiful work; but simply because our conceptions of time are so different the last part remained a little incomprehensible to me, though the effect which is produced on me without my knowing why was very powerful. It's very nice to hear from you again, and so warmly. I don't know what I shall write next, apart from a few poems which have come recently and I think are still coming, perhaps under the present pressure. I have been advised to continue the autobiography, and may do so if I feel I can do it well enough. I wrote to Gollancz about the Calvinist–Communist idea, which is still developing, but he could not offer an advance that would keep me going while I wrote it. I have the idea of a story, not a detective story this time, but that would probably be equally unproductive of advances. I have a collection of essays that could be published, but I doubt whether I could find a publisher for them just now. Hermann Broch has just finished a sort of half novel, half rhapsodic prose poem, describing the last day of Virgil's life; I've heard that it is a wonderful piece of work; but it may be difficult to find a publisher for it, and if we translate it, as he wants us to do, it won't pay us for the trouble: only bad books are any good for a translator, I've come to the conclusion. Broch is in America now, and I believe he is offering the book to The Viking Press. But I would much rather do something other than translate; on the other hand, Broch's book might interest you; that is why I mention it. Much love from us both to Ludo

Yours ever
Edwin Muir

65: TO ALEC AITKEN

St. Andrews
28 May, 1940

My dear Alec,

Thank you so much for your letter and what you say about my book. I had intended to send you a copy, but these times are so dreadful that I can't even afford presents to my friends. I am so glad you like the book so much; I had thought that you in particular would like it. For you to spot the wave echo in the roofless chapel and the little hills was a brilliant piece of literary detection—I have been pursued by these little hills often without quite knowing where they came from: I realised as I wrote the autobiography. Life is endlessly strange—but now no longer: this war takes the strangeness out of everything, and makes us contemplate our bare uninteresting bones. I'm depressed: the news about Belgium's surrender has just come in. I still think we are going to win; but what an effort, and what bloodshed it will take, and what terror to our children, and what a world of hatred and general hatefulness. Yet we are all responsible for it—I mean all peoples and probably almost all individuals in Europe—by turning away from the soul and pursuing our private ambitions and greeds and personalities, and behaving as if they alone existed. Fifty or a hundred years of that, combined with an immense development of inventive processes, was bound to lead to this. It is too awful. . . .

Yours ever
Edwin Muir

65 *my book:* The Story and the Fable *(1940; later revised and extended in* An Autobiography, *1954).* roofless chapel: *A roofless chapel near Muir's childhood home on Wyre is mentioned in* S *and* F, *pp. 14, 44 (A 15, 40).* little hills: *In* S *and* F, *p. 64 (A 57) Muir writes of 'the little green hills of childhood', after describing a dream in which he saw 'little conical hills a little higher than a man's head'. The hill near the Bu on which he played as a child and on which were the remains of an old castle is quite small. Cf. 'The Mythical Journey':*

> Wave echo in the roofless chapel,
> The twice-dead castle on the swamp-green mound.

and 'Hölderlin's Journey'.

66: TO GEORGE SCOTT-MONCRIEFF

St Andrews
13 June, 1940

My dear Scomo,

Here is the *Atlantic* and Garioch's poems; forgive me for not writing sooner; I have felt a bit troubled these last days....

I like your first poem (on the Feast of the Annunciation) more than I can say; I thought it exquisite and can imagine the pleasure it gave you in the conception. The Scots and the conceit are wedded as I don't think they have ever been before; I still think Scots is just a little too poetic in itself for poetry's daily food, but this may be a relic of my Calvinism. But you persuade me in this poem by the aptness and judgment and felicity with which you use the language. I do hope you print the poem in the *N.A.*...

I'm still thinking of you both with great affection. Much love to Ann.

Yours ever
Edwin

I liked Garioch's book of poems very much. Why not send a copy to F. G. Scott, saying that I had suggested it? I'm sure F.G. would be delighted with some of the poems and might set them to music.

67: TO STEPHEN SPENDER

St. Andrews
20 July, 1940

Dear Stephen,

I'm enclosing a subscription for another six months. I hope *Horizon* will be able to carry on. I'm rather in a quandary myself. I

---

66 Atlantic: The Atlantic Monthly *for April 1940 which contained Muir's article 'Time and the Modern Novel'.* Garioch's Poems: 17 Poems for 6d *by Somhairle Mac Ghill-Eathain and Robert Garioch. Scott-Moncrieff's 'Feast of the Annunciation' appeared in* The New Alliance *(of which he was editor, and to which Muir contributed) for June–July 1940.*

67 Nothing came of Muir's application for teaching posts, and in the autumn he went to work as a clerk in the Food Office in Dundee. Only an extract from his war diary was published—in Decision *(New York) in April 1941.*

122

don't see how we're to live on literature now, and I have no qualifications (academic degrees and things like that) which would get me a regular post anywhere. Gavin's headmaster has advised me to apply as English master for some public school, and has written to Bryanston, recommending me. I think I should enjoy teaching for a while, since writing at present is so difficult, and being published, almost impossible. I've been wondering if you or Connolly have any public school connections, and could give me any advice. Joe Ackerley has offered to do what he can for me. If you should hear of anything, or could recommend me how to set about applying to people of whose habits I know nothing, I would be very grateful. There are no translations coming in, and Harraps have refused to give an advance on a book I suggested, a war diary—which is understandable, since we don't know how long the war will last, or what vicissitudes it may pass through.

Thank you so much for the review of my autobiography, which was very generous. I've been able to write very little during the last two or three months, only a little poetry, and, very surprisingly, mostly in Scots—I expect that the present time is drawing us all back to our bases, a good thing in one way, I think. We've been terribly troubled about Gavin, whether to send him to America or keep him here, pulled to and fro in the most agonising way by two impossible choices. He gets asthma and begins to gasp and choke as soon as the thought of crossing the Atlantic is suggested to him: we have no choice at present but to keep him here. His music is going on in the most astonishing way. Do let me know if you hear or know anything about posts in public schools: I've applied to the Ministry of Information several times and put my name in the Central Register, but there, I expect, it will remain to the end of the war. I hope things are going relatively well with you. With love from us all

Edwin

68: TO STEPHEN SPENDER

[*St. Andrews*]
2 *August, 1940.*

Dear Stephen,

... I find it hard to write anything with sense in it at present; odd lines of poetry keep bobbing up in my mind, but no coherent argument will follow from them; perhaps that will come. I'm enclosing one poem which did get written, not for publication, for I don't know whether it is good or bad; it came simply out of distress of mind which I tried to deal with, and is probably far too monitory; and I distrust myself when I am monitory. As for the poem you have, if it isn't likely to be published for some time, perhaps I had better try it somewhere else. Please don't be sorry about it; I really have no vanity about it. Perhaps that is because I feel it is in its way a good poem, since it came out of contemplation and not out of distress, like the one I enclose. At any rate don't hesitate to send it back if you feel you will not be able to use it. My mind is being teased by fragmentary intimations of poems more than it has been for some time, without anything further happening, lines like

> We were a tribe, a family, a people,
> King Lear was our father,

and

> The doors yawned open in Ulysses' house,

(which has turned into a poem)
and

> He who has not been yet will be some day,
> The gatherer gathered, the finder found,

---

68 '*In a Time of Mortal Shocks*' *is here printed for the first time. The other poem mentioned had been sent to Spender with a letter on 27 April; it was not printed in* Horizon; *it may have been '*The Grove*'—the next poem by Muir to be published, in* New Alliance *(February–March, 1941). The fragments mentioned turned into (1) first lines of '*Scotland 1941*' and '*The Ring*', (2) '*The Return of Odysseus*,' (3) '*The Question.*' your poem on the air raid: presumably '*The Air Raid across the Bay*,' published in* Horizon *in September, 1940. This poem, especially the second section, was much amended before being included in* Ruins and Visions *(1942).*

(which has come to nothing). I like very much the first verse of your poem on the air raid. I like it for its admirable objectivity. But I feel—perhaps I am wrong—that the second verse would have been more effective if it had been objective in the same way, a contrast on the same level, the good things stated as concretely as the bad. I don't feel I have much right to make this criticism, since in my own poetry I am not objective at all. But I admire the virtues of objectivity. I do hope things will go well with you, and I am so glad you are busy writing; it is the best thing we can do at present. It would be nice to see you again. With love from us both.

Edwin

In a Time of Mortal Shocks

Live on through these and learn what is this life,
Pure spirit indwelling,
Live on through these,
And know they were not made to please
Heart, hand or eye or ear or tongue
Or any member.
Then fill your solitary fife
Now in the senses' sad December
And sing your silent song.
This tale is only for your telling
Who can remember
What cold flesh wreathed in its snowdrift
  sorrow
Has thought but never known,
And borrow
A song from the Silent One
To still the many,
Since there's not any
Tongue or syllable to express
Distress.
Be in the wound before
It gapes aghast, be nearer
Than the familiar bullet, clearer
Than pain searching the nerves in widening
  reaches,
Be wiser

Than learned loss that baldly teaches
Letter by letter what could have been,
Dull difficult history. Be slyer
Than Terror the Great, the gaunt ten-foot-
    long guiser.
Be closer
Than the tongue-shaking lie is to the liar.
Lose to the loser.
Be at the root
No fear can find, the foot.
There stay secure.
There is your only place of safety. Stay
There in your house and keep your day.

69: TO GEORGE SCOTT-MONCRIEFF

St Andrews
15 November, 1940

Dear Scomo,

    Forgive me for being so remiss about your letter... We haven't anything you could call a home here now. I'm working in the Food Office in Dundee, and Willa is teaching in Gavin's school. I get the 8 o'clock train every morning and don't get back till 6.30. Willa's hours are better, but her work is much more exacting. The house is empty all day: and at night we don't feel like doing much more than resting in comfortable chairs. We've both had very bad colds on top of all this; and so my own morale, in matters concerning correspondence, has sunk completely. Literature, as far as we are concerned, has flopped. I still do reviewing for *The Listener*, but that is almost all. There are many other people, I've heard indirectly, who are in much the same position.

69 Ann's book: Auntie Robbo, *a book for children, by G. S.-M.'s wife, published by The Viking Press in U.S.A. in 1941, reviewed by Muir in* The New Alliance *for December 1941–January 1942; now in the* Penguin Puffin books series. *Colin Walkinshaw (J. M. Reid) did a programme for Radio Eireann, one of a series arranged by G. S.-M. as a bridgehead between Scottish and Irish writers. Vonier: Anscar Vonier O.S.B. (1875–1938), Abbot of Buckfast, author of many theological works, one of which (perhaps* The Personality of Christ *(5th imp. 1939)) G.S.-M. must have recommended to Muir.*

I'm so glad to hear the good news about Ann's book in America. It will mean a good deal to her, and to you both. My poor auto has sold very badly, but I've had some really nice letters about it from all kinds of people. What you say about the Colin Walkinshaw programme sounds exciting—I'm looking forward to it; but when I think of Scotland, and when I come in contact with it, as I do now every day (this is one of the advantages of my new job), I do not—forgive me—feel very hopeful. Perhaps this is due partly to my way of life. The curse of a personal discouragement is that it makes one discouraged about general things—but then, it seems to me, looking at Scottish life, that discouragement is everywhere in it. My own discouragement is relative; for I have hopes less idle than my first hopes, but I am not convinced that our hopes for whole peoples are very securely grounded. I've all these things to think out yet; probably my work gives me leisure to think, though not to write: and that may not be an entirely bad thing either. Numerous lines of poetry keep occurring to me; but I have not the time or the energy to follow them out into the poems that should follow them; and this is what I regret most.

... I'm sorry to say I haven't got on very well with Vonier. Whether it is that I'm an intractable heretic I don't know, but that approach does not recommend itself to me. I've been reading St Augustine's *Confessions* with intense attraction and repulsion: it seems to me one of the greatest of all books; the description of the ecstasy unsurpassed by anything else I know. An enormously great and passionate mind: the only thing that nears it in elevation and power being some of Beethoven's music. And what an artist! But probably you know the book well.

We would love to see you again sometime, if you could come for a week-end—we're out all the rest of the week.

The raid didn't do much damage to us; knocked a few panes out of the back windows—which were fortunately open; and tore the back door off its hinges. A quite mild business altogether—we saw the raider leaving across the roofs without realising that he was the offender. Love to you both.

Edwin

70: TO HERBERT READ

St Andrews
16 April, 1941

Dear Herbert,

Forgive me for not replying sooner. Some time ago I strained my heart, and I have been laid up for some weeks, unable to undertake any exertion at all without causing the most disagreeable sensations in my chest. I had been working in the Food Office in Dundee and trying to keep up my literary work in the evenings and week-ends. A sharp pain in my chest attacked me one morning as I was hurrying to my train; the same thing happened next morning; I sent for the doctor, and he told me I must lay off everything at once. I've given up the Food Office, with relief; I am managing to get my *Listener* reviews done; and meanwhile I am slowly recovering; the doctor says there is no reason why I should not recover altogether if I follow his orders.

I tried to get your autobiography for review from *The Scotsman*, but was not successful; but I have since read it and like it very much. I like the first part best, which is natural, perhaps, as far as I am concerned, for that period of life is the one which appeals most to my imagination. Your plan of the autobiography is very different from mine, and I think in some ways preferable; you are objective, even in the childhood chapters, where I was (I feel sometimes painfully) subjective; you give the generalised content of experience where I tried to get at the particular. Both methods are equally good, I think; when they are combined, as in Augustine's *Confessions*, they produce something terrifically impressive. I do feel that in the latter part of the book you generalise too severely; I should have liked to hear you telling by what steps you reached your present position; but on the other hand when I try to trace how I came to such convictions as I have now about life, I find it terribly hard to distinguish a road, or to explain the jumps (often jumps in the dark), which took me to my present unsatisfactory position, where somehow or other I manage to keep a precarious balance. My belief in immortality is of course an immense help in steadying me (as well as being the main experience of my life), but on the other hand it makes whatever is unstable in this life seem even more unstable. But I am talking about

70 Read's autobiography was Annals of Innocence and Experience *(1941; incorporating* The Innocent Eye, 1933*).*

myself instead of about your book. I was very much impressed by it, by the second part where you stated your beliefs as well as by the first where you described the imaginative and sensuous foundation for them. My own beliefs are different, or at any rate diverge from yours at certain crucial points, coming back every now and then and joining yours for a while. I felt throughout, again and again, your truth to your own experience at its most essential; and I felt that in some ways the experience was very like my own, though the positions we have reached, starting from it, are so different....

Yours
Edwin

71: TO ALEC AITKEN

St. Andrews
12 June, 1941

Dear Alec,

I feel guilty at not having written to you before, but you will forgive me when you know what we have been doing. All winter

---

71 *The poems sent with this letter were 'The Finder Found' (later called 'The Question'), 'The Guess', 'The Prize' and 'To the old Gods'. The last of these was considerably revised before publication; so this earlier version may be worth giving:*

To The Old Gods

Old gods and goddesses who have lived so long
Through Time and never reached Eternity,
Bound by slow wasting wood and hollowing hill,

You should have left our mortal dance and song,
The mound, the well, the memory-haunted tree.
They are forgotten, yet you linger still.

Goddess of caverned breast and channelled brow
And heart slow hollowed by millennial tears
And endless autumns fading in your eyes,

Eternity cannot match your fabulous years,
And kingdoms deep in Time, nor yet allow
Its chosen thoughts so pitiful and wise

As yours beneath the ever fading bough,
And vast compassion curving like the skies.

Willa was teaching in the school that Gavin goes to, and I was working in the Dundee Food office. We found it a hard strain—we're no longer young—to get up at 7 every morning and go through a settled routine all day, after keeping no times for twenty years. It quite exhausted us, and about three months ago I broke down with a strained heart (from which I am now recovering), and Willa, after enduring it longer, followed my example about a week ago. So that now we have, almost literally, one heart between the two of us. We took these jobs because at the time we could get no others—for myself, particularly, I found that my lack of an academic degree is a most astonishing obstacle: in Scotland nothing but a certificate of some kind seems to be recognised as really meritorious—a curious example of the preference of faith to works, for surely by this time I've done some work that should count. But there it is. Our winter was passed in mere existing, mere enduring: we had quite given up living, as if that were a leisure-time employment, and we had no leisure: we merely worked and went to bed. Thank God that is now over; but I shall presently have to look out for a job again—what I want is something as mild as milk, and lasting for about three hours a day: but that is not a likely expectation. I'm negotiating for a post as publisher's adviser, but I am not very sanguine about it: still, it may come off, in a few months' time. It would mean flitting to some place near London; but we should have to put up with that.

The doctor told me that, if I went on as I was doing, I should kill myself off in a year or two. He told me I was not to over-exert myself or to worry, and the last part of his advice seemed quite fantastic at the time; yet I found to my surprise that, if I set myself to it, it could be followed. So I've been living in a state of enforced tranquillity, and because of that my illness hasn't been altogether to the bad: it made me realise that I had been rushing on like a madman, past my true self, living my own actual unique life as if it belonged to anyone at all, or to someone whom I had no concern with, someone who did not matter in the least to me. That at least is over now, and whatever job I find to do, I shall try to make sure it never returns. The result of my tranquillity—or rather one of the results—has been a little freshet of poetry: I'm enclosing some of it, not knowing how you will like it, for it seems to me different from most of my poetry: there is no effort in it, for at present I'm unable to make such things as efforts; and I'm afraid it lacks intensity, but it may have some other quality that makes up for that: I don't know. The war I've put behind me as much as possible, along with my personal worries; it's a justified precaution, indeed almost a duty: though I must confess it's a duty I rather take to, unlike most duties: not at all as stern a daughter of the voice of God as W.W. would have given his august approbation to. But there it is, paradoxically enough, a duty, and all I ask from it is that it should do me good; and it does.

I wish we could see you again sometime. We should not talk of the war, but of St Andrew's Crosses receding into a completely different world, with more infinity in it than poor old stepmother Scotland can summon up. I'm glad that you are all well: I hope the trouble with your neighbours will assuage itself—nothing can be more painful. Thanks for what you say about my poetry—it was like a benediction to me—I can't say how grateful and moved I was. I hope you will be able to work again—it will mean so much to you. I can't help feeling that after this turmoil is over the old things, or rather the always lasting, always living things, will come back again, and take their quiet places. It's inconceivable that that should not happen. And even if we had a hard time for a few decades, living in an impoverished world, that would not matter so much in comparison. Love from us both

Yours
Edwin Muir

72: TO JOHN LEHMANN

St. Andrews
12 August, 1941

Dear John Lehmann,

I feel I should apologise for never having sent you the article you suggested. The reason is very largely that both my wife and myself have not been well for several months now; I strained my heart and am only slowly recovering, and she is still ill in bed with a complication of ailments. I am sorry to say that even this time I have nothing to send, but I shall let you have an article for the next

72 Muir's essay 'The Natural Man and the Political Man' came out in New Writing and Daylight, *edited by Lehmann, in June 1942, and was described by Lehmann as 'one of the most remarkable articles I ever published'. Lehmann edited also the periodical* Folios of New Writing.

issue, an article I have partly written, on the decay of the idea of man in the fiction of the present century, or rather on the supersession of the old conception of humanistic man by a new species of the natural man—represented by such writers as Hemingway in particular, but pretty general. I think this decay of humanistic man is bound up with dictatorship, and helped to make it possible. This is to put the matter very crudely, I am afraid; but I should very much like to work the idea out. I very much enjoy the *Folios* whenever they come out, and I wish you all success with them.

Yours sincerely,
Edwin Muir

73: TO RICHARD CHURCH

St. Andrews
2 February, 1942

Dear Richard,

Thanks so much for your letter. I am so glad you liked my review: I wish I had had your book by itself, instead of as one among several; but that is how poetry is reviewed, for some reason or another, as if poetry should be all alike, which it is not at all. I need hardly say that I liked and admired your poetry very much—more than anything else of yours I have read. What you say about disillusion is true in a sense—you must know much better than I if that is so in your own experience—yet I did not get a sense of disillusion from your poems, it may be because they gave such a sense of rich experience, and are so living; it may be because your disillusion as expressed in the poems is not disillusion in the ordinary sense, but only disillusion about certain things, combined with greater certainty about others. I have felt, I think without conceit

---

73 my review: in The New Statesman, *31 January 1941, of Church's* Fifty Poems, *of which he had written to Church on 15 December: 'These poems moved me more than anything else you have written: moved and delighted me with the sense of the significant living experience fully expressed, while it is most living, not merely in memory, as too much of my own poetry tends to be.' Church had acted for Dent as Muir's publisher, but now that firm was no longer taking new poetry he handed Muir over to Eliot at Faber. Muir's work for the British Council was to organise lectures, etc., for the International Houses set up in Edinburgh for foreign service men and refugees.*

(though it is hard to be sure of anything, quite sure)—I think I have felt something of the same kind in myself these last two years: a feeling which I can only describe as the throwing over of *quantity* of hope and faith and other things in favour of *quality*, or at least the willingness to do so. That may be merely a sign that one has reached a certain age: for the first half of our age we seek for abundance of life; in the second I don't see what hope there is for us if we do not try to give a quality to life. It's the only time left to do it in. I'm only half making this discovery now; I fancy you made it long ago.

I'm writing this partly to say that Eliot has taken my poems, thanks to you. I'm very grateful, I should like to say again. And now I feel, for some reason, that I'm going to write better poetry: I've written so little.

I haven't seen Ruthven Todd's edition of the life of Blake, but I shall get it, both for the subject and what you say about it. I've just got a post with the British Council in Edinburgh—the first regular income I shall have had for many, many years. It will be congenial work, and will be reassuring to my family. I'm very glad, for Willa has been very ill, and is only now slowly recovering. I wonder if we are going to see a better world before we go elsewhere. I hope so, for our children's sake.

Yours
Edwin Muir

I'm glad you met Eric Linklater; I am very fond of him; he is a genuinely sensitive and generous person beneath his rather bluff mask.

74: TO J. DOVER WILSON

St. Andrews
29 July, 1942

Dear Dover Wilson,

I am so sorry not to have written to you before. I am here in the throes of preparing for a 'flitting' to Edinburgh. Please forgive me.

As you can imagine, this half year has been an unusually meagre and dull one in the publishing trade, except for books connected with the war. I have never known a worse one. Here is the best that I can recommend to you, but with the exception of two books, one of them doubtful because it is a translation from the Chinese, I do not really think that any of them merit a prize.

The possible exception first. This is *Monkey*, a sixteenth-century Chinese story translated by Arthur Waley. It stands quite by itself, and is a fantastic, rollicking, very slightly Rabelaisian, and tremendously funny story, which I can recommend on its own account, apart from the possibility that you may consider it for your list. Though it seems to me that a story translated from such a remote language as the Chinese, and written in such excellent English, is to be considered as an English book almost.

Of the purely English novels far the best seems to me Robert Payne's *Singapore River*, which tells the story of a well-to-do Chinese family which migrated to Singapore many years ago, and what

> *74 Since the spring Muir had been working for the British Council in Edinburgh, going home to St Andrews at the week-ends, where Mrs Muir was recovering from a very severe illness. Now they were to move to Edinburgh. Dover Wilson, as Regius Professor of English at Edinburgh University, had to award the James Tait Black Memorial Prize for the best British work of fiction of the year, and he sought Muir's advice. In a later letter (17 December 1942) Muir added to his short list Dorothy Cowlin's* Winter Solstice, *and wrote:*
>
>> 'If it had been possible [Joyce Cary had had the prize the year before for A House of Children], I should have plumped at once for To be a Pilgrim, *which I think an entrancing book, though it has the fault that the scenes in the present are much inferior to those in the past. What a wonderful figure Lucy is, and her fantastic husband too, if it comes to that. You must have had a glorious time with him [Cary]; he's a delightful person.'*
>
> *Dover Wilson awarded the prize to* Monkey.

happened to the members. This book has at times an exquisite poetic quality, but tends to become a little monotonous towards the end. I liked it enormously myself, but this may be an idiosyncrasy of taste.

After this book I should put *Breakfast with the Nikolides* by Rumer Godden. This book also deals with the East: I hope you don't think my choice is dictated by that fact; actually I have a slight distaste for stories of the East; it simply happens that these two books are among the best I have struck during the last six months. This too is a delicate piece of work, but without the poetic quality of *Singapore River*. I do not think it is quite good enough for your list; but it is a genuine and skilful piece of fiction.

Another story with a real imaginative quality is *The Almond Tree* by Alex Comfort, a young poet in his twenties. It is immature, rather improbable, but the work of a born writer who should come to something as he develops. I got a great deal of pleasure out of it; but the raw parts are ferociously raw, and hardly make up for the elegiac beauty of the rest.

... By far the best novel I have received this year is *Delilah* by Marcus Goodrich, but unfortunately it is American: it is really worth reading for its own sake....

With kind regards,

Yours sincerely,
Edwin Muir

75: TO J. DOVER WILSON

8 Blantyre Terrace
Edinburgh 10
7 August, 1943

Dear Dover Wilson,

... I think I had better begin with the book which has struck me most of all, and this is *Tales from Bective Bridge* by Mary Lavin, a new writer. There is a foreword by Dunsany greeting her as a born

---

75 In a letter of 28 September, he added to his short list A Well Full of Leaves *by Elizabeth Myers. 'The first half of it seems to me filled with genius, but the second half falls off badly, though even the falling off, and the faults, are original. For myself I feel this is a real rival to Mary Lavin's book: it is not so consistent, but the quality of the first half is even more remarkable—is indeed quite outstanding.' The prize for 1943 was awarded to Mary Lavin.*

writer, and I think anyone who reads the book must agree with him. Mary Lavin, it seems, is not Irish (I expect she must be English); but the Irish atmosphere of these stories is wonderfully conveyed, the writing is very beautiful, without being fancy the form and shape of them really consummate. But what strikes one most is the purity and intimacy of the imagination. The writer is obviously young, yet she is quite mature, she makes no mistakes, and she has still obviously a world to say. Of all the fiction of the year, this, as far as I am concerned, is the easy winner....

The only book to rival Mary Lavin is unfortunately by an American writer: *The Green Veil* by Eudora Welty, who is also young and also a born writer. It is like Mary Lavin's a volume of short stories. If you would care to get hold of it for your own pleasure, I think it would not disappoint you; but of course it is outside the area I have been trying to map....

Yours sincerely,
Edwin Muir

76: TO STEPHEN SPENDER

Edinburgh
2 March, 1944

Dear Stephen,

...I was so sorry I could not get hold of you and see you when I was in London for a couple of days. But I arrived at short notice and had no chance of arranging things beforehand. I liked very much your poems in the last number of *Penguin New Writing*. In these extraordinary days I feel a hope for your generation of writers, yourself and Day Lewis particularly, and even some for my own, though there is much less time in our case to realise it. I've been going through all sorts of crises myself, which have been unpleasant and good for me, and have taken me uncomfortably near the kind of rejection of life for eternal ends which some people call religion. I'm glad I've got over it, though glad I've seen it and realised that I don't like it or want it at all, and would not have it at any price. It's very late for me to come to such a conclusion, and it may not seem a remarkable one in any way to you: I don't think it is myself: but our

76 your poems: presumably 'Three Poems' ('A Trance', 'The Statue of Apollo', 'Bridle of the Sun') in No. 18.

crises often seem to be unnecessary in a sense, or only necessary so that they may prove they are unnecessary....

Edwin

77: TO STEPHEN SPENDER

Edinburgh
21 March, 1944

Dear Stephen,

... I was much struck by what you say about death and the fortuitous snuffing out of life. I can't feel or think so clearly about it, for though I've lived so much longer I have never come in contact with it. It is the most horrible thing in the world, probably: I don't know. I shall stick to my belief in immortality, I feel that it is involved with so many of our instinctive feelings, especially the feeling that we have free will, which is simply, I think, the feeling that, in spite of the fact that all our actions and thoughts are obviously determined by all the things around us, and by our position in time, we are not completely contained by these things, therefore that there is something else in us not dictated to by time. This may appear unconvincing to you; perhaps it is only convincing if one believes in imortality as I do. And at any rate it is several removes from the experiences you have been having: therefore less real, less immediate, and of no use to you.

The problems are terrifying, as you say. The religions exist, I suppose, to provide an explanation of them. I can't accept any religious explanation that I know of, any more than you. I would rather have the problems themselves, for from an awareness of them and their vastness I get some sort of living experience, some sense even of communion, of being in the whole in some way, whereas from the explanations I should only get comfort and reassurance and a sense of safety which I know is not genuine. I don't know why, this being so, my religious experience is not without hope: I do not think it is because of my belief in immortality: I still hold it, but for some reason it doesn't mean so much to me as it used to do: whether this is a bad sign or a good I really don't know. And I don't know where I stand regarding tragedy. But may not tragedy affect us so much because it is directly concerned with these enormous and terrifying problems, without providing a solution: the beauty may be incidental. And if the dignity seems false to you, I feel all the same that it is something we should claim, no matter who it is who is blasted out of life in some horrible casual way, in a minute. Perhaps the dignity could be expressed in a different way, in which it would be more true for you.

For me too love is the supreme quality and more closely connected with immortality than any other, immortality either as you or I conceive it. And in a way I feel it is more important than immortality. If I could really love all creatures and all things I should not trouble about immortality. I should not trouble about that because I should not trouble about myself. (But that is far distant.) I've been greatly moved by a life of Tolstoy I've been reading (by Derrick Leon), and though I don't agree with him that the soul alone matters, and the flesh not at all, what a wonderful human being he was, and what a struggle he made for his idea of human love. I feel that most of the things I'm saying will seem irrelevant or theoretical to you: don't pay too much attention to them....

I'm still writing a poem occasionally, but am not much pleased with my latest ones. With love to Natasha and yourself.

Edwin

78: TO J. DOVER WILSON

Edinburgh
14 November, 1944

Dear Dover Wilson,

... The most startling exception [to the mediocrity of the fiction of the past year] is Rosamond Lehmann's *The Ballad and the Source*. It seems to me a really ambitious and very skilful piece of work, into which a great deal of miscellaneous experience and observation has gone, really poetic in its evocation of life, with a first-rate character, a terrible and fascinating woman, in the foreground, and a cunningly contrived series of scenes more and more closely encircling her, until in the end we know all that can be known about her, and yet leave her alive with her essential mystery. I think this is the most impressive novel I've come across this year: it certainly stands out clearly, in spite of certain faults—for instance the last part describing the

---

78 The prize for 1944 was awarded to Forrest Reid for Young Tom, *about which Muir must have written in an earlier letter.*

madness of Ianthe, which I found unconvincing, as also the extreme communicativeness of some of the characters. But I do feel this book has a title to be considered, along with Forrest Reid's book about young Tom. I can't at the moment decide between them in my own mind: one being small and perfect, and the other large and not quite perfect.

A quite remarkable novel, full of faults, especially in the writing, but with quite a powerful imagination is John Butt Robey's *The Innovator*, an account of life in Jerusalem in the six days before the Crucifixion. I was put off by it during the first twenty or thirty pages, telling myself that the man could not write, but as I went on I began to find a sort of Tolstoyan thoroughness and directness of eye in it which became really impressive: it's rare to find a novelist who does not turn aside from anything, and keeps his eye on the object so perseveringly. I don't feel myself this book quite comes into competition with the other two; but I do think it is worth your attention. It seems to be a first novel.

The third novel I should like to recommend is L. P. Hartley's *The Shrimp and the Anemone*; a story of childhood quite unlike that of Forrest Reid, but both very charming and very moving, painfully so. It is excellently conceived and written, and is a sort of criticism of life, essentially pessimistic, in terms of a child's life. I think again that this is worth your attention, and also that you would find it a pleasure to read....

Yours ever
Edwin Muir

79: TO OSCAR WILLIAMS

Edinburgh
19 November, 1944

Dear Mr Williams,

Your letter was a long time in reaching me, and I am afraid that this letter and the enclosures may be an equally long time in reaching you. I enclose three poems, all inspired in some way by the war; if

79 Oscar Williams had asked for poems for The War Poets: An Anthology of the War Poetry of the Twentieth Century *(New York: John Day, 1945), which he was editing. He included 'The Escape', 'Reading in Wartime' and 'The Rider Victory' (the last apparently substituted for 'The Lullaby', the third poem sent with this letter).*

you think they are suitable, please take them. 'The Escape' was suggested to me by a story called 'Corpoal Jack', an account of an English soldier's escape from prison camp, his wanderings through France, and his final arrival at Gibraltar. It occurred to me then that this journey of his was a typical modern journey; tens of thousands must have made it, hundreds of thousands must have made it in imagination in their desire to escape. These journeys remind me of the many wanderings back through Europe after the failure of the Crusades, which must have been typical of that time too. So that the escape I try to describe in the poem is partly realistic and partly symbolical. 'Reading' has already appeared in *The Listener*, but the other two poems have not appeared anywhere....

Yours sincerely
Edwin Muir

80: TO WILLIAM MONTGOMERIE

The British Council
39 Dlouha Trida
Prague I
Czechoslovakia
6 March, 1946

Dear Bill,

... I have been lecturing twice a week to the English class at the Charles University (I call it a class, but it is more like a demonstration, comprising several hundred students, without books, so that I have to *create* Wordsworth, Coleridge, Blake, and the others for them—however I have hit upon the idea of getting them to type out some of the best poems, and cyclostyle them, so that we are amassing a small anthology as we go along). I have to explain the poems to them, of course, build up Blake's Tiger, find some definite meaning in the 'deeps' and 'skies', and I find this very interesting, useful for the students, and very good for myself as a critic, since it forces me to keep my eye perpetually on the object, and almost on every word. The students are an excellent lot, a bit too industrious and too deferential to facts, just like Scottish students, I fancy; but I am gradually getting them out of that, and infecting them with my own disregard for such things. I have got on to Walter Scott now, not with any great exhilaration, and look forward with some dread to Byron, who is the most venerated poetic name in English poetry here, as in most continental countries; however there will be a certain pleasure in upsetting that idol. There is a great enthusiasm for everything British here, especially among the young: there were about thirty students of English at the Prague University before the war, and there are now over two thousand. Among the very Left Wing people in the thirties and forties I have still to combat the idea that G.B. is the chief reactionary nation in Europe, and am making some progress, at least to the extent of reassuring them that the Institute, when it starts, will not be reactionary. My staff is very nice and has got the right ideas. I had a lot of trouble at the start from people who rushed to us because they disliked the Russians, or because they thought we were reactionary; but I have made it plain that I don't intend the Institute to be a centre for such people, and that we are friendly to Russia. The Institute would be a calamity otherwise....

Love to Norah and yourself and the children.

Yours ever
Edwin

81: TO JOSEPH CHIARI

26 Na Zatorce
Prague XIX
Czechoslovakia
27 July, 1946

Dear Joe,

Forgive me for being so long in writing to thank you and Margaret for all your kindness to me in Edinburgh, and to reply to your letter. I shall remember my stay with you as the one warm and comforting and intimate thing (except for my meeting with Gavin) during my two weeks in Scotland....

How are you, and are you still able to write poetry? I have written only one poem since I came, a very curious one about the thoughts of a child dying—where it came from goodness only

---

81 Chiari (1911–), poet and author of critical books, mainly about French literature, became a friend of Muir's when Free French Representative in Edinburgh during the war. 'The Child Dying': varies only in punctuation from the published version, except in line 16, which was changed to 'A flitting grace, a phantom face.' Gavin had been staying with the Chiaris before setting out for Prague.

knows. I enclose a copy of it. On the other hand I have had recently about half a dozen ideas for poems, but have never hit the mood in which I could write them: my life is too distracted. I shall not be able to write unless I succeed in putting my affairs in order during the next year; so that I am going to devote as much of my energy to that as I can. This first year has been confused and provisional; always new things turning up, and no organisation to deal with them; I and my staff too at the mercy of chance. It has not been entirely unenjoyable, but it has been wasteful. We have got a flat now; and the Institute has got a palace to work in; the bases of order are there; and so next year should be better. Prague is much pleasanter to live in than when I arrived; the people better fed: the shops better stocked; everybody more cheerful. There is a lot of goodwill towards us. But I should like to have some time and peace to write.

... I am writing to Gavin too, though I hope that by now he is on the road to us. With love to you all,

Edwin

The Child Dying

Unfriendly friendly universe,
I pack your stars into my purse
And bid you, bid you so farewell.
That I can leave you, quite go out,
Go out, go out beyond all doubt,
My father says, is the miracle.

You are so great, and I so small:
I am nothing, you are all:
Being nothing, I can take this way.
Oh I need neither rise nor fall,
For when I do not move at all
I shall be out of all your day.

It's said some memory may remain
In the other place, grass in the rain,
Light on the land, sun on the sea,
A passing grace, a single face;
But the world is out. There is no place
Where it and its ghost can ever be.

Father, father, I dread this air
Blown from the far side of despair,

The cold, cold corner. What house, what hold,
What hand is there? I look and see
Nothing-filled eternity,
And the great round world seems weak and old.

Hold my hand, oh hold it fast—
I am changing!—until at last
My hand in yours no more will change,
Though yours change on: you here, I there,
So hand-in-hand, twin-leafed despair:
I did not know death was so strange.

I've been trying for some time to write poetry that was both simple and unexpected; and if this poem is good—I can hardly tell whether it is or not—I think I have succeeded. But where it came from I simply can't tell.

E.M.

82: TO JOSEPH CHIARI

Prague
18 August, 1946

Dear Joe,

I am writing with great joy to tell you about a letter I got from *Orion* yesterday, accepting your longest poem. . . .

My dear Joe, I can't tell you how delighted I am by this. I knew my own opinion of your poems, which I told you about in Edinburgh, but I knew also how various can be the opinion of writers about the same poetry and when I sent the poems to *Orion*, I simply did not know what to expect. And so you will appear first as a poet in what is really the best literary miscellany in Great Britain; and this is what I am so glad about.

Gavin has arrived at last; yesterday morning. I must thank you over and over again for all your kindness to him. Willa got Margaret's letter yesterday, and will reply to it to-day or to-morrow. We might have got both letters, Margaret's and the one from *Orion*,

---

82 letter from Orion: *from D. Kilham Roberts, expressing admiration for Chiari's 'White Temple by the Sea' and accepting it for publication in* Orion IV. *Orrs: Professor John Orr of Edinburgh University and his French wife.*

some days earlier, but we had been away in the Tatras, in the east of Slovakia, for a week, and just got back yesterday morning in time to meet Gavin's train. We went through some curious adventures to do that. Our car (or rather the Institute's car) had three punctures between the Tatras and Bratislava, where we arrived at 4 o'clock in the morning on Friday. Between Bratislava and Prague we had again three punctures, and were left without a spare wheel in lonely forest country early on Saturday morning: Gavin was going to arrive at the Wilson station in Prague, we were told, at 8 o'clock. We stopped a car that was passing, a huge car of a semi-racing type, and asked for a lift to Prague. The driver, a handsome, opulent-looking man, said he wasn't going to Prague, but that he could take us to Tabor (fifty miles from Prague), where we could get an early train to Prague that would get us there in good time. We both got in, leaving the chauffeur with the Institute car. The car into which we got was an open one. The driver set off at about 150 miles an hour. Willa was in front with him; I was in the back holding a jar of honey which we intended for Gavin's first breakfast with us; it had only a thin paper cover on the top. We came to various cross-roads marked Tabor, but in spite of what Willa said, the driver swept past them all, saying airily: "Tabor! All roads lead to Tabor'. He took us at the same breakneck speed over half of Bohemia; it was quite dark, no moon; we passed through huge mountains, across great plains, round dizzy corners (still at about 150 miles an hour at least). Finally, when we found we were in quite a remote part of Bohemia, the driver shot past a car that was driving in front of us, and suddenly drew up across it, and asked for Tabor. We found we had to turn back for twenty miles; finally we arrived there after haring for more than three hours through the most wild and magnificent scenery, lit up brilliantly by the head lights. The driver (and he was a magnificent driver) was obviously half-mad and in command of a wonderful car; he was trying half to impress and half to terrify us; if we had shown any signs of alarm heaven knows to what lengths he might have gone. He turned every now and then to Willa and asked: 'Are you not afraid, gracious lady?', and when Willa said, 'No, why should I be afraid?' he was distinctly disappointed. At some points he would wave his hand negligently and say, 'I went over that wall once; the car was smashed to bits'; but he still failed to impress us; that is why he gave up at last in despair and actually took us to Tabor. Now and then he would take out a revolver, and tell us that he had been stopped by a man before he reached us; the man had asked for money, and he had shot between his legs, and rode away. The car as it leapt on bumped so furiously that the honey leapt up through the paper covering and was splashed over my trousers and all over the back seat; I was bathed in honey, and sitting on honey. Meanwhile I held the honey pot in my hands and decided just where I should hit the man on the head with it if he became really dangerous; I decided that behind the ear would be most effective. When we got to the Grand Hotel in Tabor, I apologised for the honey spilt and smeared on the back seat, and the driver took out his revolver again and put it melodramatically to his head, and said to Willa: 'Honey on the back-seat: shall I shoot myself because of that, gracious lady?' Then we found that there was no early train from Tabor that would get us to Prague in time, and at this point Willa broke down and began to weep loudly. But there was a very nice nightwatchman in the hotel who took us in; I got out of my trousers, by now steeped in honey, and put on another pair; and the nightwatchman managed to get us a taxi (between four and five in the morning), and on that we set out on the fifty mile stretch to Prague, and arrived at last. As soon as I arrived I had a bath to get the honey off me; I'm not sure whether it is all off yet, for it sticks like anything. And so that is our most curious adventure since we came to Czechoslovakia. I should have mentioned that while we were going at this incredible speed, the driver had a habit of taking both hands off the wheel to gesticulate or make one of his silly remarks or to light a cigarette. The curious thing about this Walküre ride was that it was extraordinarily exhilarating, in spite of being alarming; I hadn't known what speed was before; it is something that literally carries you away, so that you aren't in the least concerned when you turn a sharp corner with all the tyres screaming on two wheels. Willa felt exactly the same, she told me after (We hadn't time to compare notes while the hurricane drive was on. Actually the man told her that he was going to take part in a race two days afterwards). No, the only thing that really alarmed us was the man himself, his shouts, his whistles and hoots, his remarks and his revolver.

We are a little bit exhausted after these strong sensations, and want nothing more than to remain motionless, and rest. My dear Joe, I still feel so happy about the poem. I see I haven't mentioned the name of the man I got the letter from; it is Denys Kilham Roberts, the remaining editor, along with myself, if I am still regarded as one of the editors. I do hope you will keep up your poetry, whenever the mood seizes you. I like your poems very much, as you know. Will I try some of the others on John Lehmann, whom I know? And have you written any more? I want to thank you again for all you have done for Gavin. We intend to keep him here until the beginning of October, when the new term begins: I think it would be foolish for him to return for that examination in the beginning of September; and he needs our care for some time. He arrived perfectly all right, and enjoyed the experience, though it rather alarmed him in prospect: it has been very good for him. I shall write to you again soon. With thanks again and love to Margaret and yourself, not forgetting the children. I am typing this, for my writing, I know, is an infliction on my friends, Give my kindest regards to the Orrs. I'm very very sorry that Harry Wood has been ill; do give him my kind regards too, and the hope that he will soon be better.

Yours ever,
Edwin

83: TO JOSEPH CHIARI

Prague
14 September, 1947

Dear Joe,

Forgive me for being so long in writing. I have been away for a month's holiday in Marianske Lazne (once Marienbad), and I spent my time writing poetry there mainly: I had had a number of poems dammed up in me for some months, with no chance of coming out; and there by good luck I found the means and the right moment for them. I have almost a volume, but not quite, by this time; I intend to call the poems *Symbols*, or something of that kind, for they all deal with symbolical human situations and types; and I hope this will give the volume a sort of unity, and at the same time that it won't cause the contents to be monotonous. To get these poems out was a great satisfaction to me, but I was disappointed that I didn't get out all the poems I wanted. On the other hand new ones appeared, which was gratifying, and so I found myself partly in a state of poetic

83 Chiari's early poems were published in The White Temple by the Sea *(Moray Press, 1951).*

resolution and partly in a state of flux. But the holiday hasn't given me as much rest as I really should have had, but instead excitement partly pleasant and partly painful. I can't say yet what I think of the product; I'll send you some of it when I've gone over it again.

I've been over your poems several times, and I've taken the liberty of making some notes and suggestions in pencil, which I hope you will not mind, for they were set down in friendship. I'm as convinced as ever that you have an original poetic gift, imagination, sensibility, and a profound feeling for essential things. What you lack up to now is an intimate sense of the language; it shows in these poems sufficiently for them not to produce the effect they should produce....

All good to you all, and love to you all from us both.

Yours ever,
Edwin

And love to Gavin too, dear boy, when you see him. I hope he has passed his examination.

84: TO PATRICIA SWALE

Prague
13 July, 1948

Dear Pat,

Do accept this as a kindness to us, and an act of goodwill, and a friendly greeting between two people who enjoy spending money, and above all in thanks for your royal birthday feast, which I can't think of your paying for all by yourself. And do spare my feelings (which are very sensitive) by just accepting and saying nothing.

With love
Edwin

84 Miss Swale was Registrar in the British Council at Prague. She writes 'I gave a dinner party in grand style, but couldn't really afford it; and although he gave no indication at the time of knowing this, he took it all in and insisted on paying half the cost with this note, though he and Willa were my chief guests.'

85: TO MISS SPENS

Prague
23 July, 1948

Dear Miss Spens,

I hardly know how even to begin to ask you to forgive me for not replying before (or rather replying at once) to your letter. My only excuse is that I have been troubled by miscellaneous things, that I have been unwell, and that I have had to make a great number of preparations before leaving this country. I shall be leaving now in a few days....

What you say in your letter interests me very much. I know nothing of the literature of the Transfiguration, and in writing the poem probably did not see where it was leading me. On the other hand I have always had a particular feeling for that transmutation of life which is found occasionally in poetry, and in the literature of prophecy, and sometimes in one's own thoughts when they are still. This, I think, is one of the things which have always been with me, or more exactly, which have persistently recurred to me, and I suppose in this poem it has found a point of expression. But that is the total of my learning on the Transfiguration. I still remember how as a child it filled me with wonder. The idea of Judas going back into innocence has often been with me. But I seem to have blundered into something greater than I knew, though as it grew the poem became clearer and clearer in my mind. The ideas you mention move me very much; I hope to become more familiar with them. One lives and misses so much one does not know about.

Thank you for all the kind things you say. It's a great joy to me that the poem has brought joy to you.

Yours ever
Edwin Muir

85 Miss Maisie Spens, author of Receive the Joyfulness of your Glory, *had written to Muir about his poem 'The Transfiguration.' Later he said in a broadcast 'I had always been deeply struck by the story of the Transfiguration in the Gospels, and I had felt that perhaps at the moment of Christ's Transfiguration everything was transfigured, mankind, and the animals, and the simplest natural objects. After the poem appeared I had a letter from a lady who had made a long study of the subject, and to my surprise I found that the idea which I had imagined in my own mind possessed a whole literature, and that in some of the Russian churches it was often represented pictorially.'*

86: TO JOSEPH CHIARI

The Hermitage Guest House
Silver Street
Cambridge
8 September, 1948

Dear Joe,

Do, do forgive me. For months now I have been suffering from both physical and nervous exhaustion, and to have them both put me in a curious blind dejection for days at a time—a thing I haven't suffered from since a bad time I had as a young man. The physical side is much better—I've been here a month, doing nothing but nothing; the nervous side I haven't yet quite got cured, though fits of almost cheerfulness are at last beginning to break in. I've stayed here in Cambridge not because I wanted to avoid Scotland—I have a keen longing for it, and strangely enough (for I was there only for three years) for Edinburgh in particular. But I felt I had to be in reach of London until the Council had come to some decision about me. They have been nice to me, and I think they are likely to find me a university post; I must not say where at the moment, for I do not definitely know yet. A post of that kind would give me a good deal of more leisure than I had in Prague, and I feel at present that I would like leagues and leagues of leisure, for as one gets older the questions that life asks seem to become vaster and vaster and stretch into endlessness. I have got some comfort in the last few weeks in the thought that there is forgiveness in the universe, that everything is not a mere play of forces and wills: I am beginning to understand faintly the Christian idea of forgiveness, very faintly, for it is surely one of the greatest of all ideas. I know so little about it that I shall say no more about it. That I can come to the point of writing at all is a sign that I have been helped to forgive myself at least, and to feel that in a far larger sense I am forgiven; so do you forgive me too, for I have been a sad burden on your patience and goodness.

I have read your poems, and I have made notes on the margins, and in a few days, when I have gone over them again, now that I feel more myself, I shall send them on to you. I know you are a poet, I feel it when I read these poems; I feel still that your language does not always fit what you have to say, though sometimes it fits it exquisitely. I cannot quite make up my mind, dear Joe, for at present I have nothing that can really be callèd a mind. So will you wait for

another few days, until I have improved a little—and I am now really improving. I saw Eliot last week, during a Council visit to London, and he spoke very warmly about you, and said how much he liked you. I must make a supreme effort to come to Edinburgh; I feel I simply must breathe the air of Scotland before I go away again. Fabers have accepted another volume of my poems; I really think it is the best I have done yet, but that is a hard question to answer, for one is partial to what one has just been doing. I am very moved by some of your poems, and find a very unusual beauty in many of the lines. At odd moments I am reading *Don Quixote* to comfort me; it is the sweetest, most universally kindly book I have ever read, almost a kind of human Bible. Forgive this rag-tag of a letter, which is very like me at present. With much love to Margaret and yourself,
Edwin

87: TO NEIL GUNN

[*1948?*]

I add my greetings and my congratulations on such a wonderfully delightful book, a book with a sun of its own (a very old sun—since reading it, Neil, I've got the quite novel feeling that the sun is a very old and very experienced star and has looked upon us and our fathers and been above us and about us and in us for a long long time). It's a mature book, steeped in time and in your own experience and acceptance of things: it's like a harvest. I feel myself (but you know much more about it) that this last theme of yours fits your intricate and interweaving Celtic imagination wonderfully, and is as made for it: so many things brought together by such winding and yet natural ways, with the skill and craft and ingenuity of nature. The skeleton of the dead woman with her child repeated in the living woman and her living child gave me an imaginative thrill which I shall never forget: it hints at something which has haunted me vaguely before on the very verge of thought, but for which I have never found in any writing before a form. And so much is accepted in the book, and what other real wisdom is there in the imagination? I feel very grateful to you for it and for sending it to us. All good fortune (continuing). With love to you both.
Edwin

87 Sending me this page (all that survives) of a letter to him about his The Silver Bough *(1948) Neil Gunn wrote: 'I remember on one occasion* [*during the War*] *wanting to compliment him on a new book of poems, called* The Narrow Place, *and getting round to it by first mentioning a short poem which had particularly struck me. While reading it, I saw the sea water, blue-green, sunlit, in motion, before my eyes. But may I quote it:*

>   The Swimmer's Death
>   *He lay outstretched upon the sunny wave,*
>   *That turned and broke into Eternity.*
>   *The light showed nothing but a glassy grave*
>   *Among the trackless tumuli of the sea.*
>   *Then over his buried brow and eyes and lips*
>   *From every side flocked in the homing ships.*

Edwin told me that the poem exactly described a dream which he had had. I know we talked of the wonderful clarity and radiance of the light—of the sea—which remained in our minds from early boyhood years in that northern world. But I cannot remember if I mentioned a word in the poem which had affected me, that word "homing". I may have been diffident about mentioning it because I felt that such a word gave a warmth to radiance, appeared to add human experience to austere vision, and that some of his poems might gain by having it here or there, if only in the sense of gaining more readers. I know this kind of criticism is difficult if not dubious, but possibly it contains the one point I could look at here for a moment in a personal way. I don't want to repeat words like eternity, austerity, symbol, heraldic, which keep recurring in appreciations of his poetry, as if what he emotionally experienced or saw was always given a timeless shape, was translated from the fluid movements of life in the living moment into a permanence that abides where time and eternity cross. We know he had that kind of vision and could himself abide for moments in that place. But when we cannot enter into that place, into that condition of being, where what is fixed is not fixed but held in dynamic suspension, in the radiance of revelation, then we may find his poetry strangely static, lifeless, carrying life like a memory to the place beyond, where it remains forever "frozen". Hence the apparent lack of human warmth, so that a word like "homing" stands out and is received somehow with gratitude.

But that the lack is only apparent can be seen from a letter which I got from him after he had read a novel of mine, The Silver Bough. *I'm afraid I am not a keeper of letters, except by accident, and this one fell out of the book, where I had left it after checking some point in his letter, I suppose. Its extravagant generosity embarrasses me over again, but I cannot think of any more authentic way of showing his human warmth in action, its depth, even its height all the way to the sun! Here he is being naturally himself and as naturally generous to another. Clearly, too, concepts like time and acceptance are not in the nature of philosophic abstractions but realities experienced in his inner being. A poet's essence must also be the essence of his poetry. And in fact*

88: TO RAYMOND TSCHUMI

Lungo Tevere Marzio 10,
Rome
10 June, 1949

Dear Mr Tschumi,

... It was very considerate of you to send me your essay on my poetry, and I feel very grateful to you. I can say quite sincerely that it has given me a fresh view of my work and made me more aware, I think, of what I have been doing. In the moment of writing one is not clear, except about immediate things, and I fancy that on the whole that is a good thing. A writer is perhaps the least able to judge his own work, except, again, on the immediate point, where his mind and his feelings are a guide to him, and he has an immediate intuition of what is right and wrong. But it is a great help if he can stand back and have a look at his work as a whole, and I found your analysis of the poems extraordinarily interesting, and also illuminating. Your study of them gave me the feeling, which I have rarely had before, of seeing them simultaneously from the outside and the inside. I know in myself that I have been, I suppose, unusually concerned with the problems of time and eternity, but I hardly realised until now that it came out so clearly in my poems. So that I owe this realisation to you, and feel very grateful for it.

... In two cases only I disagree with your interpretation of particulars, particulars about which you could not possibly know the inward history. On page 29, 'Written in memory of a friend who was killed in a motor accident'. It is a plausible reading. Actually he did not die in a motor accident, but by natural means. What happened was this. One day, after an illness, I was walking out in the little town of St Andrews in Scotland, when I saw a young soldier,

88 Raymond Tschumi, *Professor of English at St Gallen University, had sent Muir the chapter on him which was to be published in Tschumi's* Thought in Twentieth Century English Poetry *(1951). The poems referred to are* 'To J.F.H[olms]' *and* 'The River'.

---

the essence is always there, any "lack" being due to the reader's blindness. I am tempted to say more about this, because an intelligent reader may well be blind, until, reading on, he forgets himself, then sees, and enters in. I know of no poet of my time, not even Yeats, who so intuitively pierced through human obscurities to this ultimate light.'

so like my dead friend that he could easily have been mistaken for him, dashing by on a motor cycle—he too had been in uniform the first time I met him. I was in one of the curious moods which sometimes come with convalescence: at any rate I did not know for a moment where I was; the worlds of life and death seemed to fuse for an instant. It was a curious feeling, and no one but myself could know that in it lay the genesis of the poem.

The other point is your interpretation of the frontier walls falling down on page 33. This poem was written during the war, soon after the invasion of France, which brought images of universal disaster to so many of us. Frontier walls seemed to be beyond saving just then, and I had an image of a Europe quite featureless, with all the old marks gone.

... Thank you again for your generous imaginative understanding of my work, and all good luck to your book.

Yours sincerely,
Edwin Muir

89: TO KATHLEEN RAINE

Rome
24 August, 1949

Dear Kathleen Raine,

I should like to thank you for your very understanding review of my poems, the review that comes far nearest to my own feelings about them. I feel very grateful to you. I was interested particularly in what you said of the ancestral imagination which you said was still found in Ireland and Wales and Scotland. I hope it is also in England—I feel you yourself have some of it. I think I got some from Orkney ...

Yours sincerely
Edwin Muir

89 review: in The Observer *7 August 1949, of* The Labyrinth.

90: TO JOSEPH CHIARI

Rome
20 December, 1949

Dear Joe,

Forgive me for being so long in writing. I've been in rather indifferent health for some time, perpetually exhausted, and at the same time kept too busy here with miscellaneous work. I've had two pieces of good fortune, one I feel due to you and one to the goddess of good fortune; but even they have failed to lift my present weariness, which has been troubling me now for weeks—perhaps its simply due to growing old. The first was the doctorate from the University of Rennes in the second half of November, the second the Foyle poetry prize, which has just been instituted this year, so that I'm the first to get it. I couldn't travel for either of these honours and had to get them *in absentia*. I'm very glad of them both. I seem quite unable to acquire honours in the usual way, and have to have them given by an act of grace.

Dear Joe, I'm sorry to be writing to you in a phase of weariness. I've put a good deal into the work of the Institute, and the result is that it is going very well now, and attracting large audiences. But I shouldn't have said 'the result is', for it's not my doing, or only partly; for I have a staff I should thank God for; it is great good luck that I happened upon them. It is great good fortune to work along with people you like and who like one another: it makes all the difference between happiness and frustration. I like the Romans too—those I know, those who come about the Institute. I'm much struck with Rome, and all its wealth of associations; you feel the gods (including the last and greatest of them) have all been here, and are still present in a sense in the places where they once were. It has brought very palpably to my mind the theme of Incarnation and I feel that probably I shall write a few poems about that high and difficult theme sometime: I hope so. Edinburgh I love, but in Edinburgh you never come upon anything that brings the thought of Incarnation to your mind, and here you do so often, and quite

90 The poems referred to at the end of the second paragraph are 'The Days', 'Night and Day' and 'The Shrine', the last of which has not been reprinted since its appearance in Botteghe Oscure V *(1950). Poems on the theme of incarnation written soon after this were 'The Son' and 'The Annunciation'.*

unexpectedly. I'm rather afraid of writing on such a theme and though it occupies my mind whenever my mind is free from daily affairs, I feel nothing is ready yet to be written down. I haven't written much at all, a poem about the first seven days, and one about day and night, and one, with which I'm not very pleased, about the gods hanging round a ruined temple. But I hope things will emerge in time. . . .

I met Douglas Young in Venice (at the PEN Conference), and also in Rome: I met George Scott-Moncrieff in Rome too, and Auden, and Pritchett, and Rex Warner—everybody seems to come here: its a sort of thoroughfare all the world passes through. I wonder if you will ever appear on our doorstep some day: how nice it would be. From Douglas I got the feeling that the Lallans poets weren't doing as well as they expected. I have no ill-will towards them, but they never seemed to me to be very gifted, except for Grieve. I'm going down to Capri for Christmas if the weather holds good—Willa is needing a holiday too. With a Happy Christmas and New Year to both and to the children, and much love

Edwin

91: TO EDWARD SCOULLER

Palermo
19 May, 1950

Dear Ned,

Forgive me for being so long in writing, after getting your very very kind letter. The fact is that I've been ill for a considerable time, with gastritis and neuritis simultaneously. . . . It's the first real illness I've had for years, so I mustn't grumble.

Two months ago the B.C. fixed up a lecture tour for me in Sicily, so I've come here along with Willa, who is going to lecture too (in Italian). I feel better already, being out of Rome. It's not that I hate Rome; I like it better than any other city I've ever been in; but it's nice to get away, all the same. You ask about the Catholic lure. Rome does have an effect, priests and churches and processions

91 Edward Scouller and his brother Bob had been friends of Muir in his Glasgow days. Active socialists, the three had formed a branch of the National Union of Clerks. Now a teacher, active in adult education, Scouller had supported Muir's appointment to Newbattle, where he later gave occasional lectures.

are so almost continuously before you. Rome is supposed to give you a scunner at Catholicism, or a temptation to join. I haven't any scunner (except at some of the politics), or any temptation to join (I couldn't), but what a religion it is, how much it takes into itself, and how much more human Catholics are, at least in Italy, than Protestants anywhere. I'm immensely impressed with Romanism, on the whole I like it, and the carelessness of it, and all the imaginative ritual and richness; but I could no more join it than I could fly to the moon. Almost all my staff are Catholics; the Director of Studies is a very nice chap from Glasgow called Joe O'Brien; they're all very easy to get on with, the Italians particularly; I think they're wonderfully good people. But this is all gossip.

... I'm coming back to Scotland in the beginning of July, and shall probably be back there on the 7th.... Czechoslovakia, in the months after the *Putsch*, left me with a breakdown that lasted for about six weeks, and I'm grateful to Rome for curing me, and setting me up. Even so I'll be glad to get back. And I think the work at Newbattle will be very interesting and worthwhile.

I must stop now. All my best wishes to you all and Bob.

Yours ever
Edwin

92: TO DOUGLAS YOUNG

Newbattle Abbey College
Dalkeith
Midlothian
15 July, 1950

My dear Douglas,

... As for your list of poems for the Anthology, I don't suppose anyone who writes poetry would agree with any proposed list. In Rome, in a spare moment, I did make out a list, lost it, and then found no time to reconstruct it. My dear Douglas, just please yourself. I think you've weighed me down too much with Scottish themes. Actually, in my own judgment, the most Scottish poem I

---

92 Douglas Young (1913–), Scottish poet and classical scholar, was editing an anthology, Scottish Verse 1851–1951 *(1952), in which he included eleven poems by* Muir *(but only one of those mentioned here, 'The Transmutation'). The Scotsman for 7 July contained a letter from him about the Scottish Covenant.*

ever wrote is the 'Ballad of the Flood,' which appeared in *First Poems* and is written in Scots (whether Lallans or not I can't say, but Scots at any rate). I'm fond of it myself, but it's very long. It's more or less in ballad Scots. I don't care much for 'The Refugees.' Among the sonnets I like best 'Transmutation'. I would prefer 'The Human Fold' entire; otherwise it loses its meaning. I think 'The Combat' (from *The Labyrinth*) is one of my best poems, and I'm fond of 'I've been in love for long,' at the end of *The Voyage*. Now these are things I should have said long ago, when you wrote to me first. Pay no attention to them, if they come to worry you now....

It's very nice to be back again, in such a delightful place, and with such a kind welcome from everybody. I hope you'll come to see us whenever you can. The morning we arrived in Edinburgh I bought a *Scotsman* and read it at breakfast in the Waverley Hotel. What a difference from the *Times*. Controversy going strong, and you among it: it was refreshing; I like to read it; I shall probably not take part in it. But it's a form of life, though not mine. With kindest wishes, my dear Douglas,

Yours for Orkney
Edwin Muir

93: TO T. S. ELIOT

Newbattle
31 May, 1951

My dear Eliot,

I'm so glad, and so grateful to you, that you are going on with the volume of poems. I've had a look over John Hall's introduction, and I like it. I've returned it to him to-day. I hope you will think it is the sort of thing that is fitting.

As for the terms, these are quite satisfactory, so far as I'm concerned. But John Hall has done a great deal to get the poems together, and has supplied all the enterprise and carried through all the arrangements, for which I'm the more thankful, as I had never met him when he made the suggestion first. I feel sure his expenses have

93 volume of poems: Collected Poems 1921–1951. *J. C. Hall, a young poet working in publishing, had written to Muir suggesting that it was time for a collection to be published and offering to do the preliminary work. £6.10.0: this was all Hall wanted, but Muir insisted he should have more— out of royalties. In the end £25 was agreed to.*

come to more than £6.10.0, for he came up here particularly to see me. I think a percentage of the royalties would more or less express my gratitude to him. Do you think a 25% of them would be proper? I have mentioned that I should like him to have a percentage, without mentioning the amount; but whether he will consent to this or not I do not know. With kind regards

*Yours
Edwin Muir*

94: TO ALEC AITKEN

*Newbattle
28 June, 1951*

Dear Alec,

Forgive me for not writing sooner; the last term with all the students always on my door-step, or in my room (nice, quite delightful students, but so continually there!), visitors, reports, God knows what, quite wore me out, and as soon as the term ended I had to go down to London to attend to some personal as well as college things. But your last intensely interesting letter (which I shall treasure) could not be resisted. My dear Alec, how are you now? I feel you are greatly better, and I'm so glad. Is it possible for you to come out and see us some day, now that this morning promises good weather again? Do come and let us talk about the universe: if nothing else, I'll listen.

I think you made too much of my broadcast. I was trying to draw a simple distinction, corresponding to the distinction which we make normally between 'imaginative literature' and 'science'. I was perhaps unfair to science, not knowing nearly enough about it. But I was concerned with the power which produces for us a *picture* of the world and human life, in which everything moves and is

94 Aitken had written about Muir's broadcast talk 'The Decline of the Imagination', which was published in The Listener *on 10 May. In the next number of* The Listener *two correspondents challenged Muir's views, and he answered on 24 May defending his sharp distinction between imagination and science. The scientist strives towards exact knowledge, whereas imagination 'can never arrive at exact knowledge, since it deals with things, and highly important things, about which exact knowledge does not exist.' See also his essay 'The Poetic Imagination' in the second edition of* Essays on Literature and Society *(1965).*

individual; and imaginative literature (and the imaginative arts) alone does that. It is necessary for us to have a picture, an image of our life, if our life is to be of any significance; and my complaint is that the ability to produce the picture is declining, and that when it is produced it tends more and more to be confused and inconclusive; and one of the reasons I put down for this (perhaps wrongly) was that the mental energy of mankind had gone more and more into the pursuit of knowledge, more and more exact, about such things as the universe. You write in your letter, my dear Alec, about the universe; but I want to know something about Tom and Dick and Jane, and their relations to one another as they move about; I want to know something, too, about myself, my moods, my relation within myself to everything as it impinges *immediately* upon me (and that is always). This wish, followed out, creates a picture of life, or a series of pictures, drawn from experience and intuition (never demonstrable). The picture is humanly necessary and can never be complete. It has to be visual, sensible, and as far as it comes from participation in life, as far as it shows understanding, spiritual at the same time. That, I suppose, is what one understands by imaginative literature. The wider our knowledge of ourselves, the world and the universe, of course, the more sublime the picture will be. Dante was fortunate in living at a time when it was still possible to have a *pictorial* vision of the universe, with Jerusalem at its centre, and all lines radiating out from that. Science did not exist then for itself, or literature for itself, or business for itself; but all had their central point, their Jerusalem, which was the queen of sciences, Theology. But things, as Yeats said, have fallen apart since then; the centre does not hold; and we hardly know, except by an isolated act of faith, where the centre is. And it does not help me, as a human being finding his way between birth and death, to know that the universe is not the material construction erected by nineteenth-century science. I am glad it is not; I never believed it, in any case. But this life is what concerns me, and is what concerns the imagination as I conceive it, the immediate life of sensation, feeling, divination, attraction, repulsion, enjoyment, suffering, with whatever meaning can be wrung out of it (and meaning it has, perhaps too many meanings). Science is a wonderful thing—I realise this, for I know you and can guess at your experience of it; guess at but not know, for my experience of life does not come to me through science but through the often blind gropings of an imperfect imagination.

And great as science is, I am troubled by the thought (often expressed) that knowledge means power, and that power falls into the hands of scoundrels and fanatics. It seems to me a real problem, and the problem of our time. Take the example of Communism. The Communist revolution should have happened in the second half of last century. There would have been 'revolutions', in Marx's sense, in the various capitals of Europe, not much more destructive than a Saturday night riot in a provincial town. But now Communism is breaking the world in two; to put it to the test would be like flinging a match into a powder magazine; it would blow us all up and the world along with us. For we have so much knowledge of things, and so little knowledge of ourselves. I am trying to gratify my plea for imagination, and my conviction that our development for the last 3 or 4 centuries has been a lop-sided one.

I think you put words in my mouth in talking about imagination as 'the mind free to create'. I'm not much concerned with imaginative 'creation', but rather with true and false imagination. Most of 'doodling' is false, though it can be of use in leading one to something more genuine. I've never had any use for 'surrealism', though some writers have come to something more real by passing through that phase: Dylan Thomas, for instance. But, my dear Alec, what do you mean by saying so mysteriously that I am being weighed in the balance? Aren't we all, and the world along with us? And what is the *verdict*, with its [?] harshness, that you cannot give me? I have never bothered much about my reputation, such as it is. But in the last few years more young writers have written about me than ever before (and the young ones particularly) and quite recently a young poet I had never met wrote asking if he could bring out a collected edition of my poetry with an introduction by himself. It was quite unexpected and touching, and Fabers *are* bringing the book out. Really all this does not affect me very much, though I feel surprised and glad that the young writers should like my work so much better than my contemporaries did. But what does it matter, in any case? We shall pass, and our works with us. Yet I should very much like to know that verdict. And do come and see us

Yours affectionately
Edwin Muir

95: TO MICHAEL HAMBURGER

*Newbattle
2 July, 1952*

Dear Michael Hamburger,

Thank you very much for the poems, the inscription, and the letter. I feel very grateful to you for all three, particularly as your sincerity (and it is an unusual sincerity) comes through all that you say. Sincerity is a matter of degrees, and I feel sure a necessary quality of poetry, and it is in that sense (not the equivocal sense in which it is often used by smart reviews) that I am speaking about it. Sincerity becomes grace (and not, again, a mere surface grace) when it is effortless and not willed; and I think your poetry has that quality at its best. It is something which you have by nature, or have achieved: I find it difficult to tell which. In any case, if you are in doubts about your poetry (and who is not in doubt about his poetry?), it is a quality which you should respect and cherish. I am not good at discussing the technical points of verse; the word technique always gives me a slightly bewildered feeling; if I can translate it as skill I am more at home with it, for skill is always a quality of the thing that is being said or done, not a general thing at all. A thing asks to be said and the only test is whether it is said well. You certainly have things to say which are your own, and from the enquiring, accepting spirit of these poems, I feel that there are many more things, of which just now you are probably unaware, which you have still to say: I go on my own experience....

*Yours
Edwin Muir*

95 Michael Hamburger: (1924–); poet and scholar, translator of Hölderlin, etc.

96: TO T.S. ELIOT

Royal Hotel
Kirkwall
Orkney
1 August, 1952

My dear Eliot,

Your letter reached me here, and it leaves me in a slight difficulty. I have no poem ready at the moment, but one is in the course of formation; this is why I have not answered your letter before; I hoped that it might have completed itself. But it is still unfinished, and I shall have to wait until I can see my way through it. I wonder if you could give me a fortnight or so; though even then I don't know whether it would be suitable. It will be nearer sixty than twenty lines when it is finished.

I'm very grateful to you for bringing out my collected poems, and I've been very pleased and surprised by some of the reviews. In reviews of the separate volumes, I've always felt that even the critics who liked my work were faintly concerned about me and wondering if my health was improving, whereas now they seem to think I've passed the crisis: I hope to goodness it is so.

I have a warmth at the heart when I think of the last time I met you in London. I wonder if you will be in Scotland some time. If you are, do come and see us, and see the Abbey, where you are welcome to pass a few peaceful days whenever you like.

Yours ever
Edwin Muir

96 Eliot had asked Muir to contribute a poem, of from 20 to 60 lines, to be published in Faber's series of Ariel Poems.

97: TO T. S. ELIOT

Newbattle
27 August, 1952

My dear Eliot,

I have outstayed my time, and still have produced nothing that seems satisfactory. I send the result, but am not pleased with it, and can scarcely think it either adequate or suitable. Dante said more in a casual line which has been running in my mind

Le genti antiche nell' antico errore

I'm sorry this is the best I can offer at the moment.

Yours ever
Edwin Muir

98: TO T. S. ELIOT

Newbattle
10 October, 1952

My dear Eliot,

Certainly, you are perfectly right in suggesting 'Zeus' and 'Eros' for 'Jove' and 'Cupid'. I don't know why I didn't use these names originally.

Your second point, too, has something in it, I think, and I shall see if I can invent a line or two to account for the last part of Prometheus's soliloquy. I don't think that the expectation of the final destruction of human life is in itself a sufficient preparation. If

---

97 the result: 'Prometheus', *without the paragraph beginning* 'The shrines are emptying ...' *and in other minor respects different from the published version. A few days later he sent to Eliot's secretary (Miss Valerie Fletcher, later Mrs Eliot) a slightly amended version.*

98 second point: Eliot had written: 'My other query is still more tentative, and may be due to a misunderstanding. In the last paragraph, Prometheus says: "a God came down long since". It is a little unexpected to find Prometheus surviving into our own epoch, since one has started with the usual assumption that one is being taken back to the era of early Greece. I don't ask you to change this, but I wonder whether a line or so (do forgive these comments if they seem impertinent) could prepare the reader for this continuity of the agony of Prometheus up to date.'

you will give me a little time I shall see what I can do; it may mean a slight or a greater extension of the poem.

With kindest regards,

Yours sincerely
Edwin Muir

99: TO T. S. ELIOT

Newbattle
20 November, 1952

My dear Eliot,

Forgive me for being so long in replying. I enclose an enlarged version to explain the reference in the last verse. I am not at all sure that it is successful, and I wish you would exercise your discretion whether to include it or not. I have made a slight change in the line which now contains 'Eros' and 'arrows', to save it from appearing a little ridiculous. With kind regards,

Yours ever
Edwin Muir

100: TO WILLA MUIR

Westway Hotel
Endsleigh Street
London
20 March, 1953

My dearest love,

It [?] me to see thy writing on the envelope and the few lines inside, a warmth even in these few words. First, for news. This is a nice quiet hotel, in a quiet street, though so near Euston Road; my room is at the back, and I hear no traffic. Second, London is *cold* compared to Newbattle, at least at present; but it seems to have had fine warm sunny weather. I enjoyed my journey down reading

---

99 'arrows': altered to 'quiver'.

100 *Transcribed from partly illegible original now, I think, lost. Janet: Adam Smith (1905–), Scottish writer, assistant editor of* The Listener *when Muir became a regular contributor in 1933 and literary editor of* The New Statesman *1952–60. Publications Committee: of the British Council. Italy: Already feeling strained at Newbattle Muir was considering the possibility of working again for the Council in Italy.*

hardly at all, looking out of the window at mostly flat and uninteresting scenery, but just enjoying the looking: two possible poems cautiously emerged, or rather provisionally presented themselves: I really seem to need a tram or a train of my own for versical purposes. I had dinner in the hotel, then wandered out to get the feel of London, Tottenham Court Road, Charing Cross Road; they seemed much the same as in the old days, except that there was much more traffic, and hosts of cheerful, silly nick-nacks in the smaller shops. I wandered into a cinema, 'The Astraea', and sat through a very silly American film about the atom bomb, and the preparation of the American airman who was chosen to drop it—impossible, silly nobility attached to his *choice*, whether or not. I think a little bit of American bad conscience behind it—hence the nobility.

Next morning I did a little more wandering, and had lunch with Janet at the Little Acropolis. She told me a lot about the *N.S.*, which I'll retell when I see thee. She asked me out for lunch at her flat on Sunday, she gets nicer and nicer. Then the Publications Committee in the afternoon. How nice it is to meet these people: Bonamy Dobrée, John Lehmann, Day Lewis, Laurence Brander all so friendly, so naturally civilised, everything discussed sensibly.... This committee made me think of others which I needn't mention. I fixed up nothing for last evening: I was glad to have a rest, which I spent in my room, lying on my bed and falling asleep over a 'tec by Day Lewis which I had picked up at Foyles. Quite a good one. I'll bring it back with me.

This is how I'm fixed up. Today, lunch with Terence Kilmartin at some restaurant called the York Minster in Dean Street. Tonight dinner with John Hall at his flat. Tomorrow lunch with Laurence Brander at his club. Tomorrow dinner with Kathleen Raine at her flat. Sunday lunch with Janet, as aforesaid. Sunday evening free. Monday, lunch with T.S.E. I haven't been able to get hold of Joe Ackerley yet, but will manage to see him sometime, I hope. I mentioned the idea of getting young poets to Newbattle to Janet and John Lehmann, and they didn't look on it as a wild idea. I'll do it to Kathleen Raine and T.S.E. as well. Perhaps something will come of it.

I'm feeling all right and behaving sensibly. I hope thou as well, my love. It *is* cold here; but I imagine it's a general cold. No fog, but a general greyish mist, and as far as I can make out a north wind.

I'll sound Kilmartin about Italy, and Laurence Brander too when I see them tomorrow.... I've booked my seat for the 10 train on Tuesday morning, which arrives at 5.15 in Edinburgh, so if Webster could call for me then I'll be back before 6. Much, much love to thee, my darling

Edwin

101: TO GEORGE BROWN

Newbattle
13 May, 1953

Dear George,

Forgive me for not writing before. I've been terribly hadden down with committees and other troubles. I am wondering how you are recovering now, and whether you are feeling better and more cheerful....

The term is grinding on, and to-day I was talking about James Joyce. A writer to be admired (and sometimes enjoyed) but a sad chap altogether. I wish I was talking to the students about poetry instead of prose. I only half believe in prose, it's a sad fact. But the course made me read *Clarissa*, which was a thrill which I don't think I succeeded in conveying to any of the students, not even you: you don't know what you have missed. Still, it is not a book for reading in bed. I've been looking over my shelves, and I must say I have been struck by the number of dismal books which in my perverse pursuit of 'culture' I've managed to accumulate. Hardly one that would even raise a horse-laugh. It's quite extraordinary. Have you ever read Osbert Sitwell's four volume autobiography; now there's an exception, and if you would like to read it, I'll send it on to you. And there's Fournier's *Grand Meaulnes*, an interesting book which I think would be completely in your world. I love it. But so much of modern literature has come out of hatred, or disgruntlement, or what people call sophistication, which seems to me the most vulgar thing in the world....

I don't think I can get to Orkney this summer—I should have liked to come to see you. But I've been commissioned to continue my autobiography, and I have not managed to write a word so far.

101 *George Mackay Brown (1921–), Orkneyman, poet and writer of fiction, was a Newbattle student 1951–2; suffered from tuberculosis.*

Also I've been stung by the Income Tax people and shall have to economise strictly. I've been given a Heinemann prize for the *Collected Poems* by the Royal Society of Literature, which will help me to pay my tax, thank goodness. I was invited to Dublin as a guest of honour to attend the international PEN Conference there, but I shan't be able to go. But I'm not grumbling, and I shouldn't grumble to you. I'm still writing an occasional poem, thank goodness for that too. I saw Stanley Cursiter the other night, and both he and Phyllis are now very much better in health.

Willa and I send our love to you, my dear George, and our hope for a quick recovery.

Yours sincerely,
Edwin Muir

102: TO DOUGLAS YOUNG

Newbattle
24 June, 1953

My dear Douglas,

Thanks very much for what you say about the poem and the Coronation Honour, which was a great surprise to us, but particularly about the poem. Nevertheless I don't agree with you about the 'heavy bump' in the middle. I was not trying to give a correct account of what Odysseus was doing, but conveying the anxiety and bewilderment of Telemachos and his mother, and I think the picture of someone wandering about in a circle gives a better impression of persistence and frustration over a long stretch of years than any nautical image could possibly give. At least that is how I see it: I think I have read the Odyssey about twenty times, so that I was not floundering about at random. Some day when you are in the neighbourhood do come and see us. . . .

Yours ever
Edwin

102 Young had congratulated him on his C.B.E. and on 'Telemachos Remembers', printed in The Listener *on 18 June; but had objected to the lines:*

> Far away Odysseus trod
> The treadmill of the turning road

on the ground that The Odyssey *is a nautical affair.'*

103: TO JOSEPH CHIARI

Newbattle
7 June, 1954

Dear Joe,

Do forgive me. I've been very worried for a long time about Willa's health, and last February she at last agreed to go into a hospital in Edinburgh. There the surgeon operated upon her, but found that he had to make two operations instead of one: an older growth behind the one shown by the X-ray. Two days later internal bleeding was still going on, and another operation had to be made to stop it. For some days she hovered between life and death, but then gradually began to recover. Then pleurisy set in, throwing her back again, but at last she began to come back to life. She has been back home now for several weeks, steadily improving, but still not able to make much effort. All this is the last phase of a long illness, which has cast anxiety over her and me. Now that the operation has been successful, I think she will be better in health than she has been for years. I feel as if we were beginning to emerge out of a long dark fog of anxiety into light again. I hope this will help to explain and excuse my long silence. And in addition there have been worries about this college too. I haven't written more than two poems this year—28 lines in all.

I've heard that you have been having your troubles too, and I'm so sorry about them for the sake of both of you and your family. I'm enclosing a testimonial and do hope the post will be yours. I've learnt a great deal about what fear means during the last few months, and what a purely destructive thing it is, and how right Christianity is in setting up faith and hope as great virtues. Fear is the mood of the world just now, and the single human being has to make a deliberate effort to overcome it. I hope you are not too worried by it; I am, myself, whenever I let my attention ramble. The world has changed a great deal for the worse since the time when we used to meet and talk in Edinburgh. But it will change again, sooner or later, perhaps not in my lifetime, but probably in yours. I have grown quite old now, and would like to leave some testament in verse before I leave this scene. All good fortune with the Liverpool post. And in spite of my silence, my love to you both

Edwin

103 two poems: I think 'Milton' and 'The Great House'.

104: TO JANET ADAM SMITH

Newbattle
25 October, 1954

My dear Janet,

I am sending you these three poems in doubt and trembling, for I have been writing prose so long, finishing my autobiography, that verse is new and awkward to me: one seems to write prose and poetry with different hands, and whether the right or the left is the poetic one is hard to say. But I think in any case that I shall be writing more poetry now, though these last three poems, I must say, look rather strange to me. If you like them I shall be glad; if you don't just send them back to me. I would like them to appear together if possible, but if you omit the second one I won't mind, for I don't like it as well as the others. You mustn't think I am unhappy because the poems are; they came from I don't know where. But I feel like a novice, after all that prose, and you may not like them at all.

It would be very nice to see you again. I'm kept very busy here, and tied to the place.

With love from us both

*Yours
Edwin*

105: TO MRS SMALLWOOD

Newbattle
1 November, 1954

Dear Mrs Smallwood,

I want to write and tell you how very pleased I am with the way in which the Hogarth Press has presented my autobiography. It is

---

104 three poems: 'Effigies *1, 3 and 5' (as numbered later) appeared in* The New Statesman *on 27 November.*

105 Mrs Smallwood is a director of The Hogarth Press, *which published Muir's two earliest volumes of poetry and most of his books of literary criticism as well as* An Autobiography. *Virginia Woolf's diary (2 April 1937) shows a resilient response to Muir's criticism: 'Quite set up and perky today because I was so damnably depressed and smacked on the cheek by Edwin Muir in* The Listener [*Vol. XVII (31 March 1937)*]*.*

very beautifully done and I feel most grateful. I do hope the book will sell, and repay all your care and labour and mine. . . .

I want to tell you how moved I was by Virginia Woolf's diary, and how sorry I was to realise that I once reviewed one of her books, *The Years*, in such a way as to give her pain (I am glad to think that it was my sole bêtise, so far as I know, for indeed I was and am a great admirer of her work). It makes me realise what a hangman's job a reviewer's is, or at least what things we do without realising the effects; though, thank goodness, there is the other side as well. But what a wonderful woman Virginia Woolf was, what an artist, and how willingly she suffered for it, and how much. I met her only twice, and cannot claim to have known her; I realise, after reading the diary, how much I lost, along with many other people, by that. But what a wonderful human being comes through these personal notes and entries.

I hope we shall see you again sometime soon, and please give my kindest regards to Leonard Woolf.

Yours sincerely
Edwin Muir

106: TO KATHLEEN RAINE

Newbattle
6 December, 1954

Dear Kathleen,

Thank you for your letter and thank you for your review, in which you were far too kind to me. No, my struggle hasn't been heroic, as you said there; it's only that there has been something stubborn in me, perhaps peasant, though I would have been a bad farmer, as my father was—and I'm thankful for that too; he had all the good qualities of the Orkney peasantry, without the bad acquisitive ones that narrow life down. But you know the life that I knew as a boy and still know, and it will come back to you again, perhaps quite unexpectedly: I feel this from my own experience. We all feel that we shall never write another poem, and feel it sometimes for long stretches: I think it is a common experience, and very painful, and very unpleasant, until the gates open again. I know how unpleasant the world is growing. I can feel it here as you feel it

106 review: of An Autobiography *in* New Statesman *27 November.*
three poems: 'Effigies 1, 3, 5' in same issue.

in London, though not so thickly, for I'm not in that dense atmosphere and not meeting intellectuals. The three poems in *The New Statesman* are affected by it—a little infusion of poison in them except for the third, which comes from an old memory. I have a few more satisfactory poems in my mind, but not written all these weeks because I'm so occupied here. It's taken me quite a long time to recover from the thought that Willa might die (she was very near it), and I'm still very tentatively, and slightly fearfully, attempting poetry. But something will come. Do believe that it will happen with you too.

Actually here things are very difficult. A party in the Committee (this is private) have been trying to get rid of me for some time, and to turn this into a short-term college: courses for week-ends, or weeks at most. I like the work with the students, but the perpetual [?] has spoilt everything; and I've got tired with fighting back (successfully so far); I hate fighting. That is why I've been thinking for some time of throwing the whole thing up: the worry and dissension gives me pains in the chest at the least occasion, and all sorts of other silly complications. So that there's disintegration here as well as in London. That is partly why I've been half-thinking of going there or somewhere near there; if I'm to make my living again by writing, I shall have to be in the neighbourhood. Thank God Willa is getting well again and in a few months should be quite recovered. I'm unresolved at the moment, and cannot decide what to do....

I'm sending the Ariel poem, and glad Michael Hamburger liked it so well, but I'm not satisfied with it myself at all, or only a little.

With love from us both, my dear Kathleen

Edwin

107: TO T. S. ELIOT

Newbattle
8 July, 1955

My dear Eliot,

I am perfectly willing, after what you say, to return to *One Foot in Eden*. I had a sudden feeling that the title might appear a little ridiculous, but that is perhaps unjustified. I agree entirely with you that it is a more striking and memorable one than the other, and so I think we should let it stand.

I am very glad that Djuna Barnes has written something again. I admire her book *Nightwood* very much indeed, and would like very much to read her new play. I met her once in London many years ago, and I think I shall try to see her in America when I go there; I liked her very much. I think anything she writes must be remarkable. ... So I am looking forward very much to seeing the play once it is in its final form.

We are leaving for America on the 26 August by boat, and I feel sure that my time at Harvard will be very interesting and enjoyable and surrounded with kindness. I hope I shall be able to write some poetry there; here, I have very little time for it.

With many kinds regards,

Yours ever
Edwin Muir

107 In January Muir had sent a new collection of poems: 'I do hope you will like them, and that if you think some would be better out than in you will tell me.' Eliot had replied that he liked them very much indeed. 'I have seen nothing which seemed to me of inferior quality and better out.' Muir had then suggested changing the title of the projected volume from One Foot in Eden *to* The Succession, *and Eliot had asked him to reconsider.*

Djuna Barnes: had written a play The Antiphon, *and was revising it. Eliot had asked Muir to write a reader's report on it.*

108: TO KATHLEEN RAINE

Newbattle
12 August, 1955

Dear Kathleen,

How can I thank you? It would be a godsend if the Bollingen foundation gave me a fellowship, but whether or no I shall never forget your kindness. I feel your letter to them has been peculiarly timely, for a few weeks ago I got the idea for a long poem, after re-reading a miscarried attempt long since published, a 'Chorus of the Dead', and realising that I could do it better now and in quite a different way. It has made lines and passages come more readily than I have known them to come in the past years. Do you remember that you told me when I was in London last that I would not write any poetry in America? Herbert Read told me the same. I don't know whether it was a cunning trick of my peasant unconscious that gave me beforehand something that would occupy my mind in America, or whether it was a real movement of my imagination, but I hope the last; really I think it is, for such things don't make themselves known except at their time. Forgive me for speaking of these large plans, but they have excited me, and everything is still in movement. But I am glad, remembering what you said, to have the idea to take with me to Harvard.

We are coming to London on the 22nd of this month, and shall be staying for a few days at the Westway Hotel in Endsleigh Street. I do hope we shall see you then, and we are looking forward very much to the party which you and the Frasers so kindly intend for us. We are sailing on the 26th.

During part of this year I have had a great number of letters from Tom Scott, sometimes three in a week; but I haven't heard from him recently. I hear he and Elizabeth have been in Skye for a holiday.

---

108 Tom Scott: (1918–   ); poet and critic; knew Muir at St Andrews and was a Newbattle student 1953–4; his projected poem, never completed, was 'The Tree', suggested by his reading of Johannes Erigena's De Divisione Naturae. *He writes 'The gist of it was a poetic recapitulation of animate life forms from the amoeba to Man and perhaps beyond. . . . Behind it all was God's purpose of producing a species perfectly adapted to life on earth—and only earth. The experiment leads on to Man, potentially the successful species, in whom all other forms are subsumed, and Man is subsumed into Christ, the perfect Man to whom all mankind aspire.'*

His last idea for a long poem is quite magnificent, and I wrote to tell him so. I have asked him to wait for lines which will give an image of the various sections, and will produce other isolated lines round which he can build in the poem. I think it is in lines that the poetic idea becomes imaginatively embodied; until that happens nothing but the bare idea is left; and I feel that is Tom's danger. The idea of this poem of his is wonderful, all the same. I wish he had the means and the absence of care to be able to sit down to it. But again it is a great pity he feels compelled to write it in Scots, which hardly anyone reads. Difficulty on difficulty.

Thank you again, my dear Kathleen, and I hope the muse will visit you some time when you least expect her.

Edwin

109: TO TOM SCOTT

Newbattle
20 August, 1955

Dear Tom,

I am in the middle of packing, but I must write to you before I go. You have had strange and wonderful dreams, and I feel sure that dreams are propitious. You have to take your own road, and, I feel, through many difficulties, practical and other. I wish I could help you in your practical matters; but I am not very practical myself: things seem to happen to me. And I can't help you in your spiritual difficulties, and perhaps help is the thing you least want. I wish we had seen more of each other since you left Newbattle: it would have been good for us both. I agree that Scotland is hard to put up with, and difficult for a poet. But there are good people in it; and I think it is a pity that your craft is failing. You are a man who needs to be a great deal by yourself.

Your dreams say strange things: for instance that I may write your poems, and you mine. That is beyond conception, for we have all our separate pasts behind us. My own 'long' poem is very different from the one you once described to me. It will be (if I can bring it off) in the form of a chorus, varied between united and single voices, and the voices will tell of their life on the earth in a

109 craft is failing: probably refers to Scott's depression over his inability to complete the poem referred to in 108 above.

place where their life is behind them. I attempted the theme once when I was much younger, and not at all successfully. Now I feel I could do it better, with some experience of living. The characters will tell their mortal experiences good and bad, wretched and happy, and what I hope will come out is some sort of image of life, and some sort of justification for that strange experience. I don't want to go into it too fully in case I should fix it too rigidly in my mind; it is quite fluid, yet lively enough, throwing out lines and situations which I shall try to build round. I may be mistaken, but I feel that it is in the line that the intellectual idea takes on flesh and reaches incarnation; and I am depending a good deal just now on lines coming. I wonder if this is your experience too.

But I don't want to write about the poem—you would hardly credit how shapeless it is in my mind just now; it might become anything. The important thing is that it is working.

I wish you everything good, and light widening. Probably I shall not see you for a long time, but write to me whenever you feel moved to it. I should like to say before leaving that I have no doubt at all of your high gifts: may they come to early fruition. We shall be staying, for some time at least, at the Hotel Continental, Cambridge, Mass., but I can also be found at Harvard University, Cambridge, Mass. With love from us both to Elizabeth and yourself.

Edwin

110: TO T. S. ELIOT

Hotel Continental,
Cambridge,
Massachusetts
13 January, [*1956*]

My dear Eliot,

I feel I should have written to you before about Djuna Barnes's play. On the other hand I thought I had better see her first and discuss it with her, and I did this about a week ago when I was in New York for a poetry reading. Her health, as you know, has been wretchedly bad; during the two or three hours I spent with her she had to stop twice and take something or other for her asthma. I had met her only once before, about twenty years ago in Chelsea, and I did not recognise her. But she has great spirit and was surprised but not greatly offended by the extensive excisions I had marked on the margin of the first act. I hope she was not dejected by them after I left. After all she took four years to write the play, and is living now what seems to be a lonely comfortless life in a street and house which would cast most people (I know they would cast me) into hopeless depression.

About the play, I do feel that the first act is impossible. I pencilled in brackets the passages which I thought should be left out, so that the line of action might be left comparatively clear. To bring this about I left out (as I told her) whole passages, almost pages, brilliant in themselves, but which did nothing to advance or explain the action, or tell what the play was about. I wasn't able to go over the whole action of the first act with her. I think, if she accepts the excisions, the first act will be quite clear, and probably effective. She doesn't expect the play ever to be acted, she says; though I think it could be, and that some time it is likely to be. The difficulty about the first act is that it obstructs even the reader; he doesn't know where he is, there is such a furious marking time. The idea has occurred to me that, if someone could be got to tailor the play, it might appear on the Third Programme with success. That might enrage Djuna Barnes, but it might also encourage her. She asked despairingly while I went over part of the first act with her: 'Have I got to rewrite it *again*?', and I reassured her by saying that all she had to do was to leave out some splendid but irrelevant matter. She promised to read through the first act after I left, with the excisions. I had done that myself several times. I haven't heard from her yet. With the excisions in the first I think the second act follows quite naturally. We talked a good deal about the 'exposition', which she thoroughly detests. I hope she will see that my excisions really do give movement and shape to the first act. I know very little about dramatic art myself, and could never write a play; but I do know, as a reader, what can be understood and what cannot, what moves and what does not; and that was my sole justification in suggesting these omissions.

Considering that she has spent so much time over the play, and considering the genius poured out in it, I feel myself that the second and third acts should stand as they are. I have actually marked one or two passages for omission, but nothing like the wholesale omissions in the first act. I had the feeling that she was near the point of giving up the whole thing in despair. She may decide, on reflection, that my suggestions are all wrong, and she may be right. But the first act is certainly very wrong as it stands: I don't think anyone could deny that. I do hope in any case that I have managed to be of some help to her, for I feel myself that *The Antiphon* is one of the greatest things that have been written in our time, and it would be a disaster if it were never to be known.

The plot itself, once one gets into it over the obstruction of the first act, seems to me very effective (I mean I was deeply moved by it), fantastic as some of the details are. The mother, the two evil playboys her sons, Miranda herself, all convince me on the plane where they are shown. Jack Blow is impossibly garrulous; I excised a great deal of him. The cruel game of the two sons with Miranda and her mother I thought a wonderful image of evil, and the Noah's ark very strange and moving. But as for my excisions, I don't know yet whether Miss Barnes will accept them or reject them.

I am enjoying my life here. I have seen a good deal of Harry Levin and like him very much. I have seen Robert Lowell and Robert Frost too, and some of the young poets. Everybody has been most kind. I haven't been tempted to eat or drink too much (I had been warned against this before I left). I've given three of my six lectures, and they seem to have gone well. (I'm very pleased that the Poetry Book Club have shown my book.) I do not know much about America yet, and it would take a long time to know anything essential about it; but I like very much what I have seen of New England. I hope that you are keeping well now. With many kind regards,

Yours
Edwin Muir

P.S. Kathleen Raine spoke to some people in the Bollingen Foundation before I left, saying that I should be given a grant. I have not taken any steps yet, and I wonder if you could advise me. I resigned my post as Warden of Newbattle before I left, for the committee were moving to turn the college into a short term college, with which I could not have done anything serious. I can easily make my living by miscellaneous writing when I return, but would dearly like to write poetry.

III: TO KATHLEEN RAINE

Hotel Continental
28 February, 1956

Dear Kathleen,

Forgive me. I have often been on the point of writing to you, remembering all your kindness, and my own great admiration and affection for you. It is no excuse that we have been involved in an apparently almost inextricable system of social relationships since we came here: kind, considerate, warm, intelligent, discreet, almost everything, but in some way, and apart from a half-dozen people we are genuinely fond of, not what critics call *significant*. Everything is so enormously *close* to one here, in the spatial sense, and everything else so far away: England and Scotland, for instance. And Europe and the world too. And yet I know hardly anything of this country yet, though every day reminds me of it, almost always in the most friendly way. It has great merits and obvious ones: more charity I think, than we have, hope that fills me with astonishment, with alarm, and faith—there I get quite lost. I think the effort to understand, more than the thing to be understood, is what daunts one most. I must not give the idea that we have not enjoyed ourselves in many ways, or that we are ungrateful for so much kindness and consideration; that would be absurd. And the stay here has given Willa a providential chance to recover herself; and she is much better than when you saw her last.

A letter from John Hall has brought me at last to write the letter to you which I should have written, for other reasons and long ago. He wrote about the Bollingen Foundation. I was in New York two weeks ago, and saw Barrett then by appointment, and he gave me an application form. I had written to him beforehand, saying that you had spoken to his secretary about me in London, and that I would like to apply for a grant so that I might be able to have more time for poetry. I told him also that I had wanted for some time to write something about Hofmannsthal, who is now regarded in Germany and Austria as the greatest writer of his time, greater than Rilke. But it seems that the Bollingen had sponsored a volume of translations from Hofmannsthal, and that it had sold very badly; and Barrett recommended me to apply for a grant for poetry instead. I

---

111 Herbert: Sir Herbert Read.

think I could get recommendations from Eliot and Walter de la Mare, from you, I hope, and perhaps from Herbert, though I do not know whether he likes my poetry or not. On the other hand, it is clear that I am not certain to produce the poetry the grant is intended to bring, and that the mere expectation of it might be a hindrance rather than a help. In any case I have another idea, closer to me than Hofmannsthal, much as I love him. The Ballads, especially the Scottish ones, have meant a great deal to me for many years. I am fascinated by the world they live in and the world that produced them and kept them alive for so many centuries; the transmission of poetry for such a long time by the peasantry, and some of it great poetry; the light this throws on poetry itself; the effect it had on romantic poetry and the romantic movement; the part of the supernatural in all this, its acceptance and its realistic delineation. The department of Scottish studies has been doing a great deal in the way of enquiring into the present state of the ballads in Scotland. I should have to take that into account, and also study the German and French ballads, the American ballads too. All this would give me a great deal to do which I would very much like doing. I would like most of all to recreate imaginatively the whole world of the ballads, which I don't think has been done yet. I was born into it, for the ballads were still being handed on in our house in Orkney when I was young, and in the other houses there as well; there is very little of it now, I'm afraid. Does this strike you as a possible proposal for the Bollingen? Do tell me, and as soon as you can. My application must be in before the first of April and I shall have to get some recommendations before that. Could you get Herbert's advice? I actually think that, among other things, the enquiry would encourage my writing of poetry; I love these old things so much. Forgive me for landing all this upon you so suddenly.

I have actually written eight or nine poems since I came here, mostly from lines that came when I was wakening in the morning. There is no knowing when such things will come, or where. I do hope that you are writing poetry again. I have just got your collected poems from *The Observer* for review, and I am looking forward to writing about them: what strikes me again is the absoluteness of vision in them; I don't know of anyone else who has it, or maintains it in its purity. I depend myself too much on invention, which is a weakness.

I have met Robert Frost twice since I came, and am very much impressed by him; he is really a great man and a very wise man. I think I got on with him so well because his mother came from Orkney; he likes to talk of us Orkneymen, which endeared him to me. I have met Robert Lowell too, and like him very much, and a perfectly delightful young couple, Richard and Charlee Wilbur, and a wonderfully warm and gentle and natural Irish-American, Jack Sweeney. I have been twice to New York, reading poetry, and once to Washington and once to Chicago (a terrible place), and once to Bryn Mawr, which is very pleasant. But mostly we have been here.

I hope you have been enjoying your stay in Cambridge. Have you met there a young man called John Holloway? We knew him in Scotland and like him very much; in fact he is looking for a house for us somewhere near Cambridge, where we could settle when we get back to England this summer. My troubles with the Newbattle committee have made Scotland a sore place for us. And in any case, if we are to make a living by writing, we shall have to be somewhere near London. But if the ballad project comes off, I shall have to visit Scotland fairly often, and that would be a pleasure too.

Dear Kathleen, Willa and I send our love, and every good thing to you.

Yours
Edwin

And I am sending my love to you also by *direct* lighting, as well as through Edwin's calm radiation!

I have been looking at your poems too, with delight,
Willa

112: TO T. S. ELIOT

Hotel Continental
13 March, 1956

My dear Eliot,

I am so sorry you have been ill, and I hope you are well again now. The weather must have been very hard to bear; it sounded alarming even from here. But the latest news seems to indicate that the cold is messily going away. I hope it is so.

I am glad that Djuna Barnes has sent her new version. I would very much like to see it. I should have written to her, but I have been busy getting together my lectures, and lecturing and giving readings in various places. I think the States unsettle one. In any case I have been writing some poems which seem quite queer to me, whether good or bad I find it hard to say. But to return to Djuna Barnes, I hope the new version is a possible one; I have no idea how many of my deletions she has accepted. As for the fee you mentioned, I don't care whether I get one or not, and should prefer to think that I did what I did out of love of the work. I should prefer to leave it at that.

I have taken the liberty of speaking about the play to the people who run the Poets' Theatre here in Cambridge, and as they are young and eager I think they would love the chance to put it on. They produce their plays quite well, and have an intelligent audience. I wonder if it would interest or encourage Djuna, or perhaps make her see the need to alter or omit some things in the play, if she were to see it on a stage. The Poets' Theatre holds only fifty people; you might call the audience almost a private audience, which in this case would be all to the good. I think they would almost certainly put the play on, if she were to consent; but I shall not write to her unless you think it would be advisable.

I want to ask if you would act as a reference for me in an application for a grant which I intend to make to the Bollingen Foundation. Kathleen Raine last summer mentioned my name to the secretary of John Barrett, the Vice-President, who was in London at the time. I saw Barrett last month when I was in New York giving a reading, and gave as my reason for applying for a grant that I wanted to have more time in which to write poetry. He gave me an application form which I must send in before the first of April. Later I discovered from Herbert Read that the Bollingen rarely give grants for such purposes, and that some project—which means some enquiry—is far more preferable. Now I have been interested for a long time in the Ballads, and their transmission by word of mouth for such a long time: in fact they were still being handed on in Orkney when I was a boy, and I know them from that time, and the conditions of their transmission and what may be called the technique. We had only one book of poetry in our house, that is Burns; but there were scores of ballads that we knew: it was the same in the other farmers' houses. I have been interested for long in the world of the ballads and the world out of which they came; the fact that they solved the problem of the audience for poetry, which is so impossibly difficult to-day, (there is great poetry, as you know, among them). I want to study the question of the audience: the ballads and folk-songs had their audience, which among the peasantry was everybody, and the court poetry (I can't find a more adequate term) also had its audience, which did not interfere in the least with the other; and all this happened in a sense naturally. This all has a bearing on society, and the difference between the society in which this could happen, and our own. I want to deal too with such things as the beliefs, natural and supernatural, in the ballads, and the curious and yet apparently congruous mixture of Pagan superstition and Christian belief. Then there is the fairly clear presupposition that the ballads did not degenerate but were often improved in transmission, showing that the audience was not merely receptive but critical and inventive. And there may be in the whole process something of Jung's Collective Unconscious, though here I am on uncertain ground. There is also the possibility of demonstrating that poetry is not in its primitive nature a rarefied thing but a natural expression, where it is allowed to be, of imagination even among people who have never thought what poetry is. I am sure that the theme will expand in all sorts of directions. There has been a great deal of enquiry by the Department of Scottish Studies of Edinburgh University during the past few years, and I could draw from this information not only about the ballads but about the ambiance in which they grew and perpetuated themselves. I give you this outline of the theme so that you may be able to decide whether you can stand as a reference. If you can, will you let me know soon, for my application must be in before the end of the month, and if you allow me to use your name, I must do it before then.

I think we shall try to be back in England by the beginning of June, and after that we shall try to get a house in the country not too far from London. My wardenship of Newbattle is over because of a difference of opinion between myself and my committee on how the college should be run. Willa and I will have to depend for a time on making our living by writing. To have a subject for a book, and a grant to enable me to write it, would be a great help.

We have enjoyed ourselves here, almost entirely because people have been so kind. But we are still puzzled. We have met your cousin Miss Hinkley several times and find her very charming.

With many kind wishes,

Yours ever,
Edwin Muir

I liked very much the appearance of the new poems.

113: TO GEORGE BROWN

Hotel Continental
9 April, 1956

Dear George,

Forgive me for not writing sooner. I have been in the stress of writing out and giving the last three of my lectures, and I have been entangled as well in a web of hospitality, not really insistent, indeed so kind and considerate that it was impossible to escape. The Cambridge people, the Harvard professors, are almost the kindest lot, I think, I have ever met: not offensive, rather quiet, and very considerate (I must come back to that word). The New Englander has a very strong English tradition, a kind of delayed allegiance. An Englishwoman who has lived here for 17 years shocked an old Bostonian lady a little while ago at a tea-party where they were discussing who was the worst character in history. The Englishwoman suggested Queen Victoria, thinking of all the crimes against art committed in that reign, and the old Bostonian cried: 'Olivia, you, an Englishwoman, to say that of your Queen! You should be strung up.' There is great urbanity of manners, great insistence on custom; when you are invited out for supper the table is always lit by candles (I found that very pleasant): and when supper is over the ladies retire, and the men sit over their wine for a while longer. Not what I had expected at all, but we're told that Harvard and Cambridge are not like the rest of America. However we shan't be able to see much of that. We've been twice to New York (I had to give two readings there), to Washington, a really handsome, I'm tempted to say beautiful city, to Bryn Mawr, a woman's college near Philadelphia; and I undertook an expedition by myself to Chicago, an unspeakable place, flung down in every conceivable style, all of them bad, on the border of a great lake. I won't return there again. We stayed in Cape Cod, the most lovely bit of America I've seen yet, for a week-end with Edmund Wilson, a rather tough but kind man whom I like very much. And we've to go down to Connecticut

---

113 The poems by G.M.B. mentioned appeared in Loaves and Fishes *(1959)—except 'The Masked House', which was discarded. G.M.B. comments on the letters to him, only a small proportion of which are printed here: 'You can see how consistently kind he (and Willa too) were to me in the last seven years of his life. But for him I think I'd never have had the courage to send any of my poems anywhere.'*

to two colleges there where I've to give two more readings. We expect to return towards the end of May or beginning of June. In spite of all the kindness, and lots of good conversation, I could not live in this country for good; it is not my atmosphere, and Willa feels the same. But why it remains so strange to us I cannot tell.

I've taken the liberty of sending a selection of your poems to Mrs Alice Morris, the literary editor of *Harper's Bazaar*. I hope you don't mind: I've appeared in it myself, I know that it pays exceptionally well; that really is the reason for my choice. It has published most of the best known American poets, and some of the English. So that if you should hear from Mrs Morris, I want to save you from the shock. I admire these poems of yours more and more the more I read them: you have a feeling for words which I sincerely envy! and the feeling and imagination in the 'Elegy', 'The Masked House', 'The Old Women', 'Thorfinn', 'Hamnavoe', to take a varied selection, are very moving. The genius is there, my dear George, and I wish you all that it offers you. I still think you should prepare a volume of your best poems up to now.

I'm going to write to Robin Richardson of the Scottish B.B.C., asking him if he will commission Willa and me to pay a visit to Orkney and Shetland and write a script on the lines of 'Revisited'. I would love to see Orkney again this summer. Perhaps it will come off and I shall see you again. . . .

Love from us both,

Edwin

114: TO KATHLEEN RAINE

Hotel Continental
10 April, 1956

Dear Kathleen,

Thank you for your letter. I have heard from Herbert too and framed my application according to his and your advice. I have added, as you suggested, that I fancy the work on the ballads would give me something for my own poetry and perhaps something to other poets too. I do hope the project will come off; for it will give me time for something which I shall enjoy doing and take me back

114 The Bollingen Foundation did give Muir a grant, and extended it after his death to Mrs Muir, who wrote Living with Ballads *(1965)*.

again into the roots of poetry, where we should all be, and away from fashion. I have made a genuflection to Jung, as Herbert and Eliot, these wise men, advise. I have taken the liberty of giving you as one of my guarantors or referees: the other two are Herbert and Eliot. Please forgive me if I have gone too far: I mentioned the matter in my last letter, and you did not object.

One has to be an Oxford graduate to become Professor of Poetry at Oxford: so John Holloway told me. I think it will be good for Auden to be back in England again: I don't think America has been good for his poetry: it has been getting more and more rootless. I know I have been writing some very queer poetry since I came, with a good deal of new horror in it; why, Heaven alone knows, for every one here has been extraordinarily kind, and considerate at the same time. But I am not at home here, in spite of the consideration and the kindness: I was far more at home in Italy. You say that for poetry Cambridge is a spiritual desert, but I want the landscape, the soil (I hope that some of it is left), things shaped by generations with affection and made into a human scene. I shall try to get up to Orkney this Summer if it can be managed at all. I suppose what is wrong with me here is that I am hungry. Horrible thought: I don't know whether Eden was ever here.

I have heard from Tom Scott only once since I came: announcing his conversion to the Episcopalian Church: it seems to have been a real experience, but it has failed him. I have never been able since I left the Presbyterian Church to enter any other one; I can't take the step and I feel I never could. I am so glad that David Gascoyne is so much better. If he has started writing again, I think he will write poetry. I wish he would; I wish you would too; but I am getting tiresome. I can't tell you how your *Collected Poems* moved me: I could say only a little about that in my review.

We have seen quite a lot of the Wilburs and the Sweeneys and are very fond of them both. We have seen not so much of the Richards, and I feel we haven't come actually to know them, except to the extent of seeing what an extraordinary creature he is. We like the MacLeishes too, a really warm and human pair: I feel a great affection for them, and for Harry Levin too, a gentle sensitive creature with a razor-sharp intelligence, a touching combination.

I do hope that you are finding Cambridge congenial in itself; it is so beautiful, even if a desert. The modern world seems to wither everything; why, it would take a hundred years to find out.

I have given the last of my lectures, which I do not much like. I hope this does not sound too dejected. Willa is being put to rights by the Harvard Medical School, which I believe is the best in the world. And if that can be done, it will be an infinite happiness.

With love from us both

Edwin

115: TO JANET ADAM SMITH

Priory Cottage,
Swaffham Prior,
Cambridge
22 September, 1956

My dear Janet,

Thank you so much for your letter. I agree with you about the second poem. It started from something a Harvard student said. She had attended a lecture of Ivor Richards, and he had set off in one of those wonderful inspired passages of his, so that the poor girl was left, as she told me, and as she told him, 'in bewilderment'. And his reply to her struck me as very fine, and seems to have struck her too: 'That's splendid. That's where one should start'. But the poem is not at all equal to that. I may attempt something later, more adequate, for the incident sticks in my mind. Ivor Richards is a wonderful creature; I saw something of him at Harvard, but not enough. You are an old friend of his, of course, and must know better than I do what I've been saying about him. . . .

With much love from us both

Edwin

115 second poem: 'The Poet' ('And in bewilderment').

116: TO JANET ADAM SMITH

Swaffham Prior
26 September, 1956

My dear Janet,

George Fraser's anthology arrived from *The Observer* by the same post as your letter; I was sorry to find it there, and now I can hardly send it back. The publishers, I think at George's instructions, had sent me another copy more than a week before. I am not looking forward, frankly, to reviewing the book, and find as little to inspire me as you do, yet I feel a certain sympathy for these young people, though they are so cautious and, so it seems to me, so sad, and so careful not to hope. A strange generation; I wonder sometimes if something unique may come out of it yet.

I *have* had an idea for Books in General, but whether it is a possible one or not, I can't say. The idea is to make a short general comparison between *Godot* and *Mother Courage*, and between Beckett and Brecht as represented by these plays. I was in Cambridge a little while ago, and picked up *Mother Courage* in German at Bowes & Bowes, and later I got hold of *Waiting for Godot*. I have quite a number of ideas on these strange plays (Brecht is not so strange as Beckett). Brecht I did not expect to like much, but he does have a striking talent, quite apart from the political slant; and his humanity is more evident than his politics. I don't think *Mother Courage* has been translated yet, but would that matter? I leave it to you.

I enclose the bewilderment poem, but not for publication. It is only a note for what might turn into a poem, as I see it now. I think if I found an 'objective correlative', it would come to life; and I think I have found one, the poet Hölderlin in his half-mad prophetic phase. There is something in Plato's idea of 'divine madness', in Shakespeare's too, and Hölderlin is the great

116 Muir reviewed Fraser's anthology Poetry Now *in* The Observer, *14 October 1956. After praising the high level of accomplishment, he went on: 'One begins to suspect that most of the younger poets are content to do the lesser thing neatly rather than attempt the greater thing clumsily.... Empson moves us by the spectacle of a shocking struggle for control. In his followers the control is almost complete.' The projected essay on Brecht and Beckett was never written, and the 'bewilderment' poem was not rewritten.*

modern representative figure. But the poem, if it comes off, will be a different poem.

With much love from us both

Yours ever
Edwin

117: TO T. S. ELIOT

Swaffham Prior
17 October, 1956

My dear Tom,

I am so glad that you have managed to get Djuna's play into reasonable shape at last; it has been a long struggle. I would be very glad if you would quote that sentence of mine, if it will be of any help. I do admire the play enormously, and should be able to admire it still more now that it has been given a shape. That reading in the Poets' Theatre made me realise that in my repeated readings of the play I had remained quite unaware of quite obvious impossibilities; I suppose I was beguiled by Djuna's imagery.

Willa is much better than she was, although here she has a great deal more of house-work than I like, cooking, and innumerable other things. She moves better and has less pain. The little house is very charming, and we have fallen in love with it. It is in a pleasant village, and looks out on two ruined church towers, each set on a little knoll of its own; one of them damaged by lightning sometime, and the other by time itself. The neighbours are kind, and the village shop is next door. I confess that sometimes I have a slightly sinking feeling, knowing that now I have nothing to do but write, and must depend upon it. But I feel that it will be all right.

I didn't see the quotation from Horace Gregory, but I feel it would have run better if it had said, 'Since ... no Orkney poet has made so impressive ... as Edwin Muir.' Celtic origin is hard to establish, and the Orkney people are a mixture of everything. My

117 sentence: in his letter of 13 January about The Antiphon *being 'one of the greatest things that have been written in our time'. Poets' Theatre: both Eliot and Muir had been at the reading of* The Antiphon *there in May. Horace Gregory: had written that 'since the death of W. B. Yeats, no mature poet of Celtic origin has made so impressive a contribution to modern literature as Edwin Muir', and Eliot had asked how 'an old Viking like yourself' felt 'about being called "a poet of Celtic origin".'*

father came from an island filled mostly with Muirs, and my mother, whose name is Cormack, from a parish where there is still the ruins of a chapel erected to Cormack the Sailor, a follower of Saint Columba. And probably there was a faint mixture of Vikings somewhere unknown in the story, but I hope not. What nonsense nice people write.

Yours ever,
Edwin

118: TO TOM SCOTT

Swaffham Prior
2 November, 1956

Dear Tom,

... I intended to write to you before, but I seem to have been busy with all sorts of things, among them getting this house in order. And I have begun, after a longish interval, to write poetry again, trying to hammer out a style. I notice you are taking up the old Celtic gods: I don't know much about them, and can say little therefore. But I notice that your poem comes to full life when you write of the Scotland we know (about the middle of the second page) and that after that everything goes splendidly. I think it is a very fine poem, but that it owes little to the Celtic gods; I have no doubt that they are well worth enquiring into. I am trying, at long last, to bring my own poetry up to the present and the future (the future not seen, I may say, in any Utopian light). I don't know how it will go, and so I can't advise anyone else. But the present and future are themselves a dream of a kind....

With love from us both,

Yours
Edwin Muir

119: TO GEORGE BROWN

Swaffham Prior
20 December, 1956

Dear George,

... I hope you aren't having this detestable fog in Edinburgh. We are having the second day of it here: the roads almost blind.

118 your poem: 'Fergus'.

And up to now we have been enjoying the loveliest weather (almost like early spring), the thrushes singing like mad, and a robin in the back garden with a sweet never ending song. I think this must be very unusual; I have never heard the birds singing before at this time of the year. But now all is blanketed, curiously silent, and soporific. I expect things will waken again in a day or two.

I agree with you very much about Edinburgh in general, though there are some civilised people in it too: but there are everywhere, and I'm merely repeating a platitude. It is curious that I felt almost the same thing about Glasgow when I went there first as you do about Edinburgh now, though far more blindly; I wasn't able at that time to explain to myself why I disliked things. I think what disconcerted me was the aggression, the assertiveness, the lack of courtesy, as you call it, a kind of courtesy one had got used to as a natural thing. I'm glad you're meeting the old Newbattle crowd, and it warms my heart to think they talk of the days 'before the fall'. There was some faint air of Eden about the place then. . . .

Willa and Gavin and I send our best wishes for a Happy Christmas and a Good New Year, and our love.

Edwin

120: TO KATHLEEN RAINE

Swaffham Prior
24 January, 1957

Dear Kathleen,

I would like to give a talk some time to the literary Circle (is it a Girton or a Cambridge society), but I would prefer to wait until the warm weather comes—the later spring—for this bothersome pain in my chest has been troubling me whenever I move about, travel even a short distance, and it is not only a great nuisance in itself, but when it comes on it more or less immobilises me. I feel I shall be much better in a few months; I think if I'm careful now that is quite probable.

I'm looking forward very much to seeing you and Miss Brad-

120 Bradbrook: Fellow, now Mistress, of Girton College, Cambridge; author among other books, of The Growth and Structure of Elizabethan Comedy *(1955). Holloway:* The Minute *(1956). two poems: perhaps 'After 1984' and 'The Strange Return', published in* The New Statesman *22 December 1956. The third poem is 'The Brothers'.*

brook next Wednesday. Do tell her I enjoyed very much her book on Elizabethan Comedy. I liked John Holloway's book of poems better, I think, than you did. There is something impressive in them, a clear-sightedness, a resolute biting on the nerve. And a strangeness too, and I like strangeness. And I felt, as you did, the reminiscences of Aberdeen: I think he was fond of the life there. Actually I felt that he may do something quite extraordinary in the style of imaginative speculation and speculative imagination. Do you feel that?

I'm glad you and Miss Bradbrook liked (if that is the right word) my two poems. They're certainly what Eliot, I think, used to call Purgatorial. I'm trying to write one now about a dream I had recently about my two brothers, Willie and Johnny, dead fifty years ago. I watched them playing in a field, racing about in some game, and it was not a game which either of them was trying to win (there was no winning in it), and because of that they were infinitely happy in making each other happy, and all that was left in their hearts and their bodies was grace. It is very difficult to convey this in a poem. I had not thought of them for a long time. And when I did know them (I was little more than a boy then) there was affection, but also little grouses and jealousies, assertions of the will, a cloud of petty disagreements and passions which hid their true shape from me and from themselves. In the dream it seemed to me the cloud was dispelled and I saw them as they were. I'm sure Blake could have told me everything about it.

Edwin

121: TO JOHN HOLLOWAY

Swaffham Prior
10 May, 1957

Dear John,

Thank you both. The Russell Loines Award was a great surprise to me, and a very welcome one: and so near my birthday: Willa and

121 The Russell Loines Award was awarded by the American Academy of Arts and Letters. Holloway's sonnet sequence was 'The Gates of Janus,' later published in The Fugue *(1960). Muir had given a talk on poetry at Queen's College, Cambridge. Holloway writes: 'His being "afraid" afterwards perhaps related to how, rather delicately in fact, his sense of how different the poet's world was from the academic one came through what he said'*

I feel that the heavens are smiling on us. May they smile on you too.

I have been reading your sonnet sequence, John, and I think it is a very remarkable work, but still so strange to me that I have not made peace with it yet. I would like to read it again a few times; to me it has a sort of objective strangeness, outside my orbit; indefeasibly yours, a landscape of your own which I enter with trepidation, it is so powerfully evoked. A strange, very strange country of the imagination, beyond sadness or the comfort of sadness. I think that your very plain colloquial use of language is most effective, but occasionally that it jars like a false note. The imagery is wonderfully evocative because of an extra precision; the precision sometimes of nightmare. Some things, quite clearly set down, I did not understand: they were vividly before me but I could not account for them: I do not think this is a fault. I remember that Eliot wrote to me about my last volume of poetry that he liked it very much, but he found some of it obscure (this from *him*!); and it may be that I am repeating his error in this letter to you. But I have no doubt at all about the poem itself and am very much impressed by it.

I'm so glad that the students liked my talk so much. I was afraid afterwards that I might have said things I should not have said. I'm glad that it went off so fortunately. I shall be seeing you both tomorrow, and I'm not sure whether this letter will reach you before then or not. I do hope so.

All good wishes to you both, and thanks to Audrey for all her kindness

Yours ever
Edwin

122: TO BETTINA LINN

Swaffham Prior
9 June, 1957

Dear Miss Linn,

... Your novel is by far the best contemporary novel I have come across. Is it your first one? If so, it is all the more remarkable

122 Bettina Linn: American novelist, author of A Letter to Elizabeth *(1958), the novel referred to here, and of* After the Wedding Anniversary *(1965).*

for the mature and experienced art, applied to such a difficult human problem. The problem itself reminds me of the Henry James of *What Maisie Knew* and two or three other novels; and you seem to have too his naked sensibility, so moving in these books; but the whole thing is your own, the imagination, the mood, the style, the inflection: I most sincerely congratulate you on such a success—I mean an imaginative and real success. I suppose the mark of a true writer is complete devotion to the truth of the human situation he or she deals with: that is very rare, and like all rare things not a mere matter of choice but a gift. You seem to me to have it in an unusually high degree, and it is a thing very hard to find in the novel just now. As for the writing, I find it sometimes very beautiful without being ostentatiously so, and in general precisely what the situation demands. I should have thanked you long ago for the great and unexpected pleasure the book gave me, and for sending it to me....

Yours sincerely
Edwin Muir

123: TO GEORGE BROWN

Swaffham Prior
5 December, 1957

Dear George,

Forgive me for being so long in writing. It is partly because I have been out of sorts, and partly because I have had too much to do. I have, again and again, started to write to you, and being stopped by the one reason or the other. I feel, have doubtfully felt recently, that I have begun to deal practically with that matter of breathing which gives me the chest pains, and am consequently more hopeful and assured. In any case it has been a most uncomfortable time. Willa is improving too, walks better, and so we are both more comfortable about ourselves.

I have read your poems several times, and again before I began to

---

123 Muir was extremely pleased when The Hogarth Press accepted Brown's poems, which were published in 1959 in Loaves and Fishes. *For Eyre and Spottiswoode's* New Poets 1959 *Muir chose poems by Iain Crichton Smith, Karen Gershon and Christopher Levenson.* election: *Muir had, rather unwillingly, allowed himself to be nominated by some ex-Newbattle students for the Rectorship of Edinburgh University. He got only 61 votes, the winner being James Robertson Justice.*

write this letter. I am greatly impressed by them: you write better and better, it seems to me, as you go on. I like particularly 'That Night in Troy', a splendid poem, both for its imagination and its language, 'The Shining Ones', for a sort of dark splendour: 'Thorfinn' and 'Hamnavoe', which I have read many times before, I like as much as ever after the last reading. I am picking out the greatest ones. But there is none that I don't like: there is some element of delight (that rare quality, and growing rarer and rarer), in them all for me, except 'The Eve of the Corn God', which I find cold and abstract and theoretical compared with the others: I may be wrong about this, but I feel that the theme has not inflamed your imagination, that you have not entered into the figures in the poems, except intellectually. That, at least, is the impression the poem makes upon me. But in all the others I feel a vivid sense of delight such as I feel from hardly any of the other poetry that is written now, and not only that but beauty as well. I admire these poems more than I can say.

I have been urging you to publish, and now I have been delaying unforgivably: I must excuse myself with what I said at the beginning of this letter. Now about the publication. Would you like me to send the poems to the Hogarth Press? I mention them, for I am more at ease with them than with Eliot and Faber's, and would receive an earlier reply from them too. They published Norman MacCaig, as you know. If they refuse, there is always Eliot to fall back upon. And there is a possible other chance, even after that, which I can only indicate now in confidence: please don't mention it to anyone. I have recently been asked by Eyre & Spottiswoode to select and edit a volume of poems by poets who have not been published in book form (this, at my request, included poets who have been published locally: I was thinking of you). The book is to include the work of three poets, and the whole scheme is to be advertised in the press in January. You could be published in this book, for I know that I cannot hope to find anyone as good as yourself....

What a flop I had in the rectorial election! The results weren't published in the English papers, thank God, but Gavin went in to the general library in Cambridge and got hold of a *Scotsman* there, and the awful truth came out. Not that I much care. I wonder who this man Robertson Wisdom is? I hope you didn't get involved in the fights, and that the whole thing was enjoyed by the Newbattle contingent.....

Willa and I send our best wishes and are longing to see you.

Edwin

I've written a few poems recently.

124: TO JOSEPH SUMMERS

*Swaffham Prior
26 October, 1957*

Dear Joe,

I don't know how to thank you for your essay. So far as I can judge myself and my work, it seems to me extraordinarily intimate, understanding, and right; indeed it has told me things about myself which I hardly knew, and which I realise to be true. I was especially struck by 'translation' in Simone Weil's sense, applied to the poetry: I wish I could become a perfect translator of that kind. That gleam of light, I think, will be a great help to me, at least a great encouragement. It expresses something to be striven for rather than ever achieved, for a perfect translation is almost impossible. It seems to be the thing that Rilke—and he was a great poet in spite of his naive cleverness—strove for so long and achieved only here and there in the *Duino Elegies*. But it is a wonderful thing to attempt.

124 Joseph Summers, then a Professor of English at the University of Connecticut, had met Muir in America and had sent him an essay, 'The Achievement of Edwin Muir', which was published in revised form in The Massachusetts Review *(Winter 1961). The passage from Simone Weil he quoted is: 'The effort of expression has a bearing not only on the form but on the thought and on the whole inner being. So long as bare simplicity of expression is not attained, the thought has not touched or even come near to true greatness ... The real way of writing is to write as we translate. When we translate a text written in some foreign language, we do not seek to add anything to it; on the contrary, we are scrupulously careful not to add anything to it. This is how we have to translate a text which is not written down.' The passage from* The Three Brothers *is David's nightmare vision of the worm in his hand and his subsequent meditation (pp. 269–74). It may have been this reminder of* The Three Brothers *that started Muir writing his poem 'The Day before the Last Day', which is largely based on another passage in the novel (pp. 333–7). Summers and his wife (U.T.) were living not far from Swaffham Prior during 1957–8.*

I had forgotten that passage from *The Three Brothers*, and I was surprised to find that I wrote anything so good so long ago, in that very unequal story. I have not read the book for more than twenty years, and do not even have a copy of it now; my last remaining copy was lent to someone long ago. But the quotation does bring the past back very vividly, and not sadly; you were right—though how could you know?—that my main nausea was over at that time. I read the passage as if it were almost out of a book by someone else, and only gradually recognised it as my own: time plays strange tricks with us. I was glad to see it again.

I like particularly what you say about my poetry, but I like your words about my criticism almost as well. The only thing I think I would have liked out is the reference on page 24 to the 'careerists': I am sure young poets get involved in poetic fashions often quite innocently, and cannot help wanting to be 'in the swim', even if only as a kind of protective element, and not with an eye on success. That is my one mild suggestion.

I have learnt things about myself from your essay, and how can I thank you? Perhaps by acknowledging your very rare perception, but that is not much to say. The essay is a fine thing in itself; I could not wish a word altered except that one word 'careerists'. So thank you again.

Willa and I want to thank both U.T. and yourself for that day we spent with you. We are still enjoying the chocolate cake; it's lovely. Come, both of you, to see us some day soon again. We send our love to you both.

Edwin

125: TO LIONEL KNIGHTS

Swaffham Prior
27 December, 1957

My dear Knights,

... Thank you for your very kind and very clear letter. Now as for the lectures on modern poetry, I suggest two on Eliot, one on his critical theories and one on his poetry; and another two on Yeats, the first on his ideas, and the second on how they are expressed in his

125 L. C. Knights: then Professor of English at Bristol University, where Muir had been appointed visiting Professor.

poetry. Would this be suitable, or have you any further ideas to suggest?

Then the talks on 'The need for Literature': I think of them like this:

> The Use of Poetry and Imagination.
> The Present Decay of Poetic Imagination, and its Causes.
> The Poet and his Audience: the Ballads.
> Examination of some poems, including 'Tyger, Tyger', 'Tears, Idle Tears', and 'The Ecstasie'.

I think this might provide a scheme for trying to convey what poetry is for. If you have any ideas that would help, I would be very grateful. As for 'descriptive matter', the nearest I can come to it is my belief that imagination is the main faculty by which we comprehend human life, however imperfectly, and are able to know the people we know, including ourselves. It is employed at every level from the lowest to the highest, by people who never read a book, and by the great novelists and poets. The knowledge it gives is not practical knowledge; yet as it is purely human it includes that too, and in the individual who possesses it, has an effect on practice. Will that, or something like that, do? . . .

Yours sincerely
Edwin Muir

126: WILLA MUIR TO EDWIN MUIR

Swaffham Prior
18 February, 1958

My dearest love:

. . . I had a wonderful night's sleep and feel all the better for it. The removal of Peerie Breeks's Tensions (not to mention Glands, Tubes, and Tummy) has given me a wonderful feeling of relaxation,

---

126 Written the day after Muir left for his four weeks' stay in Bristol. Peerie Breeks's: Mrs Muir wrote in Belonging *(p. 34) of the early days of their marriage: 'We began to apply the tender Northern adjective "peerie" to nearly everything around us, and to ourselves. "Peerie" is used to describe what is lovable as well as small: it is a very affectionate diminutive. I became "peerie Willa" and Edwin reverted to his mother's name for him, "peerie Breeks". Popsy: the cat.*

197

I might almost say relief. By the time thu comes back I shall be very fit, I swear, and able to cope with any or all of them. But I do hope, my dear lamb, thu will be a bit unwound by that time, I doubt thu's not a domestic animal at all, and should not be let become one: much less than Popsy, who has been walking all over this letter, making it somewhat disjointed in style. She looked for thee last night and wowled a bit after she had failed to find thee in any corner, but I managed to head her out of the bedroom.

It's a bright sunny day with a bitter, bitter cold north wind. And although I am relieved of thy tensions, I love thee very much, tensions and all, and think of thee a lot, (as well as thinking a lot of thee!)

A peerie cuddle—how I wish I could provide it—and if thu must have a concubine I shall look the other way—but I want to give thee a peerie cuddle all the same.

Love from
Bad Willa

127: TO WILLA MUIR

The College Close Hotel
College Road
Clifton
Bristol
20 February, 1958

My darling love,

Your letter has made me so glad. So the removal of my Tensions has begun already to bring relaxation to my darling Peerie Jewel! That's more than I could have thought or expected, but I'm glad from my very heart. And now I'm beginning to feel more myself as I used to be too. Last night, after the lecture, and a meeting with students at Knights's house, I slept on almost to 9 o'clock, and had breakfast in bed. A double set of ailments in one house has been getting us down; I do feel now that you will be quite enormously better and different when we meet again; and I feel that I shall be

127 Anne Stewart: wife of W. C. Stewart, Professor of French at Bristol, earlier Lecturer at St Andrews when the Muirs were there. Isobel Artner: had known the Muirs at Menton in the twenties before her marriage to C. F. Powell, Professor of Physics at Bristol. misons: should be mesons.

very much better too. In fact already I'm not bothering nearly so much about myself, and accordingly am feeling more like a normal being. I've been unwinding quite a lot; and I only realise now how great a trial I must have been to thee, poor lamb, in all these months. Forgive me. I don't know whether I'm a domestic animal or not: I've certainly been worrying a lot, and needlessly, and worrying thee too, my poor poor lamb, more than I can bear to think of. So forgive me, and expect me to be another Peerie Beek when I come back. I really think I shall be. But I'm so glad that thu is feeling relieved and released now, and without the anxiety I brought thee. It will all be different, and my very tummy, not to mention my solar plexus, is behaving better already.

The lecture went very well; everyone was very pleased with it, and there was a big audience, some people standing. So that is all right. I felt nervous for a few minutes, but that soon passed over. The Knights's have been very kind. To-day I've taken a sort of holiday, beginning with breakfast in bed, then with a walk round Clifton, a rather lovely place, then lunch, then reading *Buddenbrooks* in bed (it's far better than I thought), and now writing to thee. I saw Anne Stewart at the lecture, and she told me that she had been cured of arthritis in Germany by injections made from an extract of mistletoe. She had arthritis in the knee, and it is quite gone. She has invited me to her house on Saturday week, and I'll find out from her then all about the cure. She is looking well. I met Isobel Artner (Powell) there too, and I'm to have an invitation from her presently. Her husband, I've been told, is a very distinguished physicist, and got a Nobel Prize a few years ago. His subject is misons, whatever they may be, and he spends part of his life on the Mediterranean, sending up balloons, which the Italian Navy picks up for him when they fall in the sea. He seems to be one of the main authorities on misons, and Knights says he is a very nice person.

I shall treat this month partly as a duty four weeks and partly as a holiday and relaxation, and not worry about either part of it. Thank thee again for what thu says in thee letter. I won't forget about the cups and the necklet (is that what it is called?).... My dearest lamb, I am truly feeling better, and had begun to feel better before I got thy letter, and much better after it. We'll have many a peerie cuddle after I come back. And my dearest love to thee.

from
Bad Beek

128: WILLA MUIR TO EDWIN MUIR

Swaffham Prior
1 March, 1958

My dearest P.B.

The coffee cups have come! How pretty they are, and how like thee! By that I mean, for instance, that they must closely resemble the sky-blue tie thu has bought thyself. Well, I thank thee for them: they will be a credit to us if ever we have a visitor for luncheon or dinner. (We might even use them ourselves.)

We are back in spring weather here, and the daffodils and narcissi will be coming out in a week's time, by the look of them. I am still doing quite well; this Saturday morning I got up and opened the house and got the cup-parcel from the postman, and paid the milk and the papers, all with much more competence than I would have shown once. I feel I have been lacking in gusto for too long, lacking in that *joie de vivre* which every act of living ought to have, a natural sense of thrill in being alive, even if one is only washing dishes; well, I have seen the light, as it were, and I am going to have much more Gusto. I think I muted myself too much for fear of upsetting thy solar plexus, so I warn thee, I am not going to be so muted in the days to come. The more I enjoy living, the more I get a kick out of it, the better I shall be. Perhaps thu was needing some such 'kick', and Bristol has provided it. Perhaps a sick solar plexus can be better cured by being swung into a new rhythm than by being tranquillised. Can it be, I asked wildly, that Toynbee is partly right? and that one needs challenges?

I have been thinking over the amethyst question and realise that I asked no questions; are they simply amethyst beads? (which I don't much want) or are they a *Garnitur*—stones set flat in metal settings? ... If so, I would like them, yes—and all the more if they are a deep colour, not pale ones. If they are just beads never mind them. ...

But thy dear letter has just come, and it's no use my going on about necklets! thu will have bought the amethysts—which I am sure are beads!—and I will NOT be ungrateful. I have torn up the rest of my letter, for it is now irrelevant.

The success of thy lectures, although I expected it, is none the less pleasing. I am certain that there is none like thee, none, in being an inspiration to students. It's rather a waste having thee blooming all alone in Swaffham Prior, isn't it? Perhaps thu should lecture, weekly at least, to me and Popsy, to keep thy hand in. I find that in thy absence I greatly lack conversation. . . . I did have one intelligent conversation with Eliz. Looker on the telephone, and realised that that is what I miss. I am becoming a Silent Woman, seething with unspoken comment. . . .

I hear Gavin stirring, which means tea-making time. Bless thee, bless the necklet, bless the blue cups, and bless that telephone call when thu makes it.

Much love from P.W.

129: TO WILLA MUIR

*Bristol
3 March, 1958*

My dearest,

What a lovely letter I got from thee this morning, full of loveliness. It makes me feel we are both going to be better and better, and happier too. I'm doing well, like theeself. I get one of the stomach upsets now and then, but I pay little attention to it, and it passes quite quickly in consequence. It likes to be noticed, I suppose, and now that I cut it dead, it's getting discouraged. I can feel the *gusto* coming back in thy letter already: I'm going to play back by acquiring *carelessness*: I've acquired quite a lot already. I feel I've been a dull, dull dog for a long time: a pain in the neck. So don't let thyself be muted, my dear lamb. I can assure thee I've got free from part of my care, by being conscious how much I've worried, and deciding that the worry was not only wasted, but bad in itself.

I'm not sure about the amethysts—they're beads, I'm sorry to say, not a garnitur: they're quite pretty, but clearly not what thu wanted. I'll have another look, and see if there is anything else I can find that is more likely. I bought them on Saturday, but the shopwife, a nice woman, would exchange them if I could find something else. I'll see.

I'm afraid thu must have lacked conversation a lot for the past fortnight. I'll try to provide a lot when I get back. . . .

With all my love

P.B.

129 He was able to exchange the amethyst beads for a silver necklet, which pleased his wife very much.

130: TO WILLA MUIR

Bristol
12 March, 1958

My dearest Lamb,

Happy Birthday to Thee, and better and better ones as the years go on for us. I love thee, I shall always love thee, and I'm so happy that I shall see thee the day after thy birthday, so keep it for me. I would have preferred the 13th (dear old 13th) to the 14th: I put out a tentative feeler, but in vain. I must lecture to the students on the 14th at 10 a.m., and on nothing more exciting than T. S. Eliot. I shall get the 11.45 from here; if I'm lucky and the train is up to time I shall get the 2.24 Liverpool Street train to Cambridge, arriving at 3.24. If I miss that I shall have to put up with the 3.48 arriving at 5.15. Blessings on thee, my Jewel, and my love to thee. It's been very cold here: there was a fresh fall of snow on the ground this morning; now (I'm writing this before 12) it has all melted away, and the paths and the ground are wet and sopping. This milder weather is on the way to thee, and will reach thee, I prophesy, by the blessed Thirteenth.

How wonderful to think I'll see thee on Friday

Thy P.B.

I hope the necklet has arrived and that thu likes it.

131: TO NORMAN MACCAIG

Swaffham Prior
23 April, 1958

Dear Norman,

... I keep seeing poems by you everywhere, with friendly envy (if there is such a thing: I hope there is). How lovely to have the spring flowing freely (you are really to be envied) and not monotonously either, but with more variety than ever before. I've been rather daunted in the last year or two by the fear that I am keeping on writing the same poem, and I fancy that it has inhibited (horrible word) the flow. I have written very few poems lately, but many parts of poems which ceased when they seemed to be taking the same old course. Some of the parts are quite good, I think, and perhaps

131 longish poem: 'The Last War'.

the best thing I could do with them would be to integrate (another awful word) them in a longish poem: I don't know: that may be what they are best suited for. Time will tell. *The Waste Land* was made out of splinters.

Willa and I are living a quiet life here. We see some of the Cambridge people occasionally: Kathleen Raine and John Holloway mainly: we like the peace. I am still taking notes for the book on the Ballads, and I hope to be in Edinburgh again sometime this summer to make enquiries. I have almost enough poems, now, to make up another volume, and one half of them I intend to put under the heading of 'ballads', though only one or two will be in strict ballad form: they will be mostly on half-narrative, half-legendary themes. I think there is still a great deal to be learned from the ballads, especially a tight attention to the theme. By the bye, Norman, have you a copy of a book of mine called *Latitudes*, and if so would it be a bother to let me have it on loan: I haven't a single copy myself. The Hogarth Press have asked if I could add some essays to the *Essays on Literature and Society* they published some years ago, and it occurs to me that there may be things in that older book which might be re-written (It has long been out of print). I've been writing on Dickens and Jane Austen recently too, and other things....

We all send our kindest wishes.

Yours
Edwin Muir

132: TO NORMAN MACCAIG

Swaffham Prior
22 May, 1958

Dear Norman,

I don't know how to thank you for your kindness over *Latitudes*. I have just been sent A. S. Neill's copy, and so I'm returning yours and the library's, with thanks—and thankfulness—for I don't want you to have any further trouble. I hadn't read the book I should say for thirty years, and it was a humbling experience. So much mere nonsense combined with overweening confidence, arrows clumsily

---

132 'the same poem': MacCaig had said that though Muir's poems pointed to a common centre, each did so from a different direction.

notched and shot mainly into nothingness. And yet there were things here and there, choice forlorn fragments, that seemed to be worth doing something with again (I had quite forgotten these particular strays). So that I shall have something to add to the book the Hogarth Press want, but not very much. . . .

I've been reading Malory's *Arthur* again in the last week; I had read it first when I was in my early twenties. A wonderful down to earth nobility in it: one thinks of nobility as having some high kind of refinement in it, but there is none in Malory. I had been bored by the quest of the Sangreal when I read the book first, but this time found some wonderful things in it (though it is occasionally boring): the last part, with the destruction of the Table Round, is high tragedy. Gawain suddenly becomes a wonderful complex mixed character: I wonder if a tragic character has necessarily that particular mixture of attributes, that unusualness in the mixture. But you probably know the book better than I do. I have only the advantage of coming to it quite fresh again; the combats, frankly, become a little monotonous and tiresome.

I've just finished a poem called 'The Last War', made up partly of fragments of 'the same poem' you mentioned in your letter, and I hope the unity will be there, as you said. Willa and I have our aches and pains still, but sometimes I think not so badly as before. Gavin has a job now as a tutor for Wolsey College in Oxford. It is a correspondence college, and he can do his work at home, correcting mathematical papers and sending them off. He has been attending lip-reading classes in Cambridge for a good long time, and he has now a really reliable hearing-aid, and he has made a great deal of genuine progress in the last year. It is a great satisfaction to us. And this job will mean a great deal to him, and give him hope, which he had little of before.

Willa sends her love, and I look forward to seeing you this summer. Thanks again for the book.

Yours
Edwin

133: TO DEREK HAWES

Swaffham Prior
7 July, 1958

Dear Mr Hawes,

Forgive me for being so long in replying. I have been ill with water on the lung, ordered to rest, and undergoing injections to draw off the water. I am now slowly recovering.

I agree with much that you say about my poem, and am very glad that it moved you so much. I am still not well enough to write at any length. I think the poem is to some extent 'engagé': it began as that anyway, and then developed of itself. I think you have gone wrong in thinking of the horses as wild horses, or as stampeding. It is less than a year since the seven days' war happened. So the horses are good plough-horses and still have a memory of the world before the war. I try to suggest that they are looking for their old human companionship. As for the 'tapping': have you ever listened, on a still evening, to horses trotting in the distance? the sound is really a pretty tapping. The drumming sound indicated that they were drawing nearer: the hollow thunder when they turned the corner meant that they saw the village or farmstead and found their home. I think I am right in the choice of verbs here. And the apparent contradiction between the lines you quote afterwards is not a real one. For the horses are seeking the long lost archaic companionship, accepted in former times by man as an obvious right, so that it never occurred to them that there was anything surprising in using and owning horses. It is the surprise of the return that makes them realise the beauty of that free servitude. I wonder if I have explained myself.

The many fine things you say about the poem I feel very grateful for. I think there is genuine understanding there. I hope you will go on with your criticism, and I hope these few remarks of mine will be of help.

Yours sincerely,
Edwin Muir

133 Derek Hawes, then a student, had sent Muir an essay on his poem 'The Horses'.

134: TO T. S. ELIOT

Swaffham Prior
1 August, 1958

Dear Tom,

I am willing to agree to anything you may think to be advisable about the inclusion of new poems in the new *Collected Poems*. As you asked me, I am enclosing some of these extra poems, most of them very dark, I'm sorry to say, except the two about women, and the one about my brothers, the subject of which came to me in a dream. The poems I enclose make up almost half of those I have in hand. I feel, as you do, that it would be better to keep them until I have enough poems to make up a small volume.

I find that I have very few alterations to suggest for the present *Collected Poems*. There is nothing to be done with that stiff language; I was comforted in reading on to see that my language began to reform itself. In *One Foot in Eden* I have decided to leave out four of the religious poems, which seem to me now to be quite inadequate. I have made a few alterations in other poems in this volume, but I take it this will not cause any bother, for the whole lot will be reset in the course of things. I shall send the two books on in a couple of days. I want to have a last look at them.

I am taking care to follow the doctor's instructions, and have been almost a model patient for the past few weeks. I have to go to Newmarket for another X-ray on Tuesday, to test my lungs for water again. I have been breathing almost freely for more than a fortnight, and I had not realised for quite a while that breathing could be such a pleasure. With kind regards,

Edwin

134 Muir had been asked whether he wanted to make any corrections for a new edition of his Collected Poems. *Eliot had suggested that* One Foot in Eden *should be included, but probably not new poems written since then if there was a prospect of there soon being enough for a new volume; but he had said he would like to see the new poems. The two poems about women are presumably 'Penelope in Doubt' and 'The Two Sisters'. The four religious poems left out of* One Foot in Eden *are 'The Christmas', 'The Son', 'Lost and Found' and 'The Lord'.*

135: TO PHILIP O'CONNOR

Swaffham Prior
19 September, 1958

Dear Philip O'Connor,

It was very stupid of me; I should have sent you the questions when I sent the answers. I have found them now, and enclose them in case they should still be of use. Thank you very much for sending me your autobiography. I have read the childhood part and been very impressed and moved by it; not merely by the honesty, though that is unusual enough, but by the insight and the violent humanity. Reading about the strange chances of your childhood, I can understand your questions better now, just as you do my answers on the class question. You are much better versed in that question than I am, simply because our lives have been so different. You had it thrust harshly on your notice when you were very young, and I have remained only half absentmindedly aware of it; but your book gives me a real idea of it. I think it is a remarkable book, and I thank you again.

I am sending this care of Faber & Faber in accordance with your second letter. I spent my first fourteen years in Orkney, where I was not aware of class, and in Glasgow I was conscious only of the rich and the poor, the Scottish division; it was not till I came to London when I was 31 that I heard people talking about the English social divisions: 'He's pure middle class', 'She's pure lower-middle class', 'He thinks he's upper-middle class', and so on. The Scottish division —money in the bank or being on the dole—is no better and probably worse.

With kind regards,

Edwin Muir

135 For O'Connor's questions and Muir's answers to them see O'Connor's The Lower View, *pp. 180–7.* autobiography: Memoirs of a Public Baby.

136: TO T. S. ELIOT

Swaffham Prior
19 September, 1958

Dear Tom,

I am sending with this letter my copies of *Variations on a Time Theme*, *Journeys and Places*, and *The Voyage* as well, in case that may be out of print. I have typed out three poems from *First Poems* which I should like to go in: 'October in Hellbrünn', which should follow 'Autumn in Prague' in the existing collection; and 'Ballad of the Soul' and 'Ballad of the Flood', which should come after the 'Ballad of Hector in Hades'. These complete all that I want to include of *First Poems*.

I would like the whole of the *Variations* to go in, and all of *Journeys and Places* except for one poem, 'Judas'. Also I would like all of *The Voyage* to be there, except for two poems, marked for omission on pages 19 and 42. I feel that there were one or two poems in *The Narrow Place*, omitted by John Hall, which I would like to recover; if the book is out of print and difficult to get hold of, then it can't be helped. I used to have a copy myself, but it seems to have vanished; perhaps loaned to someone and never returned. *The Labyrinth* was included intact in the present edition of the poems. I have marked two or three poems in *One Foot in Eden* which I want to omit. . . .

The only thing that remains now, I think, is the matter of *The Narrow Place*. If it can be found, then I shall feel that the collection is as complete as I can make it, but I hope that too much trouble will not be taken to find it; and please do not send me a copy of the extant *Collected Poems*, for I have a copy here. One thing more: *Journeys and Places* is prefaced by an 'Author's Note', which should not be included. I think that is all I can think of. I hope you will like

136 It had been agreed that the new Collected Poems *should be not just John Hall's selection plus* One Foot in Eden, *but a complete collection of all Muir wished to preserve. The poems left out of* The Voyage *were 'Dialogue' and 'Song' ('Here in this corner'), and out of* One Foot in Eden *the four religious ones mentioned in the letter of 1 August and 'The Choice'. breathing: In a letter of 8 September he had written: 'My breathing has not become quite unconscious yet; I think I must have been breathing wrongly for so long that it may take me some time to get into the right habit. But the pleasure is there, and the lungs are dried.'*

'The Ballad of the Flood' in ballad-Scots, which is so different from that of Burns. The 'Ballad of the Soul' is very imperfect; its source was a waking dream which came out of my course of psychoanalysis over thirty years ago, and scared Maurice Nicoll, who was concerned for my sanity, I think. I told him I could stop such things if I deliberately tried; I had had one or two of them before, but not on the same scale. He advised me to stop them, and in part of my mind I have been sorry ever since; yet as my analyst I don't see what else he could have done. They never came back.

I was very much interested in what you said about breathing. I feel actually that I have never breathed in the right way all my life— a curious habit of holding my breath at the most trivial effort, tying my shoes, for instance. I shall consult the doctor and see if he can put me in the way of breathing exercises, perhaps at Addenbrookes in Cambridge. I am very thankful for what you say.

I hope all these particulars about the poems will not be a trouble to you.

Yours ever
Edwin

137: TO T. S. ELIOT

Swaffham Prior
24 September, 1958

Dear Tom,

The Narrow Place arrived this morning, and I am returning it straight away. I have gone through it, and I would like ... to include the whole lot except for 'Isaiah'.

I think this ties up all the loose strings. Should I write a short note, referring to John Hall's collection, and thanking him? I should like to.

I would like to wish you a happy seventieth birthday, long life, continued happiness, and all that you most set your heart on.

Yours ever,
Edwin

Muir's heart was failing. He tired easily, and was not able to do much work. But his imagination was still active. His last notebook contains new ideas for poems, fragments and unfinished poems. Mrs Muir wrote: 'there were so many unwritten poems in him,—

notably one about his father and mother, which was haunting him.'
What this last might have become is suggested by the notebook
entry:

>'About my father and mother
>Realising long after their death their virtue
>   and goodness
>How could they have been what they were
>   but for Incarnation
>The incarnation of a soul in a body
>Simplicity, grace, infinite patience and
>   kindness'

His intention of paying tribute to his parents was partly realised in
his last poem, which fittingly brings his writing life to an end with an
expression of gratitude and faith. Some of the complications of the
MS are here reproduced so as to show its unfinished state and that
the received version is, in some places, conjectural:

>I have been taught by dreams and fantasies
>   Learned   the friendly and the   phantoms
>   ~~Drunk~~ from ~~the minds of phantoms of the dark,~~
>   (And knowledge gathered
>   ~~night and chaos~~
>   ~~night~~   ~~day~~
>   From ~~the light and dark~~)

>And got great knowledge and   ?   from the dead
>   ancestors
>   Kinsmen and kinswomen, ~~enemies~~ [?] and friends
>   But
>   And from two mainly
>   Who gave me birth

>Have learned and drunk from that unspending good
>   These founts whose learned windings keep
>   My feet from straying
>   deadly
>   To the ~~fatal~~ path

210

>   That leads into the sultry labyrinth
>   ~~glares~~ [?] is bright
>   Where all ~~is bright and false~~ and the ~~false~~ flare
>   Consumes
>   ~~Distorts~~ and shrivels
>   The moist
>   ~~Both flower~~ and fruit
>
>   dr?
>   H   ~~caught~~ at last   time
>   ~~But most I~~ have ~~learned~~ from ~~time which gives and~~ takes away
>   taking   right
>   And ~~passing~~ leaves all things in their ~~true~~ place
>   An image of forever,
>   The O   and
>   ~~The~~ one, ~~the true~~ whole
>
>   perceive
>   And now that time grows shorter, I ~~can see~~
>   That Plato's is the truest poetry
>   And that these shadows
>   ~~All being a shadow~~
>   Are cast by
>   ~~Cast by a truth~~ the true.

He died on 3 January 1959.

Supported by the Bollingen Foundation Mrs Muir picked up the task of writing a book on the ballads. Muir had been able to do no more than make some notes, and her *Living with Ballads* (1965) is entirely her own. With J. C. Hall she edited Muir's *Collected Poems* (1960), adding a final section to those he had himself selected. She then went on to write an account of their life together, *Belonging* (1968). She died on 22 May 1970.

APPENDIX

The anthology The Modern Poet (*Sidgwick and Jackson, 1938*), *edited by Gwendolen Murphy, included Muir's poem 'The Riders' (No. II of* Variations on a Time Theme), *and the editor quoted extracts from two letters from him (pp. 168–70)*

Mr. Muir writes to me about 'The Riders':

'the point round which the poem crystallised was the beginning:

> At the dead centre of the boundless plain
> Does our way end? Our horses pace and pace
> Like steeds forever labouring on a shield.

These lines came to me spontaneously, without my being conscious of the possible development they implied. The development grew from a variety of associations that would have remained isolated and disconnected but for this image, which acted as a sort of magnet, and drew them into a rough pattern round it. The Horses, as I see them, are an image of human time, the invisible body of humanity on which we ride for a little while, which has come from places we did not know:

> They have borne upon their saddles
> Forms fiercer than the tiger, borne them calmly
> As they bear us now,

and which is going towards places we shall not know:

> Suppliantly
> The rocks will melt, the sealed horizons fall
> Before their onset.

Yet the steed—mankind in its course through time—is mortal, and the rider is immortal. I stated this belief tentatively in the poem, because it was written in a mood of unusual dejection. The painful emotion in the poem comes from a simultaneous feeling of immortality and mortality, and particularly from the feeling that we, as immortal spirits, are imprisoned in a very small and from all appearances fortuitously selected length of time: held captive on the "worn saddle", which in spite of our belief in our immortality has the power "to charm us to obliviousness" by "the scent of the ancient leather".

'I was not aware, or at least fully aware, of all these implications when I wrote the poem; and I have only realised during the last year that almost all my poems from the start have been about journeys and places: that is, about the two sides of the paradox [of mortality and immortality] one of which implies the other.'

I was glad to get the following interesting reply from the poet to a query about the autumn light.

'I actually saw once, many years ago, the picture as I set it down: it is one of the few things in the poem taken from observation. It was a clear bright day in late autumn down in Sussex: the weight seemed to have left every physical object with the drying up of the leaves still sticking to the trees without burdening them. A boy was ploughing in a field, and a moving column of breath went on before him; his own breath; but the air was so light and clear, the picture so distinct, that what my eye saw was the column going in front and the boy following it. Why this struck me so much I can't say yet; but when I came to this part of the poem it seemed to be the correspondence I needed.

'"... The autumn light/We still remember" of which the "coal-black glossy hides" do not keep a glimmer. I think this is an attempt to suggest those isolated moments of pure vision which have a feeling of timelessness (and are often called timeless). My feeling about these moments (which are a common experience, though most people are unconscious of them) has always been that they do not *go into* Time; that they do not change the actual physical body of Time, symbolised by the horses. They may cast a momentary reflection on the glossy hides, but it fades almost at once. This instant fading tmakes them "autumnal". At the moment when we are aware of them we are released from the presence of Time: our limbs are "weightless." Our silvery breaths going on before us "Leading our empty bodies through the air" is an extravagant way of describing this state of freedom.'

INDEX

Abenheimer, Mrs (Irene Thorburn), 29n, 68
Adam Smith, J., 164n, 165
  Letters to, 169, 186, 187–8
Aitken, Alec, 102n, 110n, 158n
  Letters to, 102–3, 104–6, 110, 111–13, 121, 129–31, 158–60
Alain-Fournier, H., 166
America (U.S.A.), 21–2, 26–7, 32–3, 177, 178, 183–4, 185
Anderson, Willa: *see* Muir, Willa
Asch, S., 79n, 81n
Auden, W. H., 185
Augustine, St., 127, 128
Austen, Jane, 49, 203

Ballads, 179, 181–2, 184–5, 203, 211
Barker, George, 87, 87n, 94–5, 94n, 96–7, 96n, 108–9, 108n
  Letters to, 87–8, 94–5, 96–7, 108–9
Barnes, Djuna, 172, 172n, 175–7, 180–1, 188
Baudelaire, 46, 49, 50
Beaverbrook, Lord, 68, 68n
Beckett, Samuel, 187
Beer-Hoffman, R., 38
Beethoven, 85, 127
Blake, William, 96, 97, 133, 140, 191
Bollingen Foundation, 173, 177, 178–9, 181–2, 184–5, 184n, 211
Bradbrook, M., 190–1, 190n

Brecht, B., 187
B.B.C., 16, 17, 158n, 184
British Council, 16, 132n, 133, 141, 154, 164n, 165
Broch, H., 68n, 69, 76, 76n, 78–9, 81–2, 81n, 84, 99–100, 100n, 106, 106n, 107, 108, 111, 120
  Letters to, 76–7, 81–2
Brooks, Van Wyck, 26–7, 26n, 32–3
  Letters to, 26–7, 27–8, 28–9, 31–2, 32–3
Brown, G. Mackay, 166n, 183n, 184, 193–4, 193n
  Letters to, 166–7, 183–4, 189–90, 193–4
Browne, Sir T., 110
Buchan, John (Lord Tweedsmuir), 65n
  Letter to, 65–6
Bunyan, 110
Burns, John, 119
Burns, Robert, 48, 70, 181, 209
Byron, 140–1

Calendar of Modern Letters, 52n
Calvinism, 113–4
Carossa, Hans, 66n
Cary, Joyce, 134n
Cellini, B., 50
Cervantes, 150
Chapman, George, 89
Chesterton, G. K., 20n, 22
Chiari, J., 141n, 143n, 146n, 147, 149–50

215

Chiari J.—*cont.*
  Letters to, 141–3, 143–6, 146–7, 149–50, 154–5, 168
Christ/Christianity, 29, 92, 94–5, 107–8, 115–16, 148, 148n, 149, 154–5, 155–6, 168, 185
Church, Richard, 77n, 132, 132n
  Letter to, 132–3
Coleridge, S. T., 110
Comfort, Alex, 135
Communism: *see* Marx
Connolly, James, 119, 119n
Cowlin, D., 134n
Criterion, 38, 39, 39n, 81
Cruickshank, Helen, 72n
  Letter to, 72–6
Cunninghame Graham, R., 119, 119n
Czechoslovakia, 22–4, 140–1, 156

Dante, 19, 115n, 117, 159, 163
de la Mare, W., 105, 110, 110n
De Quincey, 110
Dickens, 203
Dobrée, B., 106–7, 165
Dostoevsky, 49, 50, 61, 112
Douglas, George, 27
Dresden, 24–5

Eddington, Sir A., 104–5
Edinburgh, 149, 154–5, 190
Eliot, T. S., 38, 40, 48, 52, 52n, 76–7, 88, 132n, 133, 150, 162n, 163n, 165, 172n, 191, 192, 194, 196
  Letters to, 157–8, 162, 163, 163–4, 164, 172, 175–7, 180–2, 188–9, 206, 208–9, 109
Empson, W., 187n

Feuchtwanger, L., 53n, 55–6, 55n, 61n, 63, 66n

Fournier, H. Alain, 166
Fraser, George, 187, 187n
Freeman, 22n, 24, 26–7, 26n, 27n, 28, 28n, 29, 31n, 32–3, 32n, 34n, 39n, 58n
Freud, S., 44
Frost, Robert, 177, 179–80

Garioch, R., 122, 122n
Garnett, D., 49
George, Stefan, 88n, 89
Germany, 23, 24–6
Glaeser, Ernst, 66n
Glasgow, 21, 26, 30, 35–6, 105, 190, 207
Godden, R., 135
Goethe, 29, 47, 48
Gollancz (*publishers*), 79n, 80
Goodrich, M., 135
Gourock, 90n, 91
Gregory, Horace, 188–9, 188n
Grieve, C. M., 29n, 30, 64, 70, 71, 155
Gunn, Neil, 150–2n
  Letter to, 150
Gurdjieff, 31–2, 31n

Hall, J. C., 157–8, 157n, 160, 165, 178, 209, 211
Hamburger, M., 161, 161n, 171
  Letter to, 161
Hampstead, 78
Hardy, Thomas, 31
Hartley, L. P., 139
Hauptmann, Gerhart, 39, 39n, 66n
Hawes, Derek, 205n
  Letter to, 205
Hellerau, 25
Hemingway, 132
Hofmannsthal, H. von, 30, 38, 89, 178, 179
Hogarth Press, 41n, 169–70, 169n, 193, 194

Hölderlin, 27n, 28, 38, 85n, 86, 92, 93, 161n, 187–8
Holloway, John, 180, 190n, 191, 191n, 192, 203
  Letter to, 191–2
Holms, John, 52, 52n, 58n, 63, 115n, 117
Homer, 167
Hopkins, G. M., 89
Horthy, Admiral, 72n, 74, 75
Hudson, Stephen: pseudonym of Sydney Schiff
Huebsch, B. W., 39n, 53n, 58n
  Letter to, 58–9
Hungary, 72–5
Huxley, Aldous, 31, 31n, 40, 67, 98, 99, 114

Italy, 154–5, 155–6, 185

James, Henry, 38, 83, 193
Jeans, Sir J., 104
Johnstone, William, 77n
  Letter to, 77–8
Joyce, James, 38, 42, 44, 47, 48, 50, 58, 61, 62, 67, 166
Jung, C. G., 182, 185

Kafka, 66n, 67, 69, 93
Keats, 47, 48, 57, 89
Kipling, 27
Knights, L. C., 196n, 199
  Letter to, 196–7
Knox, John, 65–6, 65n, 66

Lavin, Mary, 135–6, 135n
Lavrin, J., 34n, 36, 46
Lawrence, D. H., 27, 42, 43–4, 43n, 50
Lehmann, J., 131n, 165
  Letter to, 131–2
Lehmann, R., 138–9
Leitch, Jean, 19n
  Letter to, 19–20
Leopardi, 46
Levin, Harry, 177, 185
Levy, Oscar, 20n, 21, 22
Lewis, C. Day, 136, 165
Lewis, P. Wyndham, 50, 55, 55n, 61–3, 61n, 67–8
Linklater, Eric, 133
Linn, Bettina, 192–3, 192n
  Letter to, 192–3
Listener, 15, 80, 87n, 126, 128, 140, 158n, 164n, 167, 169n
London Mercury, 87–8, 87n, 96n, 97
Lowell, Robert, 177, 180

MacCaig, N., 194, 203n
  Letters to, 202–3, 203–4
McDiarmid, Hugh: pseudonym of C. M. Grieve
MacLeish, A., 185
Malory, 204
Mann, Thomas, 38, 199
Marx/Marxism, 84, 85–6, 98, 107–8, 113–15, 116, 160
Mencken, H. L., 20n, 22n
  Letter to, 20–2
Menton, 60
Modern Scot, 70n, 76n, 78, 81
Montgomerie, William, 88n
  Letters to, 88–90, 140–1
Moore, Edward: pseudonym of Edwin Muir
Mozart, 49, 85
Muir, Edwin: works of
  'After 1984', 190n, 191
  'The Annunciation', 154n
  'The Assault on Humanism', 27–8, 27n
  An Autobiography, 17, 52n, 166, 169, 169–70, 170, 170n
  And see *The Story and the Fable*

217

Muir, Edwin works of—*cont.*
  'Ballad of Eternal Life': see 'Ballad of the Soul'.
  'Ballad of the Flood', 157, 208, 209
  'Ballad of Hector in Hades', 39n, 40
  'Ballad of the Soul', 24n, 208, 209
  'The Brothers', 190, 191
  'The Child Dying', 141n, 141-3
  'The Christmas', 206n
  Chorus of the Newly Dead, 37, 43, 45, 59n, 173, 174-5
  Collected Poems 1921-1951, 157-8, 157n, 162, 167
  Collected Poems 1921-1958, 206, 206n, 208-9, 208n
  'The Combat', 157
  'The Day before the Last Day', 195n
  'The Days', 154n, 155
  'The Decline of Imagination', 155-60, 158n
  'The Dreamt-of Place', 87n
  'Edwin Muir and Francis George Scott: A Conversation', 31, 31n
  'Effigies', 169, 169n, 170n, 171
  'T. S. Eliot', 72
  'The Escape', 139n, 140
  Essays on Literature and Society, 158n, 203
  The Estate of Poetry, 186
  First Poems, 156, 208
  'The Great House', 168n
  'The Grove', 124n
  'The Guess', 129n
  'Hermann Broch', 76n
  'Hölderlin's Journey', 92, 93, 104n, 121n
  'Horses' (I), 39n, 40
  'Horses' (II), 205
  'The Human Fold', 157
  'I have been taught', 210-11
  'In a Time of Mortal Shocks', 124, 124n, 125-6
  'It might have been the day after the last day', 87n
  'I've been in love for long', 157
  John Knox, 65-6, 65n, 66, 68
  Journeys and Places, 97-8, 104n, 108
  'Judas', 208
  The Labyrinth, 7, 146-7, 153, 157
  'The Last War', 202-3, 202n, 204
  Latitudes, 22n, 26, 36, 203, 203-4
  'The Law', 82n
  'The Lord', 206n
  'Lost and Found', 206n
  'The Lullaby', 139n
  The Marionette, 55-6, 55n, 58-9, 58n, 64, 67
  'The Meaning of Romanticism', 28-9, 28n
  'Milton', 168n
  'The Mythical Journey', 121n
  The Narrow Place, 151, 208, 209
  'Natural Man and Political Man', 131-2, 131n
  'Night and Day', 154n, 155
  'No more of this trapped gazing', 82n
  'Novels of Mr Hardy', 31, 31n
  'October in Hellbrünn', 208
  One Foot in Eden, 172, 172n, 206, 206n, 208, 208n
  'Penelope in Doubt', 206n
  'The Poet', 186, 187-8, 187n
  'The Poetic Imagination', 158n

Poor Tom, 68n, 77, 77n, 78, 78n
The Present Age, 106–7, 106n
'The Private Place', 82n
'Prometheus', 162, 162n, 163, 163–4, 163n, 164, 171
'The Question', 124, 124n, 129n
'Reading in Wartime', 139n, 140
'Rebirth', 24n
'The Refugees', 108n, 109, 112, 157
'Remembrance', 39n, 40
'The Return of Ulysses', 124, 124n
'The Rider Victory', 139n
'The Riders', 213–4
'The River', 152n, 153
'The Road', 104n
'Robert Louis Stevenson', 70n, 71–2
'Scotland 1941', 124, 124n
'The Shrine': 154n, 155
Six Poems, 76n, 77
'The Solitary Place', 85n, 85–6
'The Son', 154n, 206n
The Story and the Fable, 100, 101, 102, 107, 111–12, 115, 117, 117n, 118, 119–20, 121, 121n, 123, 127
'The Strange Return', 190n, 191
'The Succession', 172n
'The Sufficient Place', 82n
'The Swimmers' Death', 151
'Telemachos Remembers', 167, 167n
The Three Brothers, 66n, 67, 68–9, 68n, 110, 110n, 121, 121n, 123, 195n
'To J.F.H.', 152–3, 152n

'To the Old Gods', 129n
'The Transfiguration', 148, 148n
Transition, 41n, 43n: 44, 58, 59n
'The Transmutation', 156n, 157
'The Two Sisters', 206n
Variations on a Time Theme, 103, 208, 213–4
The Voyage, 208
We Moderns, 20–2, 20n, 34n, 35–6
'The Zeit Geist', 53
works uncompleted or only projected, 17, 26, 36–7, 80, 92, 93, 113–15, 119, 120, 122n, 123, 174–5, 184, 187–8, 209–10
Muir, Elizabeth (*mother of E.M.*), 13, 103, 210
Muir, Elizabeth (*sister of E.M.*): see Thorburn, Elizabeth
Muir, Gavin, 65, 69, 81, 81n, 91, 101, 102–3, 123, 141, 141n, 143, 146, 204
Muir, James (*father of E.M.*), 13, 103, 170, 210
Muir, John, 13, 103, 191
Muir, Willa, 36, 38, 41, 41n, 51, 53, 53n, 55n, 59, 63–4, 65, 66n, 72, 81, 82, 99n, 100, 105, 107, 130, 168, 171, 186, 188, 197n, 209–10, 211; *and passim*
Letters to, 164–6, 198–9, 201, 202
Letters from, 72–6, 197–8, 200–1, 202–3
Muir, William, 13, 103, 191
Murphy, Gwendolen, 213
Musil, R., 111, 111n
Myers, E., 135n

Nation and the Athenaeum, 15, 52n
Neill, A. S., 25, 36, 43n, 53
Neumann, R., 81n, 82
New Age, 20n, 21, 24, 24n, 26, 31, 31n
Newbattle Abbey College, 155n, 156, 164n, 168, 171, 177, 180, 182, 190
New Statesman, 132n, 164n, 169, 170n, 171
Nicholl, M., 14, 209
Nietzsche, 20n, 21, 45, 119n
Nock, A. J., 26n, 27

Observer, 153n, 179, 187, 187n
O'Connor, P., 207n
    Letter to, 207
O'Neill, Eugene, 27
Orage, A. R., 20n, 21, 22, 31–2, 31n, 79, 80
Orion, 143, 143n
Orkney, 15, 21, 64, 81n, 93–4, 153, 170, 179, 180, 181, 184, 185, 188–9, 207
Ould, H., 72n, 74

Payne, Robert, 134–5
Peat, David, 90–1, 90n, 117n
    Letters to, 90–1, 117–18
PEN Club, 72–6, 72n, 167
Plato, 187, 211
Prague, 22–4, 140–1, 156
Proust, 38, 39, 49, 58, 69

Raine, Kathleen, 7, 153, 165, 170n, 177, 203
    Letters to, 153, 170–1, 173–4, 178–80, 184–6, 190–1
Read, Sir Herbert, 99, 111n, 119n, 120, 128–9, 128n, 173, 179
    Letters to, 111, 113–15, 119, 119–20, 128–9
Reid, Forrest, 138n, 139

Renn, Ludwig, 66n
Rheinhardt, E. A., 66n
Richards, I. A., 185, 186
Richardson, S., 166
Rickwood, E., 52n, 53
Rilke, 67, 89, 109, 178, 195
Rimbaud, 38
Roberts, Michael, 97
Roberts, D. Kilham, 143n, 145
Robey, J. B., 139
Romanticism, 28–9, 31, 45–6, 57
Rome, 154–5, 155–6
Ross, Mrs (Ethel Thorburn), 29n, 68

St Andrews, 86, 87
St Tropez, 59–60
Schiff, Sydney, 34–5, 34n, 39, 39n, 41n, 43n, 52n, 56n
    Letters to, 34–8, 39–40, 41, 42–3, 43–4, 45–6, 46–8, 49–51, 52–3, 53–4, 55–6, 56–7, 57–8, 61–2, 66–8, 68–9, 99–101, 101, 106–7, 107–8
Schiff, Violet, 53, 64n
    Letter to, 64–5
    And see Schiff, Sydney
Schnitzler, A., 30, 38
Scotland, 24, 29–30, 38, 41, 64, 65–6, 70–1, 75–6, 79, 80, 91, 127, 131, 149, 174
Scott, F. G., 77–8, 122
Scott, Tom, 173–4, 173n, 174–5, 174n, 185, 189, 189n.
    Letters to, 174–5, 189
Scott, Sir Walter, 140
Scottish Nation, 29n, 30
Scott-Moncrieff, A., 126n, 127
Scott-Moncrieff, G., 122n
    Letters to, 122, 126–7
Scouller, E., 155n
    Letter to, 155–6
Scouller, R., 155n

Secker, Martin (*publishers*), 79–80, 79n, 81, 81n
Shakespeare, 47, 49, 62, 89, 117, 187
Shaw, G. B., 47
Shelley, 47, 57
Sitwell, O., 57n, 58, 166
Sitwell, S., 57–8, 57n, 67
Smallwood, Mrs., 169n
    Letter to, 169–70
Smith, J. Adam: see Adam Smith, J.
Sonntagberg, 36
Soutar, W., 115n
    Letter to, 115–17
Spectator, 82n, 83, 87n
Spender, Stephen, 82–3, 82n, 85n, 92, 93n, 124n, 136
    Letters to, 82–4, 85–6, 92, 93–4, 97–8, 122–3, 124–6, 136–7, 137–8
Spens, Maisie, 148n
    Letter to, 148
Stein, Gertrude, 62–3, 67–8
Stendhal, 42, 50
Stevenson, R. L., 71–2
Strachey, L., 49, 67
Summers, Joseph, 195n
    Letter to, 195–6
Swale, Patricia, 147n
    Letter to, 147
Sweeney, Jack, 180, 185

This Quarter, 61n
Thomas, Dylan, 160
Thorburn, Elizabeth, 13, 22n
    Letters to, 22–4, 24–6, 29–30, 59–60, 68, 78–9
Thorburn, Ethel: see Ross, Mrs
Thorburn, George, 22n
    Letters to, 64, 79–80

    And See Thorburn, Elizabeth
Thorburn, Irene: see Abenheimer, Mrs
Times Literary Supplement, 96, 96n
Toller, Ernest, 72n, 74
Tolstoy, 138
Traherne, Thomas, 110
Trakl, G., 38, 89
Tschumi, R., 152n
    Letter to, 152–3

Untermeyer, Louis, 30, 32

Valéry, Paul, 46
Vogue, 57
Vonier, Anscar, 57

Waley, Arthur, 134
Weil, Simone, 195, 195n
Welty, Eudora, 136
Whitehead, A. N., 61, 61n, 62–3
Whyte, James, 70n
    Letter to, 70–2
Wilbur, Richard, 180, 185
Wilde, Oscar, 24
Williams, Oscar, 139n
    Letter to, 139–40
Wilson, J. D., 134n
    Letters to, 134–5, 135–6, 138–9
Wilson, Edmund, 183
Woolf, Virginia, 49, 49n, 50, 169n, 170
Wordsworth, 48, 57, 118, 131

Yèats, W. B., 152n, 159, 196–7
Young, Douglas, 155, 156n, 167n
    Letters to, 156–7, 167